CICERO
THE STATESMAN

BY

R. E. SMITH

PROFESSOR OF ANCIENT HISTORY IN THE
UNIVERSITY OF MANCHESTER

CAMBRIDGE
AT THE UNIVERSITY PRESS
1966

Published by the Syndics of the Cambridge University Press
Bentley House, 200 Euston Road, London, N.W. 1
American Branch: 32 East 57th Street, New York, N.Y. 10022

© Cambridge University Press 1966

Library of Congress Catalogue Card Number: 66–17061

Printed in Great Britain
at the University Printing House, Cambridge
(Brooke Crutchley, University Printer)

PREFACE

IT is hoped that this study of Cicero's career as a statesman may be of interest and, possibly, instruction both to scholars and students, and to that wider reading public which is familiar with Cicero and Rome, but has not—at any rate for some years—made it a subject of particular study.

In handling a subject such as this one is at once confronted with a difficulty; for so much work has been done by scholars both on Cicero and the last century of the Republic that a decision must be made at the outset, how far, if at all, should the narrative be equipped with footnotes. My decision was to omit them, since they would have burdened the pages immensely without contributing greatly to the narrative. References to the ancient sources for all the historical events are to be found both in *Magistrates of the Roman Republic* by T. R. Broughton and in *The Roman Republic* by T. Rice Holmes, and there seemed no need to repeat them all here; and since I was nowhere taking issue with any particular scholar's interpretation of events, it seemed unnecessary to refer to all the works of scholarship which took the same view as myself or to draw attention to those whose interpretation differed for my object is not to put forward a new and controversial viewpoint, but to write a narrative and interpretative account of Cicero's political career, which, while it may in places differ in emphasis and interpretation—as, indeed, it does—is not attempting to controvert any particular generally accepted thesis or interpretation.

A similar difficulty confronts one in drawing up a bibliography; to attempt to include all the books and articles which are directly concerned with, or throw light on, this period of Roman history would produce a bibliography as long as the book without adding to its understanding; I decided therefore to restrict it to books, and to list only those books which are fundamental for the period and the subject, and those which have a particular contribution to make to some aspect of our understanding of it. References to the many important and valuable articles are to be found somewhere among the references in the books listed in the bibliography; it is hoped that in this way anyone who wishes to pursue any particular aspect will be guided to the full literature on the subject.

I am happy to express my gratitude to G. Bell and Sons Ltd. for permission to use Shuckburgh's translation of Cicero's letters, published in the Bohn Series; all the quotations from Cicero's letters are taken from this excellent translation; and also to Harvard University Press, for permission to use B. Perrin's translation of Plutarch's Lives, published in the Loeb Series, from which the quotations from Plutarch's Lives are taken.

I must also express my indebtedness to my friend, Dr A. H. McDonald of Clare College, with whom I frequently discussed the topics as they emerged in the writing; he also read the first draft of the completed manuscript, and made many valuable suggestions for improvements; but he must not be held in any way responsible for the views expressed; that is my responsibility alone.

Finally, I must thank the Syndics of the Cambridge University Press and all those responsible, for their unfailing courtesy, advice and help throughout the process of converting the manuscript into the published work; any errors or mistakes which still remain are my fault and mine alone.

R.E.S.

Manchester
September 1966

CONTENTS

vii

INTRODUCTION

To write the biography of a great historical character is always a somewhat difficult, and generally a rather unsatisfactory, task; for one is confronted with the problem of how to handle the early years, when the subject was playing either no part or only a very minor part in the events which constitute the history of his time. If one emphasises the subject, there is very little history, and if the history, very little of the subject; yet both aspects are important, if one is to understand the later years where the character plays an important, possibly a leading, part in his country's story. For an understanding of the fully developed personality one should know what influences affected and moulded the character and ideas of the subject; to understand the problems and difficulties with which in his later years he contended we need to know their background and perhaps their origin.

Both aspects are therefore necessary, though they cannot be blended; they must exist side by side in a rather unsatisfying combination in which what one hopes is a judicious selection has been made of those trends and elements of his early life and upbringing which are significant for the understanding of the later life, and of those historical events which are significant for interpreting the later history; the two streams then, one hopes, blend together to form the single river which is the mature career of the subject in his country's history.

This is particularly true of Cicero, whose country equestrian background did not introduce him to the circles and personalities in whose hands lay the power and the government of Rome; he came from a middle-class world which looked on with awe and, possibly, admiration at the great nobles and their proud position in society and government, but had little contact with them. His passport to that circle was to be his oratory, and the story of his early life is largely the story of his developing oratorical powers, in which meetings with the 'great' tended to be few and coincidental, certainly not an essential part of his life; his early years had therefore little contact with the persons or events of historical importance.

The present biography is no exception to the pattern I have described; the first half is rather slow-moving and deals either with Cicero or with history, only rarely, as with the *Pro Roscio Amerino* or the *Verrines*, with both together; it attempts to explain the background both of the man and of the events in which he later took so great a part, and to indicate what seem to me to be the critical themes and influences of this fateful period of history. In the second half the narrative moves faster and more smoothly, for by now Cicero and the history have become one; to write of the one is to write of the other, and Cicero's central place in the politics and events of Rome from 63 B.C., even when he was not an active participant, enables the story to be written without distortion, and the tragedy of Cicero and the Republic to unfold itself without the help of the author's promptings.

The drawbacks of the biographical method are compensated by the ability it gives to focus the attention on the figure of the subject, when the subject's contribution to the events is of such importance as to warrant a central place; for in this way it is possible to show the influence he exerted on the persons and events of his time. In Cicero's case this is particularly valuable, since from 59 B.C. onwards, with rare and short exceptions, he took little active part in the events whose impact he felt so keenly; none the less his influence was known and wooed by both Caesar and Pompey, and it was this continuing influence in spite of powerlessness to act which made possible those glorious months from late 44 B.C. until his death. History must necessarily have little to say of Cicero in these years, since his importance lay only in his influence among groups in Rome and Italy, and must therefore leave largely unexplained how he was able to rally his country's forces against Antony without first having to stake a claim to leadership; it was because he had never forfeited the claim. At intervals throughout his period of inactivity men had looked to him to give a guiding lead to their own behaviour; and it is this importance which this biography attempts to explain and illumine. He was a true lover of his country, as even Augustus would later admit, and he was not without greatness; I hope that something of these qualities emerges from this story of his life in the service of his country.

CHAPTER I

THE ITALIAN BACKGROUND
AND ARPINUM

CICERO was born on 3 January 106 at Arpinum, a small country town about a hundred miles from Rome, in the territory of the Volsci, a people who had in earlier times been fierce enemies of Rome, but who had for many generations now been part of the Roman state. Arpinum itself had enjoyed the full citizenship of Rome since 188 B.C., and could thus feel itself to be politically a part of Rome and sharer of the achievements of the second century, during which Rome had risen first to primacy, then to exclusive domination within that Mediterranean world in which her destiny was cast. But to have shared in Rome's political achievement did not mean that this or other country towns had wholly absorbed the Roman attitude and outlook, or that their citizens were looked upon at Rome as truly equal to her own inhabitants, with equal opportunities of office, power and influence in the affairs of Rome and her empire. Before describing the early life and ambitions of Cicero, it will be well first to take a quick glance at Italy and her country towns; for Cicero's ambitions and career were decisively influenced by the circumstances of his birth and the forces which moulded his early years.

At the time of his birth Italy was politically divided into three: there were certain parts which enjoyed full Roman citizenship; others which had what is known as Latin status; finally there were the Italians, whose situation was by now the least advantageous. The Latins, though not full citizens of Rome, enjoyed a political status second only to that of a Roman in Italy; they contributed to Rome's legionary needs, and had the benefit of certain *iura*

4

such as the right to marry with Romans and to enter into binding contracts which were recognised in Roman law. Since they were not Roman citizens, they could not hold office at Rome, and hence could not directly influence the policies of whose execution they were the instruments; but for their upper classes at least there was a means of entry to the citizenship of Rome through the holding of office in their own communities. On the whole they seem to have been reasonably content with their situation; when the Social War broke out in 90, hardly a Latin community joined the insurgents. These were composed almost entirely of those in the third category, the Italians.

This group included the greater part of the Italian peninsula up to the river Po. Originally independent, they had for very many years been Roman 'allies', bound to her by treaties of varying degrees of sternness but following a certain number of patterns. A feature common to all these treaties was, however, a requirement to help the Roman armies with such cavalry and troops as Rome might from time to time enjoin. During the second century this requirement had been a real burden owing to the many wars in which Roman arms had been involved; the empire's growth and the immense accumulation of wealth during these years had been possible only because of the loyalty and support of the Latins and Italians, who had with hardly a murmur or protest followed Rome into wars in whose making and concluding they had no part or say, even though the cost in men and money was for all alike great, and the economic consequences sometimes grave.

Yet while they made their equal contribution to these wars, they did not equally share the profits; these went chiefly to Rome. True, the Italians found greater scope for their business and mercantile interests in an expanding empire; by Cicero's time the Italici were to be found in every part of the Roman world. But this was scant help or consolation to all those Italici who continued to live in Italy, on whom the burden fell directly, and who now began to feel themselves in a position of inferiority with respect to Rome. Subject as they were both at home and in the army to the *imperium* of the Roman magistrate, they were not seldom the victims of unjust and high-handed behaviour against which they had no appeal, and of demands to which they must unquestioningly submit. Compelled to follow Rome in a foreign policy for whose creation they had no responsibility and from which their own gains were slight compared with those of Rome, they began to feel indignant after so many years of loyalty and to demand an equality of privilege with those who were Roman citizens. With Caius Gracchus in 122 began the first phases of a struggle for this equality of status which was to end in 90–89 with the Social War and the gift of Roman citizenship to the whole of Italy as far as the Po.

For thirty years the struggle lasted, and such was the complex of conflicting interests that a solution short of war became progressively more doubtful and difficult. This is not the place to describe the details of that struggle, the different causes of exacerbation, the various efforts of the politicians to find a solution; but we must briefly consider the outlook and attitude of these people, which brought them to open war with Rome. For even though they finally achieved their object, the hatred bred by thirty years of increasingly resentful frustration could not expect to be dissipated by the signing of a treaty; for years they must feel differently from other Roman citizens; and this fact had importance for the age of Cicero.

Until they won the citizenship their position had become unenviable. Committed to policies in which they had no say, subjected to the orders and not infrequently the insolence of Roman magistrates, from whom there was for them no appeal, they could only smart, suffer and obey. Their interests were often ignored in the politics of Rome; if land was needed for allotment to the poor at Rome or to veteran soldiers, public land in allied territory was not unlikely to be used for the purpose. For although they were in theory allies, bound to Rome by treaty, but otherwise independent, the truth was very different; Rome's primacy in Italy had brought it about that by the end of the second century Rome governed the whole of Italy; whether she gave orders to the allies with tact or not, orders they remained, which must be carried out; nor did Rome allow of the possibility of ending the treaty; they were bound, it seemed, for all time. They wanted neither independence nor subordination, but equality in a partnership of centuries; only if this were denied them, were they prepared to fight for independence from the thankless tyrant.

And what of the thankless tyrant? Why was she so mulish or so selfish in her treatment of allies whose loyalty was above suspicion and to whose help she owed so much? The reasons were many, some the result of insolence and selfishness, others deeper and mirroring the greatest political problem that confronted the ancient world, a problem which Rome did finally resolve, as Greece did not. Without doubt Rome's governing class had tended to become arrogant and contemptuous of others, to regard themselves conceitedly, and to assume that their superior position gave them both opportunity and right to behave with an insolence that was often intolerable towards Rome's allies and her subjects. Thirty years before the Social War broke out C. Gracchus could castigate the barbaric insolence of Roman magistrates and others; such conduct was not exceptional, and became more common in the ensuing thirty years. Such behaviour could breed only hate and enmity in the hearts of its victims, and there is evidence enough that such had been its offspring; nor was it by any means dispelled by the reluctant gift of citizenship, extorted by a short but bitter war.

There seemed, moreover, in the circumstances of Rome's political organisation, to be a reason for her exclusive attitude towards the gift of citizenship to so many thousands, scattered over so wide an area. In the past she had been generous in this matter; but the communities to whom she had made the gift were not far distant from Rome, and could within limits exercise its privileges and enjoy its advantages. But Rome, although she was now the mistress of an empire, was still in her constitution a city-state, ruled by annual magistrates elected by all the citizens, and passing her laws in assemblies at which every citizen had the right to vote. Each allied community had similarly its own organisation for the conduct of its life and its affairs; from time to time they would receive from Rome directives, possibly couched as requests, on matters of foreign or other policy; but otherwise they ruled themselves. Their citizens' lives were centred in their own community; there was the focus of their social life, the place in which they earned a livelihood, whose property and well-being were their chief concern, whose public offices their leading citizens held. Their own community was their fatherland, as Rome was for a Roman, nor did their pride and patriotism wish to find a different country for its outlet.

The city-state presumed a limit in terms of size and numbers. Every citizen had full political rights and was free to attend the council or assembly of his city; how, then, could a citizen who lived a hundred miles or more away hope to play his part in his city's affairs, if he was seldom or never in his city? Certainly Rome herself had citizen communities at great distances from Rome, the so-called Roman colonies; but they were not indigenous growths as were the allied cities, and their relation to Rome had been defined at the moment of their birth. From the outset they were colonies of Roman citizens, building a community in some area in Rome's interest, modelling themselves on Rome, and recognising her as their true country, to whom they looked for advice and from whom they received instructions. But though these colonies were different in origin and purpose from allied towns, they could none the less serve to illustrate that communities of citizens might exist at a considerable remove from Rome. Similarly the Latin colonies, to whom the Latin rights were given, showed that there could be a development of communities more favourable than that which the Italians enjoyed, at a distance from Rome.

But so long as Rome remained in her political structure a city-state, the consequence of admitting the whole of Italy to her citizenship must appear in itself almost revolutionary. For tens of thousands of voters would be added to the electoral rolls, and this would have for the Roman plebs and noble families alike seemingly dire results; in prospect it might seem to spell the doom of that control of the elections which these noble families had contrived to establish; for while they might influence by bribery and patronage the Roman plebs, who represented so great a part of those that normally voted, how could they hope to widen that control to cover the whole of Italy? Nor would the plebs be any better pleased; their vote was worth something to them as an object for sale at the moment; but either the price must of necessity go down, or it would be beyond the powers and purse of candidates to attempt the purchase. We need not therefore be surprised that the broader vision of justice and gratitude to faithful allies should have been narrowed or obscured by meaner and more petty calculations of politics and gain. Few only at Rome had courage to rise above what seemed their selfish interests; the greater number, thinking of their own advantage, preferred to deny justice to their allies rather than risk the loss of their privileged position.

In fact their calculations were astray, for they supposed that a large number at least of these persons would, if enfranchised, come to Rome to cast their votes in the electoral and legislative Comitia. But this, as we have seen, was not their aim; equality of privilege and position was their goal, to end the humiliations they suffered at the hands of Rome and to be equal partners in the empire in whose creation they had played an equal part with Rome. This was their aim and their determination; the elections and legislation of Rome were in general of no greater interest to them than their own affairs were to Roman citizens. Only if matters of particular interest to themselves were the subject of legislation, would many of them make the journey to Rome to vote: and even then most would not come; the way to Rome was long and tedious, expensive and not always safe; most men could not afford the time and money or the retinue to assure their safety; only on rare occasions would many come to Rome.

Their civic interest lay with their own community; the Roman elections were not likely in normal times to stir them to heated discussion or angry passions; the successful candidate would, unless things went awry, be some scion of a noble family, seeking glory for his family, and profit for himself; once the Italians had Roman citizenship, his precocious temper and his immoderate insolence could not vent themselves on them; the unhappy provincials would be the victims, not they; it was not then worth a time-consuming journey to Rome to cast a vote of very dubious value on behalf of any candidate. Rome, in fact, and all the antics of its politicians left the new citizens largely unmoved; and the country-town morality would find much that went on in the great cosmopolis dangerous and alien to their simpler ways. In a world where communications were slow and precarious, unaided by all the modern means of translating men and words from place to place, there must always be vast differences between the outlook and manners of the country-town and the great capital; this was true of England until the twentieth century, and was certainly true of Italy in the first century B.C. The towns of Italy lived a simpler life, largely untouched by the political and moral corruption of Rome, governed by a moral code long superseded at Rome by one that gave a sanction to all the improprieties in politics and life that were the currency that bought success and wealth. To the countryman Rome was a rather fearsome place, likely to taint any that lived there; most of them had neither been nor ever would go there. Hearing the stories of the great city they felt perhaps a little envious of her glamorous marvels; but their roots were deep in the country, and they saw life through the country's eyes.

None the less incorporation within the polity of Rome opened the door to wider horizons for many of them; they could move about the Roman Empire as equal partners and enjoy the fruits of conquest as business men and tax collectors more than they ever had done before; they could make connexions more easily at Rome than in their own towns and find there more abundant opportunities for their talents and their energies. But the career which above all was now open to them was that of the soldier, and Italians poured into the legions both as soldiers and officers; for in the circumstances of the first century the army could offer to both soldier and officer a lucrative career, and for the officer the possible chance of entering the political arena of Rome. This was, in fact, the best, if not the only, entrance for those who could not command some initial patronage. The importance of the army will be considered later; here our concern is rather with the significance of this phenomenon in connexion with the Italians' attitude to Rome.

It was impossible that they should feel any great love for the city which had denied them what they thought their due until their arms had successfully won it for themselves. The gift of citizenship had been forcibly extorted by people with no love for Rome from a city from which they had been prepared to secede and which they had been ready even to raze. This is not the foundation of love; and though the passions of hate had smouldered down when their object was attained, the flame of loyalty had not at once leapt into life; this was still given to their own community, though they did not hesitate to profit from their new status. They joined the army, but that did not engender loyalty to Rome; the army became itself the focus of their loyalty, and if their general chose to use that army for his purposes against Rome, both officers and soldiers were ready to follow him; for it was not against their fatherland they marched, but against a city for whom they felt no great affection, to which they were bound by few ties of sentiment, and from which their general, if success-ful, could win profit and advantage for themselves. The Italians in these years took their revenge on Rome for all their slights and insults; through the army they helped to dictate Rome's policy, hastened the destruction of the Republic, and made powerless the great families who supposed they were its rulers.

The men who joined the army found a career both interesting and profitable; many country families through service as officers made valuable contacts which opened the door to a political career at Rome for themselves or their sons; and in this way Italy began gradually to play its part in governing the empire she had so greatly helped to build. The soldiers found a career more profitable than could elsewhere be found; the more fortunate who became centurions would probably retire with an equestrian fortune, thus enabling their sons to embark on a military career as officers, while most soldiers would have accumulated a fortune by no means meagre through booty and other perquisites, to which would be added the grant of land which was now customary on retirement. Their attitude to life was clear; they looked for adventure and profit during their service and a piece of land on its conclusion; if this required that they should turn their arms against Rome, they would hardly hesitate, certainly not refuse.

But what of the Italians who remained at home to ply their crafts or till their fields, or to lead the lives of country gentlemen in their own community? We hear little of them, for since they played no part in the affairs of Rome they pass almost unmentioned by Roman writers. Cicero gives us an occasional glimpse: he tells of his own early life at Arpinum, of the simple morality of his grandfather and his parents, their conversations and their ideals. We seem to be living in an earlier Rome, the simple tenor of whose life was matched by an equally simple moral code, uncomplicated by the worries of empire or the reasoning of philosophers; right and wrong were easily distinguishable, and right was what it behoved a man to do. Their religion was a simpler one of faith and belief in the gods of their country and the countryside; the numerous small gods who oversaw the myriad activities of the farm, the workshop and the home had not yet been dissolved into the Stoic pantheism or the rationalist's void; they still lived and afforded their protection to their believers.

There flourished a spirit of community and pride in their city and the achievements of their sons, such as could obviously not be found in Rome. Cicero never sought to disguise his pride in Arpinum and in her greatest son to date, C. Marius; it was his ambition to equal Marius' fame, thus doubling Arpinum's. The picture that emerges in the *Pro Plancio* is of a country community, proud and delighted at the success of their sons, agog to learn of the outcome of elections in which their citizens were involved, ready in any way they could to forward their careers, which, so they felt, reflected glory on themselves. This bond of comradeship and interest gave the state a compactness and a unity which must have deeply influenced the outlook of its sons; even though they might, like Cicero, migrate to Rome, many would not slough off their early training and experience; their ideals would wear the colour of their earlier life. Cicero's upbringing was in this way profoundly to affect his attitude to Rome and the political problems that beset her; it was, in a sense, almost to blind him to the true nature of the distemper of the body politic and to show him the remedy that should, but never could, be; much in his statesman's life was rooted in Arpinum.

For his life in Arpinum had shown him the essential solidity and solidarity of the country people; different perhaps in minor foibles, they were alike in their values and their outlook; throughout Italy were to be found these communities of men, providing the strong backbone of the Roman body politic; here throughout the whole peninsula were the men to redress the balance of Rome's political excesses, to provide a moral code and saner outlook, coloured by the countryman's innate respect for work. Cicero, shocked by much of what he found in Rome, knew this; his own standards were theirs, he was one of them; and he realised that their attitudes and outlook could bring equilibrium to the dangerous rocking of the ship of state; while they soon recognised in him one of themselves, one whose ideals they admired and understood; and always throughout his long career they gave him their support. It was this bond between the two, born of their common country heritage, that guided Cicero to the solution of Rome's troubles which he always advocated, *consensus Italiae* and *coniunctio omnium bonorum*; the narrow exclusivism of the Roman families must make way before this larger vision, if they wished to save themselves and the Republic; and whether the noble families accepted it or not, Italy recognised a friend sprung of themselves.

His earliest years were spent at Arpinum and his education was largely in his father's hands, though he seems to have attended the small local school, where later stories were not wanting to show even at that tender age an intellect brilliant beyond his years and that of all his fellow-pupils. From his father he learnt much about Rome's past, her character and ideals; for the father was something of an invalid, tending in consequence to remain indoors, reading, thinking and instructing his two small sons. The family was conservative in outlook; his grandfather had been vehement to prevent the introduction of the secret ballot into the affairs of Arpinum, regarding it with horror as a modern innovation whose results could only be disastrous to their affairs. The family enjoyed locally a high repute, and though no member had yet sought office at Rome—Cicero was its first member to enter the Roman Senate—both his parents, as also his grandfather before, had connexions and friendships with important families at Rome.

Marius too was from Arpinum, the greatest man in Rome, Jugurtha's conqueror and, more important, victor over the Cimbri and Teutoni, whose multitudinous onset had terrified Italy and Rome. They had destroyed Roman armies led by nobles, and had been poised on the very doorstep of Italy; the havoc, the bloodshed and the misery their conquering advance into Italy would have wrought—and seemed likely for a time to wreak—was too terrible to contemplate. They had diverted for a time, and meanwhile Rome had turned to the *novus homo*, Marius, fresh from his African success. He had welded together an army with which in two successive years, 102 and 101, he had utterly defeated their barbarian hordes and made Italy's frontier safe for close on three hundred years from the foreign invader.

None would dispute Rome's debt to Marius; few only were minded to. But in politics things had not gone so well with him, and he had been closely involved in the serious events of 100. Himself of equestrian family, with the help of the powerful Metellan clan he had risen to the praetorship; in the atmosphere of those times this was great success, and with this achievement he should, they thought, have been content. To aspire to the consulship was tantamount to aspiring to sup with Jupiter himself, hardly to be compassed, almost impious even to think of. Yet in the disturbed conditions of Rome, with the Equites combining with those politicians who were assailing in such determined fashion the fortress of noble privilege, it could not merely be thought of, but contrived. His known military ability was a card not lightly to be thrown away; his supporters succeeded in forcing Marius into the consulship, and thus saved Rome.

But in the year 100, consul for the sixth time, he had got himself entangled with politicians whose behaviour frightened both the Equites and Marius himself, and brought Rome to the verge of civil war. Marius joined the Senatorial side and suppressed by force the commotion caused by his erstwhile allies, Saturninus and Glaucia; nor did this run so counter to his deeper inclinations as his career might at first suggest. As things then stood the only path to the highest magistracy which lay open to such a one as Marius was the path he had trodden; but his inclination was not therefore for revolution or even innovation, certainly not for violent innovation. Having broken into the exclusive group of families and become Rome's most powerful political figure, he wanted the political and social values to continue as before; because its attainment was both difficult and in his estimation glorious, he had strained his energies and influence toward it; but what if in the attainment he should destroy the glory and the fame? He would have destroyed the great ambition of his life; for the prize of victory would be no longer worth the having, if the glory was gone. He wished to bask in the warming glow of popular esteem and to find recognition with those among whom he now consorted. His presence in 100 on the side of the Senatorial order need not, then, surprise us; he was defending his own interests.

In spite of the events of 100 Marius had remained an influential figure, still able to defend his friends against his enemies, and numbering powerful families among his supporters. Then had come the Social War; Marius had been one of many soldiers summoned to their country's help, and he had been successful; but before the war was ended he had withdrawn or been withdrawn; he had enemies as well as friends, and however he might choose to regard his past, there were those to whom that past gave ground enough for deep resentment. There loomed the Mithridatic War, to whose conduct Sulla had been named. Marius coveted this command, to which as Rome's greatest living soldier he felt he was entitled; and Sulpicius Rufus, in trouble with his legislation in the new citizens' interests, was glad to enlist the support of Marius to his cause; for Marius was still in politics a powerful figure. In exchange for his support Sulpicius had the Eastern command transferred to him; Sulla immediately moved his troops to Rome, banished Marius and others, made shift to strengthen the Senate's hand against further 'democratic' attack, then betook himself against Mithridates. At once there was reaction; Marius returned and was elected in 87 to his seventh consulship.

By now Marius was an old man, embittered by his recent failure and humiliation, his mind affected by the experiences of a fugitive-exile with a price upon his head. Those who had opposed great Marius should taste the rewards of ingratitude; grimly he set to massacre his enemies; large numbers died, many at the hands of slaves. All who had thwarted the old man should pay the penalty, and many fled to Sulla's camp to escape his dreaded vengeance. The streets of Rome during those dark days were filled with blood and murder; fortunately Marius died quite soon, but even then it was too late to save his reputation. For however men reckoned his political behaviour, his schemings with Equites and others to overthrow the nobles and his patron, to an impartial eye the balance must still have tipped in Marius' favour by reason of the brilliant services his attainment of the highest office had enabled him to render Rome in her hour of need. But for the murders which he perpetrated in 86 there could be no explanation except that of revenge operating in a sick and tortured mind; and this could certainly not excuse the butchery of which it was the cause. Cicero was proud of his fellow-countryman, as was all Arpinum; proud that from here had come Rome's great deliverer and soldier; nothing could take from Marius that title to fame, and Cicero gladly gave it to him. But nothing either could take from him the reputation of a butcher, and this was no ground for pride; Cicero condemns his brutal murders, and does not seek to justify them; but they could not dim his earlier glory, and so Cicero could seek to emulate in his own way the fame that Marius had brought to Arpinum, yet not associate himself with his excesses.

The fame of Marius could serve as a flash to kindle his ambition; but the direction of that ambition was to owe nothing to him. With his country conservative background he remained throughout his life conservative in outlook and in aim; he pictured Rome and her great figures in the romantic colours of his own idealism, in which the moral code was so much more akin to earlier than to contemporary Rome. He believed that Rome was what his country family pictured her as being, rather than what she was; and even when experience had revealed the truth, he never wholly accepted it. He would sense a keen disappointment that her politicians were not animated by the high idealism with which his youthful imagination had credited them; but he could never persuade himself of the essential rottenness of much of the political system which made them what they were. The Republican form of government was the form by which Rome had grown to greatness; thus only could she, so he thought, remain great; the fault was in the individuals, not the system. However angry and dissatisfied he was to become in later life with the behaviour of some of the nobles, he never thought to condemn the system which made the nobles what they were and allowed them to continue so. Like Marius, he aspired to become a great man in terms of the polity he knew and within whose framework he designed his niche; success therefore required the maintenance of that framework and of the values according to which greatness was measured; revolution or violent change were alike inimical to his nature and his ambitions.

CHAPTER 2

HIS EDUCATION AND CAREER
TO 71 B.C.

W HEN Cicero was about ten his father moved to Rome, where the opportunities for his sons' education were far ampler than at Arpinum; and here Cicero made valuable use of the chances that were opened to him. His father had connexions with Scaevola, the augur, to whom he introduced his son; from him he learnt much until his death in 87: Cicero then joined himself to Scaevola's namesake and cousin, the pontifex maximus, at whose feet he learnt much about civil law, destined to be of the greatest value in his subsequent career as an advocate. He also studied for a time the technical aspects of oratory under Molo, the Rhodian rhetorician, who paid a visit to Rome in 88. Philo, the head of the Academy, also came to Rome, in flight from his native Athens, during the Mithridatic War; at this same time the Stoic Diodotus came to Rome, and from him Cicero learnt the principles of Stoicism. He later came to live with Cicero, and died in his house in 59.

During the whole of this decade 90–80 Cicero was reading widely, learning avidly and broadening his understanding by the study of philosophy and literature, as well as practising his oratory assiduously, and listening to every public speaker, whether advocate or politician. His later fame as Rome's greatest orator depended very largely on the hard and concentrated work of these years, aimed at the one object of becoming a great and famous orator, and during these critical years all his activities and energies were directed to this end. The broadening of his experience, the deepening of his understanding, the sharpening of his intellect were no less requisite for the attainment of his ambition than the perfecting of the technique of speech-making.

2-2

At the outbreak of the Social War in 89 he found himself compelled to serve in the army. His service was brief and distasteful; alien as it was to his nature, useless, as he supposed, to his career, he was only too ready, when opportunity offered, to abandon arms in favour of the Forum; indeed, this period of a year represented his only experience of military service until he found himself the governor of a province in 51, in charge of an army and threatened with a Parthian invasion. This was his deliberate choice, and its effect was of such importance for his career and the ultimate failure of his statesman's vision that we should pause to consider wherein lay the importance of his attitude and consequent decision.

That the military life seemed to him inferior to the life of orator or statesman is clear from what he says in several places; for that reason he was disposed to rate the greatness of Scaevola above that of Marius. This preference for the career of the Forum corresponded with his early family life, where neither his grandfather nor his father had given any long time to military service, and with the ambitions he had nourished from a very early age. His sensitive nature and somewhat delicate physique in youth combined to turn his thoughts to victories of the mind rather than to bodily exertions. Nor did there seem in 90 any great obstacle to such a career other than his family's equestrian country status, which meant that, should he decide to enter politics, the path would not beyond a point be easy. But to the young such difficulties exist only to be overcome; oratory in any case probably had the primacy with him over politics, though he almost certainly nourished undefined dreams of political success.

But the situation was in fact changing, though Cicero failed to mark the change. Marius' own career witnessed to what was possible if one allied oneself with groups and individuals hostile to the Senate; more particularly he had shown the political power that could come to the general of a great army, whose soldiers when under arms could support his political ambitions, and when demobilised could be added to his *clientes*. He had opened the

army's ranks to volunteers, whether they had the requisite property-qualification or not; hitherto armies had been raised by
the operation of the levy from among those persons only with
a certain minimum property-qualification; and each such man
could be required to serve for a total of sixteen years between his
seventeenth and forty-fifth years. This system had operated
most unfairly on the small landowner, who had often found
himself compelled to serve for long continuous periods to his
own detriment. For on his return he might well find that his
holding had suffered owing to his absence, and he might then be
compelled through lack of capital to sell his land, while he himself migrated to the city, there to exist as client to some noble,
henceforth ineligible to serve in the army, because he no longer
had the qualification. In consequence by the last years of the
second century, when military needs increased, the number of
qualified men had so diminished that the burden was falling
unfairly on the backs of those still qualified; and discontent was
not surprisingly afoot. It was at this juncture that Marius, needing
additional troops against Jugurtha, invited volunteers from all
classes, including those without any property.

The result of his invitation was all that he could have wished;
at once he found all the troops he needed; nor was any future
general likely to incur the unpopularity of depending solely on
the levy, when he could hope to find at least a great proportion of
his needs from volunteers; and this became from now the general
practice. There was a further consequence; the volunteers were
men who either through lack of property had no other certain
means of livelihood, or who preferred the soldier's not unlucrative
and adventurous life to the limited and humdrum existence
which was alone open to them in their own community. Making
a profession of soldiering they were ready and indeed anxious
to spend many years with the colours; and when armies needed
for special emergencies such as the Mithridatic War returned to
Italy after the crisis was past, they were then demobilised by the
general; and custom, begun by Marius, which self-interest was

concerned to perpetuate, gave them a grant of land. The provision of the land required legislation which the Senate was sometimes loath to promote; for the settlement of soldiers in Italy provided the general with communities of clients, whose support could strengthen him in politics at home, and Senate and general were on occasions not good friends. Then must the general procure the passage of the needed legislation; the presence of these troops could influence Senate and Comitia; and they, being under obligation to their general, would more readily support his further political sallies, if he should have a mind for such.

Further, since 88 the whole of Italy up to the Po had enjoyed Roman citizenship, and all its inhabitants were therefore eligible to serve in the legions; large numbers from the Italian countryside were attracted to the opportunities which the legionary's life afforded, far ampler than the restricted resources of their country towns could offer them. Now these men, as we have marked above, did not and could not feel those sentiments towards Rome which her earlier citizens had felt towards her constitution and traditions; men with their motives for joining were unlikely to feel the horror of the matricide if their interests turned their arms against Rome, or at least inclined them to support with those arms their general's claims, should he find himself opposed to the established government. The readiness with which the armies in this century supported their general against the government of Rome is a depressing spectacle whose basic cause lies in the fact that most of the soldiers hardly regarded Rome or her government as theirs, for whom wealth and adventure were their aims, not Rome's defence.

What was true of the soldiers was hardly less true of the officers. The only requirement for the post of *tribunus militum* was, it would seem, the equestrian census, and many families in Italy could lay claim to this modest fortune. There were many country gentlemen, the leading burghers of their town, whose wealth was derived from land through many generations, who could not hope to advance far in the *cursus honorum* at Rome;

there was also an increasing number of families in this class who had made sufficient money from this very army service to retire with the fortune of an *eques*; their sons might therefore embark upon an officer's career, and the tradition of their family would serve the son as an incentive to follow his father's career.

In the army there was for the officer a lucrative and interesting career to be had and, what was hardly less important, the opportunity to make those friendships and contacts whose value could be so very great, if he should wish to enter politics. We know of officers becoming not merely praetors but even consuls through the influence of the generals whose interests they had served; Pompey and Caesar forwarded the interests of several of their officers. In consequence these men were no less devoted to their general than the soldiers they commanded, and the whole army was likely to move as one at their general's behest.

The Senatorial families came by contrast to play a diminishing part in Rome's military system. In the second century they had provided all the officers; ten years' military service had been—and still in theory was—a prerequisite to entrance on the *cursus honorum*; men who had even held the praetorship or consulship were ready to serve as officers in case of need. But times were changed; the developing professionalism of this century, necessary indeed if Rome's armies were to match those of her opponents, made service distasteful to young politicians of high birth, who would have to mess with the rougher countrymen whose chief education was that of the army, and to whom the more exquisite pleasures and pastimes of the city were largely unknown. The young nobles might briefly serve on the staff of some provincial governor, whose influence at home could be so valuable to them in the careers on which they were embarking; but the prospect of many years in army service, learning the art of war and the minds of soldiers, was too distasteful to be essayed; they preferred Rome and the battleground of the Forum and the Senate.

The result was that the ties that had bound the army to the Senate became ever more tenuous during these years; the Senators, largely ignorant of the mind and outlook of the soldier, despised him as a man, feared him as a unit of an army, and felt a mingled contempt and dread of his officers. Few only of their members had the knowledge and experience to command an army, if an emergency arose; at such a moment they must turn to whatever man available had the ability to control and lead the army to victory. The severance between Senate and army was near complete except through the intermediacy of a general; this could be dangerous and, it might be, fatal, if they should fail to find a general well-disposed towards themselves; and this became continually more likely as fewer Senators troubled to equip themselves for the task.

None the less, as the history of this century reveals, there were men with ability to lead these professional armies to victory and to win their devoted loyalty; but these were frequently men who refused to play the game of politics according to the Senate's and the nobles' rules. From the time of the Gracchi there had developed a struggle between the Senate and those groups and persons who were either determined to broaden the basis of Roman government or to use the methods devised by the Gracchi to force their own advantage. Marius had been one such man, and his career, especially in its later stages, had shown the value to the general of his army. Sulla, although his sympathies had been Senatorial, had been able to safeguard his and the Senate's position only by using his army in 88 and by fighting a war in 83. The supreme office in which Sulla had clothed his position in the state and from which he had fortified the Senate's domination had made apparent that the road to power lay through the army. Not only had Sulla defeated his and the Senate's enemies, but all his subsequent legislation was guaranteed by the presence of his veterans in their thousands, loyal to him and to the legislation in virtue of which they were occupying land to which they had no other title. Sulla's career was a warning, an inspiration and a model: a warning to constitutionalists that arms could easily subvert the power of law; an inspiration to those frustrated by the legal trammels in which hostility could enwrap those whom it sought to thwart; a model to those ambitious men who knew that for them advantage and advance could only come from forcing the Senate and the constitution to obedience. To possess an army became matter for scheming during these years, and its possessor an object of dread to his opponents.

The opponents of government were not slow to learn the lesson; Pompey, indeed, learnt it in time to seek to threaten Sulla himself. Pompey and Caesar were the greatest of this class, so much the greatest that the rest are unimportant. But there were others; Piso and Gabinius in the 50s hoped to become important war-lords; Crassus, too, thought to be a power; but he had taken insufficient pains to become a soldier. These men realised that if they were to use the Sullan method, they must command and control an army; unlike the Senatorial families they were careful to provide themselves with that experience of an army and of warfare without which their sanguine hopes could never fructify. Caesar in the 60s without an army was as impotent as any other hostile politician; Caesar in 59 supported by Pompey's veterans could play the dictator no less well than Sulla. Pompey in 67 could command all; in 61 and 60 without his army he could accomplish nothing but his own humiliation. The army and the man were mutually indispensable; separated they were powerless, together invincible.

Cicero's country equestrian origin was respectably undistinguished; no upstart family, nor citizens of yesterday, and able to number among their friends distinguished Roman names. But no member had yet entered the Senate; and even if Cicero should enter politics, his supporters would be unlikely to help him beyond the praetorship at most; he will hardly have forgotten that Metellus did not sponsor Marius' first consulship. The nobles would never accept him as an equal; however great his abilities, however deep his loyalty to their ideals, he must always be to them an intruder from without; support for the consulship would be most unlikely, the elections to which they contrived throughout this period normally to control. Even when he did without their help become a consular, he was ineffective to sway their counsels; an intruder he remained, who had been useful and might be so again. Pompey too they would have liked to isolate; but the influence of his *clientelae* and his veterans forbade the fulfilment of that wish, as well as his abilities as soldier, which might at any time be needed.

Had Cicero's background and ideals been different, had he not been brought up in an atmosphere which exalted the nobility and the Republican constitution and stirred him to emulation of the great men of the past, in particular the younger Scipio, could he have viewed dispassionately the scene of politics, he would perhaps have sensed that the future lay not with the politicians but with the generals, and that policies, whether of reform or innovation, could be most surely implemented with the army in the background. So much was clear to Pompey, his contemporary, and to Caesar; but it never impressed itself on Cicero, to whom such conduct seemed the cause of the Republic's failure; he did not mark that the Republic's failure was in part the cause of such behaviour. His nature and his background thus beckoned him to seek to join the noble families, though this side must surely lose every engagement to which their opponents chose to challenge them. The general's art was to him inferior to that of statesman, Marius' to that of Scaevola; of Scipio, his ideal, it was his qualities of statesmanship, not of generalship, which he admired; his admiration would probably have been as great, had Scipio never led an army, though, had he not led an army, he would never have been so influential as a statesman. He failed in this to see the facts beneath the surface, to search for the truth unprejudiced and ruthless; and this was a weakness many of us share. Much of his political theory was built on a foundation of illusion which through failing to comprehend the reality was apt to apply balms and remedies which could not touch the roots of the distemper.

However that might be, during this decade he turned his

energies to the perfection of his oratory, his determination fixed
to become Rome's greatest speaker; this, rather than political
greatness, was at this stage his consuming ambition. In 80 his
first great chance was offered, at the age of twenty-six. He had
spoken in the previous year on behalf of a certain Quinctia; but
this time he assumed the defence of a man named Roscius, against
whom a charge of parricide had been infamously trumped up.
To appreciate the significance of this speech in Cicero's career
we must briefly explore the background and the details of the
case. The father of Roscius had been a wealthy landowner of
Ameria, who had supported Sulla in the civil war, fighting on
Sulla's side; the proscriptions therefore should have held no
terrors for him. But certain of his relatives, seeing in the existing
bloody turmoil an opportunity to remove their wealthy cousin
and seize upon his estates, conspired with Sulla's powerful freedman, the ex-slave Chrysogonus, at this time at the very apex of
his power, to insert the name of Roscius on the list of the proscribed; thus would his murder be a public and a legal act, while
his estates, instead of passing to his son, would be put up to
public auction; Chrysogonus would see to it that for a consideration the estates were knocked down to the cousins at a ridiculously
low figure. The conspiracy succeeded, and Roscius' son, Cicero's
client, was left destitute, but alive.

The relatives responsible for the infamous deed began now to
feel uneasy that the son, from whom they had taken both father
and property, might in his angry desperation seek to expose the
wicked crime; it was therefore resolved, with Chrysogonus'
approval, to accuse the son of the father's murder. The charge
was contemptible, but its rebuttal so fraught with danger as to
appear impossible. For the truth about the murder would need
to be told, and this would require that Chrysogonus' part in the
infamy be exposed; and such a revelation must bring to light the
injustices and excesses which had been perpetrated during the
evil days of the proscriptions. Sulla was still alive; who would
dare to criticise what he had done or call in question the behaviour

of his favourite freedman? Yet how otherwise could Roscius' life be saved?

Roscius had the support of influential families who before the revolution would have exerted themselves openly in his defence; but to do so at this moment was too perilous; for Sulla was not prepared for criticism of what he had done, particularly from those in whose favour he had done it, namely the Senatorial class. Nor did the majority want to criticise him; well pleased with the constitution he had given them, they were displeased only with the excesses of Chrysogonus and his like, whom they hated as being more influential than they. Roscius' friends, therefore, since they feared to appear in court themselves, sought for someone who would dare to assume his defence. Their choice fell on Cicero. He was young and politically uncommitted; his background was such that he could more freely criticise than they, and what he said would not give such offence as if it came from a noble's lips. His sentiment and outlook could be trusted; though he had not fought in the recent war, his sympathies had been with Sulla's side, in whose victory he had rejoiced. He seemed, then, to them to be their man; to him this seemed his chance, and dangerous though the assignment was, he readily accepted it.

His defence was successful and Roscius' life was saved. It was a brilliant and courageous achievement; for since defence required the exposure of the truth about the father's death, his murder and the sale of his 'proscribed' property, and the subsequent wish to be rid of the son, Cicero had no choice but to attack Chrysogonus openly and by name. This he did with a boldness the nobles must have envied. But he must not seem to be criticising Sulla or what he had done; he was therefore at pains to separate Sulla from his worthless freedman, to argue that what Chrysogonus had done was done without Sulla's knowledge and against the intentions of his legislation. The cruelty and bloodshed of the proscriptions were as far as possible glossed over, while his arrangements on behalf of the nobles and the Senate were commended for restoring law and order to the state. It required both skill and courage.

Yet it was in Sulla's interest to know the truth, even though Cicero might not appreciate the fact. For from the nobles' point of view much besides Roscius' life was involved. Roscius enjoyed the friendship and protection of established Roman families who, fearing to come forward themselves, had exerted their powerful influence to give him the best defence they could. Should Roscius none the less be convicted, it would demonstrate the inability of the leading families to protect those who looked to them for support and help; and this would be serious for Sulla's reforms. For these families all had their connexions among the towns of Italy, many of them in the provinces as well; Rome's relations with her allies had owed much to these patronal affiliations. If these relationships were to prove valueless in the new state, then there would follow two weighty consequences: first, the bond which existed between Rome and her communities of new citizens in Italy, which provided the best beginning for their integration in the Roman State, would be seriously impaired; for if the *patronus* could no longer help his *cliens*, then the whole structure of mutual help could well collapse, and some fresh foundation for a united Italy must needs be found. And secondly, perhaps of more immediate import, their powerlessness would be exposed at the very instant when Sulla had devised a constitution which gave them supreme control; what sorrier inauguration of the new order than to witness the humiliation of the governors at the hands of an ex-slave!

Herein lay the embarrassment of the nobles, and the importance of procuring justice and an acquittal; and herein lay the significance of Cicero's achievement in challenging successfully the insolent injustice of Chrysogonus, with all its menaces for Sulla's new order. The new and almost unknown young man's courage had contributed to the safety of Sulla's order and the nobles on whom it depended; the nobles were grateful; Sulla, who could so easily have intervened, showed by his refusal that he would not undermine his work by allowing his freedman to behave as though the only power that mattered was his.

Cicero's ambitious courage had certainly forwarded both his oratorical and his political interests; the seeds he sowed grew quickly, and the reaper as quickly gathered his harvest. So great was his reputation from this speech that no case was deemed unworthy of his patronage, and he was very active in the courts. This, however, brought its penalty; for not being at that time particularly strong in constitution he seemed in danger of having to abandon altogether the role of pleader. To put aside his great ambition to become a famous orator was more than he would submit to; in spite of the advice of friends and doctors that he should abandon the courts, he himself decided that a change in his mode of speaking might reduce the strain, and allow him to continue his practice at the bar and also to improve his oratory; in 79 he therefore left Rome to study philosophy and oratory under the leading exponents of the day. First he went to Athens, where he rekindled his interest in philosophy under Antiochus, head of the Academy, and studied oratory under Demetrius. Thence after six months he proceeded to Asia, where he visited many of the great teachers of oratory; in particular, however, he visited Molo in Rhodes, who pruned his youthful exuberance of style; he returned to Rome at the end of two years with his style improved, his health restored and his manner of delivery so much relaxed that he was able to continue without fatal consequences his profession of pleader.

Immediately on his return he found himself in demand, and during the next year he gave his attention to the bar, offering his services particularly on behalf of the Equites and *publicani*. For this he had sound reason, to build up his own circle of political support. Some support he could gain from the nobles by taking on their cases, and his defence of Roscius had accomplished much. But there was a limit to their patronage; ready they might be to support such as him for lower office, and maybe for the praetorship; yet Cicero's sanguine ambitions were not to be denied the vision of the consulship; he would remember how Marius, let down by the Metelli, had found assistance from the Equites for his first consulship; he like Marius belonged to their class, and their power and influence were greater now than then; support from them could compensate a second time for indifference or hostility from the noble lords.

Now that he was about to seek his first office from the people, the quaestorship, it was natural that he should nourish good relations with a group so powerful; throughout these years he carefully built for himself all the support he could, both with the nobles, with the Equites and with the country families of Italy, all of them now citizens. He had to construct his framework from the ground, and no material could be ignored; even at this stage he must be prepared for dislike and enmity from certain nobles, to whom his ways, his interest in Greek culture and philosophy marked him as one outside themselves. Soon there will be a contemptuous sneer for one who addressed the assembly of Syracuse in Greek instead of Latin, thus in their eyes demeaning himself by using another language; there will have been other such breaches of good taste and breeding from this brilliant and gifted outsider whose mordant wit could none the less strike deeply at their pride. Anxious he was to join their ranks, but not by fawning and depending on their condescension; he had, and knew he had, talents to contribute; his merits, not his powers of flattery, should gain acceptance for him. His oratory won him friends and supporters at this time; later it would give him influence in the Senate; but he was not yet there, and his oratory was needed to speak the 'open Sesame'.

In 76 he gained the quaestorship, elected by all the tribes, a sign that he had made himself familiar to the electorate and enjoyed their esteem; he had not sought in vain support to attain at least the first rung of the ladder. The quaestorship of Western Sicily fell to him by lot; he made it his concern while there to be honest above suspicion or reproach in all his traffic with the natives, and to treat them as equal at least in human rights; later he described the scrupulous care with which he tried to discharge his office with justice alike to the provincials and the Roman government. His conduct was not a cynical attempt to win the applause of the provincials, though this it certainly achieved; it stemmed from his qualities of character and his high sense of duty towards his office and his charges, such as his understanding of Roman history and in particular of the Scipionic circle and also his study of philosophy had taught him to expect of a good and righteous ruler. Throughout his life he scorned the opportunities that could have been his for enriching himself at the expense of those who were without defence; when most unwillingly he must in 51 govern the province of Cilicia, his self-control and scrupulous honesty where money was concerned made him an exemplary governor, quite different from so many of the noble governors who despised and plundered both provinces and natives.

His conduct so endeared him to the Sicilians that he was honoured when he left as no other official had been, and in a farewell speech at Lilybaeum he promised the Sicilians his aid and patronage should they ever need a sponsor. Four years later they were to claim their pledge and Cicero did not betray them. He also aided several young men on the governor's staff, defending their peccadiloes before the governor, thus winning friends for his future. So did his reputation and his great talents for oratory continue to serve the interests of his career, which lay now for him in politics. For one so circumstanced as he oratory and the ability to defend successfully in court were the most potent instruments he could forge; he had forged them well, and now he used them skilfully. Naturally he wished to have as fine an instrument as genius and diligence could fashion, and to be as adept in its use as skill and practice could assure; oratorical ambition was therefore natural; but his fierce desire to become a statesman now came first; the instrument was but the means to its attainment.

His return to Rome from Sicily was accompanied by a lesson. He had supposed that the reputation he had made for himself in Sicily and the provincials' high regard would have preceded him to Rome and Italy; he returned with a pleasurable anticipation of congratulations to be showered upon him, of conversations in which his honesty, ability and high repute would be admiringly discussed. The truth, alas! he found far different; no one was even faintly interested; no one knew even of his sojourn in Sicily, no one cared how he had conducted himself, no one, it seemed, had missed him while he was away. He came now to realise that to win support he must remain in Rome; 'out of sight, out of mind' was a true maxim at this time, when the nobles' predominance guaranteed to those they blessed the objects of their ambition, while the security they enjoyed from Sulla had dulled them to virtues such as Cicero was parading. It was in Rome itself and not within the empire that the contacts must be made and the influential friends found for his career: and he vowed that he would not a second time absent himself from Rome. This vow he kept; declining a province after both praetorship and consulship, only under the compulsion of exile did he leave Rome for any length of time, until the law in 51 demanded that he take a province.

On his return from Sicily he was a member of the Senate. As a junior member he had little to do but to listen and to learn, to observe its traditions and its methods and, more important, to understand the machinery by which the business of empire was conducted and the methods by which that machinery could be and was manipulated in the interests of cliques and individuals. He would have the opportunity to see with what sense of responsibility these men, to whom Sulla had entrusted the governance of an empire, addressed themselves to their onerous task; and he would come in consequence to realise that reality falls short of the ideal, and that few within the Curia were fired by the lofty notions of their responsibilities that fired his own youthful imagination. He would also come to measure for himself the difficulties that beset a *novus homo* in his relations with the aristocracy; he would feel the insolent disdain with which some of them regarded 'provincials', and the difficulties with which he

33

would have to contend in the prosecution of his career. He would also learn to recognise the cliques which devoted their energies to winning privileged positions for themselves at whatever cost to honesty and justice; and of these *pauci* he will later speak with bitterness.

We know through the accident of an inscription of one Senatorial committee on which he found a place, perhaps owing to his knowledge of the law; there may have been others. But the greater part of his effort during the rest of this decade was given to the law courts, where he continued to build political support by assuming the defence even when the client's innocence was more than doubtful. One such case has a certain interest, that on behalf of Scamander. His client was in spite of Cicero condemned; but one reason for accepting the brief was that his client's patron, a C. Fabricius of Aletrium, together with other notables of that community, asked that he should; and Cicero, in need of as much goodwill as possible, acceded to their request. He was later concerned in a further case in which his client was the man he now attacked. But the main interest of the case lay in its aftermath. L. Quinctius, a tribune of this year 74, supporter of Oppianicus who lay behind Scamander, accused the jury and C. Junius, their president, of receiving bribes to give the verdict which they gave. Junius was found guilty, and the *iudicium Iunianum* became a notorious instance of the corruption of the Sullan courts, where Senators alone were jurymen. It was one, though only one, case such as made the reform of the courts a burning issue in the programme of those whose efforts were directed at this time to overthrow the Sullan constitution and the privileged position of the Senate and the aristocracy, a position they had abused in their own interest and to suppress their political opponents.

But events of greater import for Cicero were hatching. At the close of 72 there came to Rome a Sicilian of Thermae, Sthenius by name, a fugitive from Sicily to avoid a capital prosecution, for which there was no basis or justification, by C. Verres, governor of the province. His community had sent emissaries to Rome on his behalf, and the governor's unjust behaviour was made known in the Senate—and, indeed, outside it. The Senate was deflected from passing any motion against Verres by his father's promise to see that his son did not pursue the prosecution; none the less in December in Sthenius' absence Verres found him guilty and condemned him to death. Feeling in Rome may be gauged by the fact that though the tribunes had recently laid down that persons condemned on a capital charge should not remain at Rome, yet Cicero was able to secure that Sthenius might remain, grave intimation how men felt of behaviour such as Verres'. But before we examine in greater detail this celebrated case, we must consider Pompey and the politics of Rome; for this year 71 was the confluence of several streams whose pace had been accelerating in these ten years, and the case of Verres was strongly affected by their powerful currents.

CHAPTER 3

THE POLITICAL SITUATION
AT ROME IN 71 B.C.

T o understand the political situation at this time we must
consider briefly the reforms of Sulla and their antecedents;
for the counter-revolution of 70 was in essence a return
to the conditions before Sulla's reforms. Sulla had tried to remedy
certain defects, to replace them, as it turned out, by others, and
many at Rome had come to believe that the original defects
were preferable to their substitutes. It was a period in which the
institutions of the city-state were proving inadequate to handle
the complicated problems of government which beset a large
empire; yet so wrapped round with tradition and sentiment
were their institutions that they were loath to admit of them
more than a partial obsolescence or slight inadequacy, which by
small adjustments and reforms could be made to handle the new
situation with perfect competence. No one at Rome, until Caesar
later, contemplated a form of government other than republican,
based on annual magistracies and on assemblies in which every
male citizen had a vote. Such was the Roman republican constitution hallowed by centuries of successful government and
expansion, and such it must remain.

In the second century during the years of conquest and expansion the Senate had been the effective government of Rome,
and on the whole they had discharged their task with responsibility and success. The various organs of the constitution all
continued to function, but the Senate had by differing means
contrived to exercise such control over their activities that only
seldom did they venture to erupt into independence; and on
these rare occasions the Senate had never failed to extinguish the

small flames before a general conflagration took control. They had reached an accommodation with the tribunate, which in earlier times had shown independence, and the Concilium was very seldom presented with a bill which did not have the Senate's blessing. For this the chief reason was the prestige which the Senate enjoyed as the result of her successful conduct of the Hannibalic War; after the initial difficulties with Flaminius and the early disasters, the Senate had been tacitly allowed to have the conduct of the war; and its triumphant conclusion had, as it were, sealed the compact. The following years of the second century had allowed the Senate to guide Rome's destiny during her successful wars of conquest and expansion, which she had likewise handled with resolution and success.

The Senate was in any case the body most suited to the tasks that confronted Roman government. Since it included within its ranks all ex-magistrates, there was assembled inside its walls all the experience at Rome's disposal; ex-praetors, ex-consuls, former governors of provinces and commanders of armies, all were there; whatever problem of military or foreign policy arose, always there were persons present with personal experience of the area and its difficulties, whose counsel was at their disposal; nowhere else in Rome was this experienced wisdom to be found collected. And although the Senate was in theory only a consultative and advisory body, its true position was far different. For since the chief officers of state were annual magistrates, they could not in their year acquire the confidence and the experience to take decisions on important policy without consulting those whose experience and knowledge were greater than theirs; and in the close-built society of the upper classes, who provided the senior officers, they were unlikely to want to act independently of a body composed of their own class and connexions; the Senate's advice therefore developed rather into instructions, which the magistrates normally had no wish to ignore or disobey. The tribunes might, indeed, ignore them; they had the right to introduce bills to the Concilium, which if accepted had the force of law. But during the first fifty years of the second century they showed little inclination to independence; provided that the Senate could persuade but one of the ten to act on their behalf, his veto on his colleagues could secure their interests; and during these years there was little open friction between the two groups.

The wars of the second century had, however, brought about a social and economic revolution. For Rome's permanent need of armies both to defend her provinces and against external foes imposed a burden on those eligible to serve, which over the years had robbed the countryside of countless peasants and added them to the city crowds; the framework of Italian society was thus in danger of corrosion; while with the disappearance of the peasant went also a potential soldier. The climax and solution on the military side we have seen Marius deal with, and the social and political consequences of that solution. The whole complex of problems brought about by this slow revolution required a great effort of statesmanship, if a remedy was to be applied. For Roman society was facing a crisis different from those which had hitherto defied and perplexed their ingenuity; it was not with the genius of Hannibal they had to contend, but with a slow but profound change in the basis and structure of their society, and its solution must depend on the clarity and depth of their understanding of the problem, and the sort of society at whose creation they aimed. It was on this second point that the Senate was likely to find itself in conflict with other groups; for its members would naturally wish to perpetuate the state of society in which they enjoyed the chief political and economic power; they would be conservative, even though the policies for which they were responsible had been the great cause of the present troubles and discontents.

The need for some measures of reform was apparent when the Gracchi intervened. The elder Gracchus, though he had noble support, had also opposition; the limitations of the annual magistracy became here apparent. For since he had but one year to bring about the social reforms he had in mind, he could not afford to brook opposition; nor could he rely on some successor to carry on his unfinished work; continuity lay only in the Senate, and the majority were at the moment opposed to him; he must therefore himself within one year bring about his reforms or fail absolutely. When, then, he first encountered opposition, he took his bills direct before the people, and after deposing a vetoing colleague successfully made his measures law. While we may sympathise with his sincerity of purpose, his impetuosity must be censured; for though his action was constitutional, it was out of date; whatever its merits in the past, it was dangerous and irresponsible in the circumstances of a Rome possessed of empire, and the Mediterranean's greatest power. By this independent legislation he had shown that men need not in future accept the Senate's government, that its policy could be challenged whenever it failed to find favour with a particular group; there would always be the possibility of two separate sources of government, the Senate, and a tribune working through the Concilium.

His brother Caius, faced with his brother's problems and his murder, used the tribunate deliberately to work in defiance of the Senate. The limit of time was overcome by re-election to the office; he thus emerged for two years as the centre of government at Rome, almost its prime minister, and showed during these two years the utter powerlessness of the Senate in the face of a determined tribune with a policy to implement. His hostility to the nobles he showed by deliberately bringing the Equites into importance in the life and government of Rome, which, however desirable it might have been, done in this atmosphere of animosity, could only breed antagonism and hate. Caius' example was disastrous; his brother's conduct had now become a precedent; the tribunate used thus was a sharp and fatal weapon with which to oppose the Senate, whenever it might suit some group to do so. The unity of government was thus destroyed, not by the substitution of some broader form, but by the resuscitation of a second, independent form to work, if need be, in opposition to the Senate. Whatever might be the Senate's shortcomings, it represented the most responsible body for the conduct of government; a gathering of the people in the Concilium, led by a tribune, possibly young and possibly irresponsible, was hardly a proper substitute for deciding important matters of state.

Yet this is what happened; the Gracchi had shown how to oppose the Senate, and their precedent stood unchallenged and unchallengeable. By the last decade of the century the opportunity arose to challenge once again the Senate, this time on matters of foreign and military policy. The demands of military service at a time of great strain to the state created discontent among those whose services were constantly in requisition; military disasters made the need more acute and brought into disfavour the Senatorial generals; it was an atmosphere in which opposition to the Senate bred fast, and the Gracchan method lay open to those who wished to change the course of policy. Their opponents, the Equites, having gone far to force the Jugurthan War upon a reluctant Senate for their own commercial purposes, then attacked the generals and their dispositions, when to the African war were added the disasters in Northern Italy, and forced their own candidate, Marius, into the command. Marius owed all to his non-Senatorial supporters from this stage on, and depended for the expression of that support on tribunes to pass the requisite legislation. Then came the crisis of 88, when once again a tribune, P. Sulpicius Rufus, assumed the mantle of statesmanship and, to achieve his object of enrolling fairly the new citizens created by the Social War, gained Marius' support by having the command transferred to him against Mithridates, given by Senate and lot to the consul, Sulla. Civil war had followed, and after an uneasy lull had broken out again on Sulla's return from Asia. Sulla after defeating and cruelly persecuting his enemies proceeded then to reform the constitution.

The problem was simple, though its solution might well baffle even Solomon's ingenuity. It was clear that unity of government must somehow be restored; the proper administration of the empire was impossible, if any decision of the Senate could be overturned in the Concilium. If the Republican form of government was to be maintained, it was scarcely possible to repose control elsewhere than in the Senate, which, whatever its failings and inadequacies, yet represented the only reservoir of wisdom and experience in Rome; so long as annual magistracies provided the administrative and executive officers of government, there must be behind them some body to provide that continuity of policy so essential to the governance of an empire. The only alternative was government by a man or men holding power for an extended period; no possible solution yet, since this were a denial of the Republic, itself the offspring of revolution against regal tyranny.

The Senate was therefore the only body to which it seemed possible to turn, the body to which Sulla would in any case be disposed to turn, since it was they who had supported him for the consulship and given him the Mithridatic command. Effective control of government by the Senate required the suppression of the legislative independence of the tribunes, and this must be Sulla's main task, perhaps a not distasteful task in view of what he had suffered at Sulpicius' hands. The main purport, then, of his constitutional reforms consisted in giving the Senate by law what it had enjoyed by precedent before 133; no bill might be submitted to the people without the Senate's approval; they were given effective control of magistrates and pro-magistrates, controlled military and foreign policy, and should thus be able to prevent the use of force against themselves such as had been employed in this last decade. Tribunes might not submit a bill to the Concilium without the Senate's previous sanction; and to reduce yet further the office's attraction, it was ordained that one who had been tribune might seek no other magistracy. The Equites also lost their right to man the juries; this became again the prerogative of Senators.

In theory there was much to commend in this solution; it placed the responsibility of government in the hands of those who should have been best able and equipped to carry it; by strangling tribunician initiative he silenced the one office responsible in the recent past for independent and opposed action; unified and responsible government was possible once again. But it was not to be; the nobles had been increasingly harried, criticised and obstructed since the Gracchi had shown the way; with their position had gone privilege; for fifty years with increasing acceleration the attacks had come, and they had turned to the defensive; for since their position had depended on custom, not the constitution, they had no weapon with which to parry the attack. The broader view of statesmanship gave way to the meaner, narrower glance of the politician; problems began to be seen in the light of their own interest rather than of the Republic's need; political opponents became enemies almost as deadly as the barbarian on the frontier. It could not be otherwise; when groups within a state become so antagonised in their struggle for control of government, the fight consumes too much of their effort to leave sufficient over for the problems of statesmanship which throng in on them; they are neglected, or turned to political advantage.

And when this bitterness had boiled over into civil war, the passions and the enmity had grown more bitter still; Marius' murders and Sulla's proscription left little chance for the balm of any amnesty to work a soothing influence. The Senate had through Sulla finally won, and Sulla had given them that complete control which they had sought but never had. Their opponents lay helpless; but such a situation, the result of victory on the field of war, consummated by a dictator's will, could not be the setting for a fresh harmonious start. The defeated did not concede the justice of their enemies' claims because the arbitrament of arms had decided against them; nor did they accept the rightness of Sulla's solution because a dictator had decreed it: they must accept without choice their present humiliation, while ever on the watch for a chance to recover what they had once enjoyed. One cannot in human affairs put back the clock; men who had exercised power and influence would acquiesce in its loss only while they had no choice; they could not for ever be content to stand aside in favour of the order that had been the object of all their attacks. The Equites wanted back their control of the jury courts, and they were still by reason of their wealth not without power. Ambitious men and men opposed to noble privilege, frustrated for the moment, would not be content to waste their lives in impotence or deference to the Senate; like the Equites they would remember what had been and scheme its restoration.

To assume in such circumstances the sole control of government would be a difficult task that called for qualities of statesmanship and generosity; the governors must assuage hatred and suspicion by a large-minded effort to co-operate with those who had been their enemies; for amongst them would be found a wealth of talent, whose services Rome could ill afford to lose; and there was but one alternative to unity: disunity and the perpetuation of the strife that had already nearly ruined the Republic. But the nobles had not those qualities of heart and mind so needful to the present crisis; after fifty years of hostile attack and criticism, they had all been brought up amid the acrid fumes of political con-troversy, taught to measure a proposal by its likely influence on their own position; the touchstone had been the interest of their group. It was expecting much that they should now shed all their past experience, and any such expectation was quickly disappointed. Possessed now of power and security they settled down to enjoy the fruits of their position, determined to deny their opponents the opportunity to hurt them. They behaved with a narrowness understandable perhaps, but none the less deplorable and disastrous. Some few there were with broader views; but they were swamped by the greater numbers of those determined to enjoy what Sulla had given them.

Troubles were not slow to appear; immediately after Sulla's death there was an attempt to overthrow his constitution, which with the aid of Pompey was suppressed. Then Sertorius, a Marian holding Spain, had to be subdued, a difficult and lengthy business, also accomplished only with the aid of Pompey. Attacks on the constitution were not slow to appear; the Senate's opponents, stripped of all power to act, quickly began an agitation for the restoration of the tribunes' powers. The Senate was safe as long as it was united; it might have been able to afford resistance, had the general tenor of their conduct found favour with most citizens. But it did not; recking little of their responsibilities, they kept from important tasks those who did not agree and would not accommodate themselves to the new situation; when the Mithridatic war broke out again, it was Lucullus, a good Senatorian and, as it happened, a good general, to whom the command was given; no chance now for the Populares to hand it to some other, as they had done in 106 and tried to do in 88. There was bitterness and restlessness, but as yet no means to act. In 75 the consul C. Aurelius Cotta sponsored a law to open higher offices to ex-tribunes; not in itself disastrous, it was a sign somewhat larger than a man's hand, when a consular noble conceded even this, and could persuade the Senate to concur in such a move.

Their irresponsibility was to be seen in the jury courts; for they now controlled the court before which peccant governors were tried; they therefore had the power to control injustice and impropriety in the provinces or to condone it. The provinces had suffered under the system instituted by C. Gracchus, who gave the courts to the Equites; justice abroad could be a dangerous commodity if it thwarted profits; and most governors had reached an accommodation with the equestrian interests of their province rather than risk political destruction on their return. This danger was now removed; but now the governors felt free to frolic at the expense of justice, assured of tender consideration from their peers if they were prosecuted. The Senatorial jurymen had shown a favouritism which did themselves no credit and the provinces much harm. On other juries they had shown themselves too easily swayed by bribes; in 74, as we have seen, the *iudicium Iunianum* had become a proverb. Q. Catulus had remarked this very year that the judicial corruption had provoked the agitation to restore the tribunes' rights, since in no other way could injustice be redressed; the only hope for victims of the courts must lie in an independent magistracy, that would either end the judicial monopoly or penalise corruption.

By 70 the Senatorial order was deeply unpopular with all classes at Rome, and Rome was unpopular in the provinces through the mischievous behaviour of this same order. The hatred which their behaviour had provoked, the injustices which the provinces had perforce endured, in these ten years, are mentioned frequently by Cicero in his Verrine speeches; and in the political situation then obtaining we may accept the truth of what he says. Everything had gone wrong; as it turned out, it was not to statesmen that Sulla had given control, but to one of two contesting parties who had used the time and opportunity to enjoy their luck. For ten years had they thus junketed; but now the reckoning was at hand; for the discontented sections and the outraged provinces had found an advocate with the power and prestige to confront the Senate, Pompey; and to him we must now turn.

CHAPTER 4

THE RISE OF POMPEY AND MILITARY POWER

OMPEY was an exact contemporary of Cicero, born in 106. His family had not been distinguished in the public life of Rome; one branch had provided the family's first consul in 146; Pompey's branch first attained this office with his father's consulship in 80, when Pompey was in his seventeenth year. This was the time of the Social War and the troubles precipitated by Sulpicius, Sulla and Marius; Pompeius Strabo, the father, a not unsuccessful general during the Social War, in the civil war played a dubious and double-edged game in his own interest. When his kinsman, Q. Pompeius Rufus, appeared to take over his army, to which he had been appointed, he allowed, if he did not positively encourage, a seditious attitude among the troops, which led to Rufus' murder; Strabo, quietly resuming the command, made no attempt to punish those responsible. In the following year he refused to give what help was in his power to prevent Cinna's forcible capture of Rome, retiring then with his army to Picenum to watch events, accompanied by his son; there he remained, a threat to both sides. Cinna schemed to procure his murder, to be foiled by the young Pompey; the next year illness brought about his death. The hatred of the people for him broke out at his funeral; only with difficulty were they prevented from snatching the body from its bier.

Pompey had been with his father since 89, and though his father's behaviour might provoke disgust, his soldier's skill was not in doubt; Pompey learnt much from him of military art, destined to prove its worth in the years to come; he succeeded also to the family's considerable estates in Picenum and to his father's great influence in that area and in Cisalpine Gaul. He first retired to Picenum; later he visited the camp of Cinna with the idea, we may presume, of joining him, but nothing emerged and Cinna was soon afterwards murdered. Pompey now resolved to support Sulla, who was on the point of returning, and in order to have something more substantial than himself to offer, set to collecting an army. This was quite unconstitutional behaviour, a bold step for one of twenty-two to take; for if defeated before Sulla's return he would be a ruined man, possibly even put to death. But he was a skilful and resourceful soldier, and having brilliantly defeated and escaped from the clutches of the armies sent against him, was able to join Sulla at the head of a well-trained, well-equipped and high-spirited army of three legions. Sulla saluted him as Imperator, thus giving his blessing to Pompey's illegal conduct.

Success after much bloodshed was Sulla's in Italy; he then sent Pompey to Sicily, whither Perperna and others of his enemies had fled. Sicily was won almost without a fight; and though Pompey's treatment of Carbo roused a widespread resentment, his behaviour towards the provincials revealed a quality of character seen throughout his life, considerate kindliness towards them and a refusal to enrich himself at their expense. He acquired in consequence great influence in the island, destined to prove of value later on. Thence he was sent to Africa, where Cn. Domitius Aenobarbus had rallied the Marian forces in an area by tradition friendly to the Marian cause; here too he defeated Sulla's enemies. He was now himself a powerful man, a victorious general with an army of six devoted legions; neither Sulla nor the Senate was anxious to see his return at the head of such an army in the in-flamed conditions of Italy; it could be dangerous for the recently devised constitution, which was already not without its enemies, for Italy, where Sulla's brutal treatment of his foes and opponents had created such a wealth of hatred and resentment, and for Sulla himself, who might suspect a challenge from this young, suc-cessful and popular general. He was ordered therefore to discharge five of his legions, while he himself with the remaining legion awaited in Africa a successor to be dispatched. The object was clear, to separate Pompey from his army, to bring both him and his army back to Italy in a way innocuous to Sulla and his government.

Sulla's concern was not perhaps without justification; Pompey's popularity and prestige stood high, his influence in Italy, Cisalpine Gaul and Sicily was great; such a man with such an army might have it in his power to dictate his terms of accommodation or even, perhaps, to overthrow the government; Pompey was youthfully ambitious, his attitude towards the constitution still unknown. The legions named for discharge quickly showed displeasure at the fate the government had decreed; protesting to Pompey that they had no wish for discharge but preferred to remain in his service, they encouraged him to disobey the harsh injunction and to return to Italy with all his army. This was exactly what Pompey's own ambitious spirit urged; after such splendid achievements won by courage and resource, why must he now become a mere *privatus* dependent on Sulla's kindness? Protesting therefore to the army the necessity for obedience he was careful not to succeed with his entreaties to their spirit of discipline; when he chose he could command his men; on this occasion he did not choose to, preferring to be compelled by their obduracy to do what he wished to do, return to Rome at the head of his army.

On his return he was greeted personally by Sulla and addressed as 'Magnus'; for such prudence cost nothing. Pompey then asked for a triumph, which Sulla was reluctant to allow, but once again thought well to be persuaded, since Pompey's army was intact. Sulla had thus twice ignored his own constitution in the interests of his young supporter. For Sulla had laid down with care and firmness the limits of a provincial governor's rights with his army; in a determined effort to prevent a repetition of his own behaviour, which had overthrown the government, he had forbidden a governor to move his army outside the frontiers of his province. Thus was a general prevented from returning to Rome at the head of his army, and if in future a special army was needed for any purpose, the general, who would have been given the 'provincia' in which the war was to be fought, would be required to discharge the army before returning to Rome. His orders to Pompey in Africa reflected these new arrangements; and they were disobeyed the first time they were invoked.

Secondly, Pompey was not according to the law qualified to triumph; he had held no magistracy, even though a senatorial vote had regularised his command in Africa; but not only was it unknown for a man who had held neither consulship nor praetorship to celebrate a triumph, but precedent was positively opposed to it. Now that Sulla had laid strictly down the *cursus honorum*, the rights and limitations of the magistrates, with the fixed aim of preventing adventurers and opponents of the régime from exerting improper pressure, here was his own lieutenant demanding the flagrant violation of his own arrangements, and he was supported by an army. Sulla allowed him his triumph, but not through love.

Pompey's courage and abilities had thus by his twenty-sixth year won him a place and reputation pre-eminent in the state; he had risked life and future by illegally raising an army on Sulla's behalf, his ability had won Sulla's approbation and further responsibilities; he had then successfully insisted on the honour of a triumph, though aware that neither the constitution allowed it nor Sulla wished it. It was natural that from such a beginning he should expect somehow to continue to be a public figure, ever before the public gaze, ever loved and admired, and that somehow the constitution should always adapt itself to his exceptional needs. For it was unthinkable that a former commander of armies and a *triumphator* should now bend to the humiliating task of suing for the lowest office in order to work up to the consulship; what was reasonable and proper for other young men had become an insult to Pompeius Magnus. Yet if Pompey felt thus about himself, it was not impatience with a constitution which required this of all men; it was his constant expectation that men would always make the exception in his favour. He was a loyal servant and protector of the constitution; he nourished no schemes for subversion nor had he the mind or the temperament to plan major changes to improve its inadequacies and imperfections; his somewhat unpolitical mind was on the whole well satisfied with things as they were. He wanted to be well liked and to be appreciated; he hoped that Senate and people would offer him positions in conformity with his dignity, and not humiliate him. He wanted to be regarded as the leading man in Rome, on whose behalf he was prepared to shoulder whatever burdens they might impose; and he wanted them to choose his rather than anyone else's shoulders for the burden; thus would he be the leading citizen within the Republic whose constitution he was ready to defend. Pompey never had revolutionary ideas; all he wanted was a position of primacy such as the younger Scipio had enjoyed, a position based on his achievements and the *auctoritas* which belonged to any important figure.

A certain vanity there was in him, particularly at this time; but there were not in him that ruthless determination and that penetrating insight into the needs of his case which are so remarkable in Caesar. Pompey had not in 80 a clear plan for his future and a firm determination to pursue it at all costs; he had, rather, a somewhat undefined picture of himself as an important person called upon to do important things and in consequence increasing his reputation and his influence; and always he hoped that the invitation would come from the state; he was never prepared to ask for, much less to demand, what he hoped for. Caesar by contrast knew what he wanted, and took it if it was not given. The contrast between the two was to be seen most clearly in 60; both were thwarted by the Senate; but it was Caesar who organised the Triumvirate; it was Caesar who passed his legislation in spite of the Senate and with the use of force; while Pompey stood by, an embarrassed colleague, dependent on Caesar to right the wrongs the Senate had inflicted on him.

Sulla became displeased with him; he had extorted his triumph, referred to himself as Rome's rising sun, and had in 79 supported for the consulship for 78 a man named Lepidus, whose loyalty to the new order Sulla had suspected. Sulla's suspicions were confirmed; Lepidus was soon involved with discontented elements in an attempt to seize Rome and overthrow the constitution. In this crisis the Senate, in need of a commander in whose competence it could feel confidence, turned to Pompey. Lepidus was quickly dealt with, but Pompey, having further ambitions, would not demobilise his army, as Catulus, his proconsul, ordered. This was tantamount to a threat, since the right to discharge lay with Catulus, his commander, and Pompey had no independence in the matter. He chose to regard the army as his own, and the army seems to have accepted him as their commander, hoping, no doubt, that he would find some profitable occupation for them in preference to discharge; but if they needed him, he needed them. The war against Sertorius was being waged in Spain under the command of Q. Metellus, without great success; Pompey coveted the chance to display his military skill to his own greater glory and the safety of the realm; but since Metellus was already there, and since Pompey was still without office, there was neither reason nor justification for sending him on the only terms that would meet with his approval, namely, equality of rank with Metellus. But his army in Rome's vicinity was an eloquent advocate of his cause; the Senate was persuaded to give him proconsular *imperium* and an army with which to join Metellus. Thus and thus alone, they mused, could they be rid of their embarrassment of Pompey's army at the gates of Rome; the future must take care of itself. Pompey betook himself to Spain, where he remained for the next six years, to discover among other things that military skill and strategy were not his accomplishments alone.

He was fully engaged in Spain until 71, his task made difficult by the genius of Sertorius and by the lack of support from Rome, where his behaviour had made him unpopular with the Senate.

It was not until Lucullus, desperate to be appointed to the command against Mithridates and fearful lest, if Pompey should carry out his threat to return to Italy, he would then be given this command, persuaded the Senate to send him men and money, that Pompey commanded adequate resources for his purpose; even so it was treachery among Sertorius' followers that procured his murder and enabled Pompey to end the war. On his return to Italy in 71 he was fortunate enough to encounter the remnants of the army with which Spartacus had terrified Italy since 73 until his defeat by Crassus, and was able to add the boast of having stamped out that war too.

L. Licinius Crassus is himself an important figure. He had, like Pompey, supported Sulla in the civil war, and had shown a military competence which made him suppose that he was a great general. The wealthiest man in Rome, he owed no small part of his wealth to the opportunities he took to buy the property of the proscribed at absurdly low prices. He was also an able though undistinguished advocate, ready to lend his services to those whose services he might in turn require; and by these means, his money and his advocacy, he had acquired considerable political influence among Senators, both young and old. His widespread interests in the world of business brought him into close contact with the powerful Equestrian class, whose spokesman and champion in the Senate he became. Of his two great loves, money and political power and fame, he was ready to be prodigal of the first in quest of the second. An older man than Pompey, he had looked with jealousy at Pompey's quick rise to fame and power, feeling that though his contribution to Sulla's cause had been no less than Pompey's, it had failed to find a corresponding reward; and the animosity between the two was consequently great. Pompey had then been used by the Senate against Lepidus and had then been joined in the command against Sertorius, while Crassus could only look on with impotent rage at this further advancement of the man on whom fortune seemed so frequently to smile. The rising of Spartacus gave him his chance; consular armies had been destroyed by that able gladiator, Italy was in a state of fearful emergency; Crassus had been praetor probably in 73 and volunteered to command against the enemy. He was given substantial forces and he chose his lieutenants wisely; their combined ability was successful in cornering and defeating Spartacus in 71. Speed had been necessary at the end; for Pompey's friends, knowing that his task in Spain was completed, had already contrived that Pompey should be summoned against this dangerous enemy, thus implying Crassus' inadequacy to the task. He was thus fixed in his resolve to anticipate Pompey's return, and he did; but Fortune once again favoured Pompey by allowing him to encounter the shattered remnant of Spartacus' defeated army; and Pompey, vexed that he was too late to add this victory to his laurels, boasted untruly of being the true conqueror.

Pompey and Crassus now met; both had an army, and each looked with suspicion on the other. Pompey after his sojourn in Spain saw no alternative to private life, unless he could seek a magistracy; in view of his extraordinary career and his recent Spanish command as proconsul the only magistracy which it befitted his dignity to seek was the consulship. For this office he was by the laws ineligible; he had not yet reached the age prescribed for holding it, nor had he held any of the junior magistracies which should precede it. But he was now thirty-six years old, and for seven years had commanded an army of a size proper only to men of consular *imperium*; it could hardly now be expected that he should humbly agree to start at the beginning of the *cursus honorum* and patiently work his way to the consulship; nor was his pride and self-esteem such as to commend such a course. He wished in this, as in everything, to be allowed to behave unconstitutionally without damaging the constitution; he was to be the exception, but the only exception. He wished his career to continue along the unique path on which he had ventured in 83, and he wished the exception to be made readily in token of Rome's love and respect for him; he would not extort from them the gift, for that would destroy its value; but he would be chagrined, should it not be offered.

Crassus, too, wanted the consulship, both because it was included in his ambitions, and because a consulship for Pompey would be intolerable, were it not accompanied by one for himself. They could not afford to quarrel on this issue, since each was in a position to impede the other, and this could only advantage the state. They approached Rome, therefore, careful not to disband their armies, Pompey on the pretext that he hoped for a triumph, Crassus because he did not want to be at a disadvantage.

The Senate, once again persuaded by the force of armed argument, quickly suspended the constitution in favour of Pompey's candidature, and granted him a triumph. But it could not look with favour or pleasure on his candidature; his whole career gave them sufficient cause for apprehension as to what further piece of unconstitutionality he might expect them to bless on his behalf; he had used his army in 77 to extort the command against Sertorius, and had threatened them when they were not forward in supplying reinforcements; he had now by similar tactics extracted a benison on his ambition to become consul and to enjoy a triumph, though they had wanted to grant merely a *supplicatio*; it was certain that this young man, who was not even a Senator, and seemed determined not to play according to Senatorial rules, was a possible danger; their sense of safety would urge them to oppose his candidature to the best of their ability, and they could contrive to exercise a fairly strict control upon the elections. Pompey must therefore win votes in their despite by some tempting offer.

Now it was that the sins of the last decade came home to roost; the Senate was deeply unpopular, its behaviour had been highhanded, and opposition had been impossible. Since the senior magistracies were almost entirely in their hands, opposition could come only from the tribunes, whose initiative Sulla had taken from them. The restoration of their powers had been an object of determined effort ever since; having lost their ban on higher office, the demand for their right to legislate had become more clamantly insistent as the Senate's behaviour gave ever greater offence. Pompey seized the chance to strengthen his prospects, and let it be known that, were he elected consul, he would see to the restoration of the tribunes' powers. Thus at a blow did Pompey enhance his standing with the people and his unpopularity with the nobles; and he was able to recommend Crassus to the people as a desirable colleague for himself, a step that must have been as humiliating as it was necessary to Crassus. They were elected consuls for 70.

Pompey certainly liked to be liked; he also liked efficiency in government and justice and fairness to the provincials. It was not, therefore, merely to consolidate his popularity that he asked the tribune, M. Lollius Palicanus, in early December 71 to summon the people to hear an address by him, in which he repeated his intention of restoring the tribunes' powers, and added that the provinces had been harried and plundered in recent years, that he intended to give his mind to the problem, and also to the notoriously disgraceful condition of the law courts. He realised the close connexion between the two problems, and that the answer to both could only be the radical reform of the Sullan system whereby Senators alone provided the jurymen. Such a reform would be popular with all but the Senate, and there had been a persistent demand for it in the previous years, as injustice followed injustice in the decisions given; but Pompey was now not seeking popularity so much as following the dictates of his own code of behaviour. His conduct in Sicily and Africa had been marked by consideration for the provincials; his broader, more statesmanlike outlook regarded the provincials as worthy to be treated with dignity and respect, not as inferior persons conquered by Roman superiority and now rightly exploited in the interests of Rome. Such a reform might have been expected from Pompey under any circumstances, but the hostility of the nobles made his task easier and perhaps more pleasant; easier because, had they supported him, it would have been embarrassing to seem to turn against his friends; perhaps more pleasant, because he could, in the process of doing what he believed to be right, make clear to those who had sought to frustrate his wishes that he was not dependent on them and had the power to hurt; he might win their respect, if not their love.

Before we return to the prosecution of Verres, it will be convenient here to consider the importance and implications of the army in the first century. We have already seen Sulla's use of his army, and the degree to which Pompey's career was made possible by the presence of his army at critical moments; the key importance of the army must be understood if the true nature of the crisis is to be rightly evaluated; it had brought Pompey to the consulship; it was destined to bring the Republic to its untimely end.

Armies had, as we have seen, become professional, with consequences both good and bad for Rome. On the one hand it became easier to maintain permanent armies in those frontier provinces where they were needed for garrison duties on the frontiers and for police work in the interior; during the first century there were approximately fourteen legions so disposed throughout the empire, composed of men serving generally for sixteen years; as they became due for discharge, this was normally effected in the province of their service, where undoubtedly many of them would choose to settle, since it was there that their friends—and often families—were, and where the scenes and places were now more familiar to them than Italy. Some, however, would return to Italy, still of an age to serve again, seasoned soldiers who would form the essential backbone of an army raised to deal with an emergency.

For these fourteen legions, strung thinly all the way from Spain to Cilicia and Syria, were obviously inadequate to deal with any but the normal police work for which they existed; a major war, such as that launched by Mithridates, would require far greater forces than Asia and the neighbouring provinces could muster; in such an eventuality Rome would raise a special army, for which, once the crisis was past, there was no further use. Their practice during the first century was, therefore, very close to our own, to maintain a comparatively small professional army, and to raise additional forces in time of war, to serve 'for the duration'. For this second type of army as large a nucleus as possible of experienced soldiers was needed; there was not time, once the war had begun, to bring raw recruits to battleworthiness, if the whole legion were to be composed of such; provided that such a legion contained a reasonable number of seasoned men to provide stiffening and experience, such a legion could hope to take the field quite quickly. There was therefore a possible opening for those discharged men from the standing armies who returned to Italy; and during the first century there were many occasions for their service. To the men the opportunity to serve in such an army was generally agreeable; for in the nature of the case service would be only for a comparatively short time, the duration of the war, and the chances of acquiring booty were great; while, as we shall see, it had become a regular practice to provide such men on demobilisation with a piece of land. This was an added inducement to service, but since such a grant required the passage of a law, it could involve politics and a champion in Rome prepared to sponsor the bill; and it was at this point particularly that the emergency army became a menace to constitutional government.

Marius and his supporters had promised those who volunteered a piece of land on their discharge, and the promise had represented in a sense a chance for rehabilitation on the land whence they had been dispossessed; as such it was at least a partial solution to the problem which confronted the state, which the Gracchi had attempted in a not dissimilar way to resolve. When Sulla on his return from Asia with his victorious army had defeated his enemies in Italy, he had to demobilise his by now very large army, to which he owed his success and his present position; he could not afford to antagonise them; they had supported him against the government, and they expected some reward for their loyal support. Sulla therefore settled them in colonies on land confiscated from his defeated enemies and from the victims of the proscription; it cost him little, but it served to establish the Marian precedent as a custom to be followed in the future. Emergency armies now expected on their demobilisation a piece of land; this would require that the general himself or some politician in his interest should promote the necessary legislation; and this in its turn would serve to draw the army close to the general after the war; for they not unnaturally looked to their leader to protect their interests after the war, since there was no one else to whom they could turn.

This dependence of the army upon the general was by no means unwelcome to him. For in the circumstances of first-century Rome a discharged army settled on land procured by the general represented for the general so many large groups of supporters, whether in Italy or in one of the provinces; if in Italy, men ready to support him in politics, and to serve as a recruiting ground if he should again need an army; in the provinces creating a large area devoted to his and his family's interests. As a large group of soldiers, whether discharged or not, they could represent on their return a very powerful element in Rome and Roman politics, which could exercise a considerable influence on elections and legislation by their mere presence. For this reason Sulla, it seems, concerned for the maintenance of his constitution, and knowing from his own example that no constitution was safe from the attack of a general with his army, forbade armies to be brought back to Italy except at the behest of the Senate; thus he hoped to foil any second would-be dictator.

But the power which the command of such an army conferred upon the general was too great to escape temptation. The reputation which the successful conclusion of the war conferred was equalled by the wealth he acquired from booty and the political influence he won from having so many thousands of devoted supporters, ready to help him even, if necessary, with their arms. The commander was a powerful person, and only his sense of loyalty to the state could prevent him from making nugatory Sulla's attempted defence of the constitution by requiring the discharge of the army to be effected outside Italy; for if a general chose to bring his army to Italy, and could rely on his soldiers to support him—and the great generals could—then the Senate was powerless to prevent him; they could only in such a crisis raise a second army or submit without a fight. It was an ever-present danger, which finally materialised in 49.

War and the pursuit of the military life are, except in early societies, professional occupations; with few exceptions, the brilliant amateur cannot compete with the able, certainly not with the brilliant, professional; and Rome's armies were very efficient fighting forces. The soldiers had become professional; so also, as we have seen, had the officers. The army was, in fact, a professional army, though it continued to remain in theory until the time of Augustus on a militia basis; and its commanders were men of praetorian or consular standing, that is, men who had reached the highest stages of the *cursus honorum*. Yet they might have reached these offices with but a smattering of military service and experience; a year or two as *contubernalis* and tribune, a further year or two as quaestor possibly in a province, might represent the ex-praetor's total experience of army life; as commander of a provincial army he must in that case depend heavily on his experienced officers; and he was generally careful to include such men on his staff as *legati*. But such a man, while he might, with the help of able officers, be competent to handle the largely administrative affairs of a provincial army, could not handle with success the sort of war which called an emergency army into being; the commander of such an army, since he would be involved in active war on a large scale, must be a man of military experience and proven ability; and herein lay the crux of the Senate's difficulty.

For with the increasing professionalism of the army the noble families had become ever more reluctant to give more time than they could help to the pursuit of arms, possibly because it seemed no longer necessary, since the army was becoming so professional; probably the increasing professionalism of the officer class made the service less attractive to the scions of the nobles; for instead of meeting only members of their own class in the mess, with interests similar to their own, with a body of mutual acquaintances and, possibly, connexions, they would now meet middle-class professional officers of country origin, better soldiers but less polished gentlemen; and this circumstance may have contributed towards the growing unpopularity of army service among this class, which had in the second century provided almost all the officers, and hence prevented any dangerous schism between army and Senate. Most members of the governing class still regarded the offices of the *cursus honorum* as the important objects of their ambition, and the consulship or the praetorship as its summit; they believed that political power still rested with the Senate, and within the Senate with its senior members; they failed to see that the professionalism of the army and the divorce of its officers from their own class had opened up the possibility of effective opposition to them, and that the social and political circumstances of the first century had converted that possibility into a certainty, unless they abandoned their exclusive attitude and policies; and furthermore, that even if they acted with prudence and broadmindedness, the considerable Italian element might by irresponsible behaviour and their lack of loyalty to Rome still produce most undesirable consequences, unless they could control the army.

But they remained confident that they could, if necessary, thwart the opposition of an army by political means, and that if recourse must be had to arms, they would be able to find an army and a general to carry out the task. In a less disturbed and tumultuous period they would probably have been successful; but it was part of their failure that they did not comprehend the complexity of the problems which the social, economic and political revolutions had raised and which insisted on solution; they therefore continued to fight for office and for province, leaving the army largely to others. A small number, however, there were, who realised the importance of military ability and experience, and of deliberate purpose gave several years to learning how to control and to use an army with success in the field; in consequence they became the men of real importance and the arbiters of Rome's destiny. Pompey, Caesar and Lucullus are examples; but Lucullus ultimately failed, because his aristocratic outlook prevented him from understanding or sympathising with the new, democratic army, and in the end the army rejected Lucullus in favour of Pompey.

If a sudden emergency arose in or out of Italy—and several such did arise—the Senate was apt to find no one within its ranks to whom it could entrust the task; more than once it turned unwillingly to Pompey to handle a crisis which was beyond the abilities of its own members; and on each occasion Pompey caused them anxiety lest he should use the army against the Senate. In 71 he used its threat, in 62 he hoped to gain his ends unaided by his army; too late he learnt his error, and Caesar marked the lesson. A part, therefore, of the weakness of Cicero's political ideas lay in his supposition that the only problem was the political one, and that if only the Senate could be induced to work in harmony with the Equites and the solid core of Italy, the foundations of the state would be firmly laid and indestructible; the fact that one blast from a general with an army would lay it flat was, in these earlier days, hidden from him; for he, like so many of the class he longed to belong to, despised military service and was almost without experience in the field.

Few among the Senatorial class gave their mind to the many problems which surrounded and finally engulfed them; the few that did were hardly aware of the drastic nature of the solution which alone seemed able to comprehend within itself the solution of all the separate problems. Cicero, in his earlier days like them, also failed; his country equestrian origin, his somewhat idealistic picture of Rome and the Senate, his ambition to be one of Rome's great men in terms of this early picture, all conspired to veil the truth from his eyes. He gave much of his life to the impossible task of making Rome fit for Scipio, and in this foredoomed labour he naturally looked backward, seeking by what means he could restore the earlier harmony. To him the ills of the present were explicable as diseases which, if they could be cured, would restore the body politic in all its former greatness; he should more properly have seen them as symptoms of a fatal cancer which it was beyond any remedy but that of cauterisation to cure. There is, therefore, a certain pathos in watching Cicero grapple, as he supposed, with the fatal disease, urging the application of remedies which presupposed for their efficacy precisely the basic health which was lacking, and seemingly unaware of the intractable problems which should have been the object of his concern; a shrewd and able political observer and actor, but without the depth of vision and understanding of society and its ills requisite in a statesman who was so to grapple with the problem that the spirit of the constitution persisted, even if its form must undergo some change. To Cicero the form was essential, if the spirit was to survive; he was certain that it could survive only in its present body, and that if the body could be preserved, the spirit must also needs survive; unfortunately he could not know of Lenin. But he was deeply sensitive of the spirit; and it was the spirit of political freedom as he understood it that he was so concerned to save and cherish, and to prevent whose extinction at the hands of the tyrants he gave his life.

CHAPTER 5

CICERO'S VERRINES TO THE PRAETORSHIP

ERRES was notorious while still governor for his dishonest and extortionate practices; his reputation as a cruel and greedy vulture, ready to pounce on whatever excited his cupidity and served to fill a void in his collection of antiques and works of art, was acquired even in his earlier life in Asia, and only enhanced by the scale of his operations in a sphere where his greater power gave more abundant scope to his lustful appetites. Early in his governorship he had embarrassed his father by convicting a Sicilian on a capital charge while absent in Rome, though his father had assured the Senate that he would not do so; in 71 Sicilians had come to Rome to beseech L. Metellus, the governor-designate of Sicily, to come with all dispatch and thus relieve them as soon as possible of their monstrous governor. The province was determined to institute a prosecution for extortion against him, and these same men while in Rome set to finding someone whom they could persuade to assume the task. The province had friends among the nobles, as every province did; the Marcelli were their traditional patrons, and more recently Pompey had also established ties. Cicero, the bar's most promising younger advocate, had at the end of his quaestorship offered the province his services, should they ever need his help; now they asked that the pledge be redeemed, a request in which they were joined by the Marcelli and probably by Pompey.

For Cicero the request posed a difficulty; for he had sworn never to act as prosecutor, since prosecution involved 'inimicitiae', and enemies could prove dangerous, if not fatal, to his political ambitions. For in the absence of family connexions he must depend heavily on friendships and connexions made as a result of services rendered to persons in need of his oratorical talents; and this implied defence rather than attack. In the present instance the roll of Verres' supporters was impressive; some of the noblest families, including the head of the Scipionic *gens*, were on his side; the Metelli were prevailed upon by his plundered fortune to favour his cause; and Hortensius, leader of the bar, candidate for the consulship of 69, had accepted the defence. This increased Cicero's difficulties: the risk of raising enmities, particularly in the year when he was seeking the aedileship; the fact that the defence was in the hands of Rome's leading advocate before a jury composed of men whose judicial behaviour during the previous ten years gave no grounds for supposing that they would be swayed by considerations of justice or equity towards provincials; his own decision not to prosecute, all these considerations urged him to leave the case to others.

Yet he had given his pledge, and now the Sicilians in their desperation had come to him; his honour and his word would be held as nugatory, if he failed to redeem it; the persuasions of the Marcelli and Pompey implied support at least from them, if he helped them now; and Pompey was a powerful man, whose intention it was to break the Senate's monopoly of power, and who now and always showed respect and sympathy for provincials. His inclinations and his sympathies turned him towards those who had suffered as he suffered from the insolence of the nobles. And finally, the fact that Hortensius was defending Verres was rather an inducement than a deterrent; for in all the circumstances it was clear that it would be one of the most important and publicised prosecutions of recent years; the political elements were at the moment of tremendous importance, and great political forces were involved: Pompey with his promised reforms and his consulship, the Senatorial order threatened by Pompey but brazenly determined in its irresponsibility, the future of Senatorial government, all these things were nearly involved in this case; if Cicero accepted the Sicilians' invitation and obtained a conviction, he would at once establish himself as Rome's leading advocate and win powerful support from Pompey and those who favoured Pompey's policy. All these considerations were carefully weighed in Cicero's mind, and his decision crystallised—he would be Verres' prosecutor.

Verres enjoyed the support of powerful men and the sympathy of much of the Senate; and they at once began scheming to frustrate the prosecution by political and other means. First they put forward Q. Caecilius Niger, a former quaestor of Verres', to claim the right of prosecution, instead of Cicero, with the intention that, if he established his claim, he would deliberately make a feeble attack which Hortensius could easily repulse and thus procure acquittal. This shabby scheme compelled Cicero to argue his fitness for the task before the praetor; and this he successfully did in the speech we know as the *Divinatio in Caecilium*. Now he must visit Sicily to collect the evidence of Verres' crimes, sworn statements and witnesses, and for this purpose asked for a period of 110 days, which was granted. His opponents thereupon persuaded the prosecution in another case to ask for 108 days for the collection of his evidence, thus assuring that the second case would take precedence over Cicero's, since it would be ready for hearing two days earlier; Cicero claimed that he was delayed three months by this stratagem. The object of the defence was to defer, if possible, the hearing until the next year 69, when Hortensius, it was hoped, would be consul, and two Metelli would be consul and praetor respectively. The brother of these Metelli was Verres' successor in Sicily; acceding to the Sicilians' request he had reached his province with all possible dispatch, and had at once begun to undo as much as he could of Verres' disgraceful ordinances and rulings. Then had come a sudden change; just before Cicero reached the island in quest of his evidence, there arrived for Metellus a letter from his brothers, asking him to help Verres' case in every possible way and to frustrate as best he could Cicero's search for witnesses and evidence. For this sudden request there was a reason; Verres had offered the two brothers considerable financial help in their elections, if they would persuade their brother to bless his interests; and their brother, sensitive to the need for family solidarity, had readily complied. In consequence their campaigns prospered, while Cicero's task was made considerably more difficult; only his courage and determination, reinforced by the praetor's warrant, enabled him to build his case.

Returning within 60 days he discovered that his case would be delayed because of the other prosecution, and there was nothing he could do but wait. Meanwhile in July the consular and praetorian elections were held; Hortensius and Q. Metellus were returned as consuls, and M. Metellus became a praetor; Verres' gold had not been spent in vain. Further, the lot gave M. Metellus the charge of the *quaestio de repetundis* for 69; we may either marvel that the lot should have been so discriminating in a case where the nobles' weal was so closely touched, or we may suspect the honesty of the system. By contrast Cicero was in a state of agitation, as Verres had been freely spending money to thwart Cicero's election to the aedileship; this money was, however, ill-spent; for Cicero was triumphantly returned, a measure of the people's anger with the nobles and of their admiration for Cicero's defiant courage. Verres' friends now had every reason to be sanguine; both next year's consuls were his friends, the praetor who would have charge of the court was his friend; strategy therefore required that the trial should be dawdled or delayed into the next year; and this for Hortensius should not be difficult; for between August and December the greater part of the time was consumed with various holidays during which the court might not sit. Cicero, however, well aware of their intention and his danger, outwitted them triumphantly. The first action was by tradition given to long speeches by both prosecution and defence, in which the case was handled in broad and somewhat general terms; in the second action the prosecution settled down to the detailed narration, supported by witnesses, who could, of course, be cross-examined, and a skilful barrister could waste almost unlimited time on the two actions. Cicero, however, cheated Hortensius of his chance; instead of making a long introductory speech he made a short direct attack on Verres, launching his accusations and bringing forward his witnesses; an immediate and detailed defence was now needed, and for this Hortensius was not ready; he had neither the resilience nor the resources with which to counter the attack. It succeeded; Hortensius had lost the case by default; before the second action could come on, Verres, bowing to the inevitable, had betaken himself into voluntary exile.

It was a great and well-deserved victory for Cicero, which undoubtedly would be influential in establishing his political career; he had attained his ambition to be universally recognised as Rome's leading orator and advocate; he had made important friends and connexions; his reputation ensured that he would have as many requests to act as advocate as he wanted; and the future seemed full of hopeful promise. So important did he regard both the oratorical and political implications of the case that, although Verres and Hortensius had abandoned the defence after the first action, Cicero published not only the two speeches which he actually made, but also the five speeches of the second action which he never delivered. Regarding them as a masterpiece of oratory, he was anxious to confirm his newly won position as leader of the bar; but that was not the only reason; he was equally anxious to make clear his political position, particularly with respect to the Senate. *Narrative of his position; interpretation also*

As we have seen, deep issues were involved in this case; the question of the control of the law courts, closely associated in men's minds with the restoration of the tribunes' powers, had been raised by Pompey, who was consul during the year of the action. His attitude towards the provinces, sharpened in the present case by reason of his ties with Sicily, had assured the prosecution of his sympathy and support and his friendly eye during the proceedings; the Senate, by contrast, had seemed determined to regard the case as one in which their own interests were so

5-2

intimately concerned that conviction would be tantamount to their own condemnation, and seemed firmly resolved to disregard the many clear proofs of their present unpopularity and the imminent threat overhanging them from Pompey, who had already shown the sincerity of his promises of restoring the tribunes' powers. He had in that same election speech made clear his concern for the welfare of the provinces; yet the Senate seemed disposed to seek their own humiliation and give Pompey solid grounds for taking his threatened action with the courts.

But not all of them. Even in 75 there had been sufficient men of broader sympathy and outlook to make possible C. Aurelius Cotta's law to allow tribunes to stand for higher office; and Pompey's law restoring their initiative in legislation had found support with many in the Senate. True, on this occasion the intimidation of Pompey's army might be argued; but Catulus' words showed that there were leading Senators opposed to the conduct of their peers. Cicero, determined to make for himself a great political career, could not afford to offend the powerful nobles by joining with the Populares to attack the Senate's privileged position; nor did he wish to; his ambitions were inextricably bound up with his boyhood ideas of Rome and its great men; Scipio, his great ideal, had been a great Senator. If his ambitions still centred on the consulship and entry into the exclusive circle of the nobility, they also presumed that selfsame state of affairs in which the great man's influence was exercised as Senator; it never occurred to Cicero to reject the Senate, however insolently the nobles might behave to him, and join those in open opposition to its power and privilege; and certainly at this moment such an idea could never even briefly have flashed before his mind; his career was still to make, and for Cicero that career could be made only within the Senate, not against it.

Yet the case was regarded as a critical test case, in which jurymen and Senate, no less than Verres, were on trial. The Senate was hated both because of the corrupt venality of the courts, and because of the irresponsible behaviour of its members; the prosecutor would have no choice but to expose the Senate's wrong-doings and forcefully to attack their improprieties and the shocking malpractices of Verres, who was of them and enjoyed support from some of their bluest blood. He must, therefore, use every art to win his case; for on that depended his oratorical reputation; but he must also clarify his attitude towards the Senate. His skill and ingenuity had won the case; the publication of his speeches could serve the second purpose. His attitude was clear; first, he was careful to identify himself with that order; as an ex-quaestor he was a Senator, and he constantly associated himself with that body, lest he should be supposed to be attacking as an enemy. Throughout he emphasised the odium in which the Senate lay, the bad behaviour which had generated and nourished this odium, the dishonesty and corruption of some of its members; all these were important elements of his prosecution. He warned the jury of the hatred felt for their privileged position, and pointed out that a verdict in Verres' favour would certainly spell the end of their control; for Pompey had given fair warning. He emphasised in pleading rather than menacing tones his association in the humiliation which was threatening, and made clear the importance for Rome of having the Senate as its governing body, and the consequent necessity that they should be ready to purge themselves of their unworthy members rather than, to maintain a solidarity that harmed their best interests, to condone what was manifestly unjust and inexcusable.

He went further; for he stated in many passages that the Senate was worthy of its responsibilities and powers, but was frustrated and brought into contempt and hatred by the bad behaviour of a small faction, the 'pauci', whom he mentioned frequently. It was this small group, he contended, who were responsible for what had happened; it was only these 'few' who abused their position and opportunities in their own selfish interests, who were prepared to go to any length to increase their wealth and to protect their fellows from the consequences of their behaviour. Among these 'pauci' were to be found Verres and his present protectors, the Metelli, Scipio Nasica and others. The conviction of Verres would therefore at once enhance the Senate's good name as honest jurors, and also strengthen them by dealing a hard blow at those whose every activity brought further disgrace upon that body. This line of attack enabled Cicero both to strike hard at Verres and his defenders with untempered vigour, and also to show himself as the Senate's champion, concerned for the privileges and good name of the body to which it was his honour to belong.

There was a large measure of truth in his contention; for, as we have seen, there had been quite considerable Senatorial support for the two pieces of legislation in favour of the tribunes; but the greater part of them were its less distinguished members, who like Cicero must for their future success find some powerful support, but who unlike him had no commodity to offer so valuable as his oratory. The attitude of these 'pauci', all of them nobles, towards Cicero served as a spur to his attacks; they were insolent and exclusive, contemptuous of 'outsiders', sneering at Cicero's educated interest in philosophy and Greek, now and at all times disdainful of his middle class country background. They had little but their birth and their ancestors' prowess with which to bolster their superiority; but this they found an ample and sustaining support. To Cicero, who admired Rome's earlier ideals, who was desperately anxious to become a noble, and who would have given strength and vigour to their fast evaporating ideals, this was humiliation hardly to be endured, an insult which stung keenly. For he was conscious of his talents and knew that by any but their twisted scale of values he was the better man; better in talent, in education, in understanding of the true tradition, which, could they but be prevailed upon to embrace its standards, would, so he thought, give Rome a government as good as in the second century, and introduce that sense of responsibility into the governance of her empire which it was being left to men like Pompey and the Populares to bring about. Their behaviour towards Cicero was their behaviour to others like him;

he had talents which gave him a certain power and independence; they had not, and must succumb. Thus these insolent and ignorant 'pauci' were a force of corruption, whom Cicero would like, in the interests of the Senate, to root out.

If the Verrine speeches revealed something of Cicero's ideals and ideas for the government of Rome, they also made clear the limit of his understanding of the problems which beset the Republic. Responsible Senatorial government, guided by high-minded and honest nobles, was his idea of what it could and should be. It was the picture of Scipionic Rome translated to his own day, with the injection of such 'novi homines' as himself; and this picture was marred by the bad conduct of the 'pauci', who lived unworthily of the nobles' code. This missed much, but Cicero, bound, sometimes almost fettered, by the background of his youth, never really came to terms with the facts. The animosity which had since the Gracchi grown between the Senate on the one hand and on the other those able but sometimes irresponsible men who sought to wrest the initiative of government from the Senate, and the Equites, had raised an issue which must be resolved and resolved beyond hazard of doubt: who was to govern Rome. Either the Senate governed, or the tribunes; if the former, they must realise that their responsibilities were not to the maintenance of their own position but to the good of Rome and all her empire; if the latter, it must be based on something more than the aspirations of a young and possibly irresponsible man, holding office for a year, and prepared to seek to forward sectional interests or to bribe his way to votes by popular legislation.

So inflamed had become passion that it had blazed out into murder and civil war; Sulla had practised drastic surgery on the body politic, hoping that health would be restored. But it had proved vain; the past could not be exorcised nor men made to think and to behave as though the past had never been; and now in 70 everything was as it was before, with nothing solved and animosities as keen as ever. If the Senate refused to behave like statesmen, and if individuals behaved as they had done before

Sulla's reforms, then the situation could grow only worse; the end could only be disintegration or a second Sulla, who would control the Roman world by virtue of his army. Herein lay the danger; Sulla had won control by reason of his army; Pompey in 77 and 71 had had his way by reason of an army; if men were ready to use an army against the government, and armies consented to be so used, then government was in permanent jeopardy, whatever group was in control, and however responsibly that group might seek to govern.

Cicero had now established himself as the foremost pleader at the bar, and had, in spite of his opponents' efforts and Verres' gold, been triumphantly elected to the aedileship, the second step in the sequence of offices which might—and, Cicero hoped, would—lead to the consulship. The aedileship was itself not very difficult of attainment; but it was a necessary stepping stone, and Cicero might well be satisfied that his talents and his oratory had won him a goodwill and respect among the voters which had made something of a triumph of his election. He might further reflect that the attitude he had shown in the prosecution of Verres towards the political problems of the day was a major cause of his high standing with the people. A country *eques*, he had dared to challenge openly that hard nucleus of nobles whose chief concern was the maintenance of their privileged position, which their behaviour proved them unworthy to hold; and though he now had the support of distinguished men, it was none the less true that it was he who had taken the lead. A fund of goodwill was built up for himself which was to assure his equally triumphant election to the praetorship and to the consulship; the ordinary people and the Equites recognised in him a person who embodied and reflected their own attitudes towards Senatorial misgovernment and the possible solution; where he diverged was not yet apparent. Many members of the Senate were also his supporters; not everyone in the Senate came of distinguished lineage; few could hope for the consulship, not a great number for the praetorship; they must have smarted under the insolence of the 'pauci' as much as did Cicero. The type of person who had voted for the Lex Aurelia by which the tribunate was opened to higher office would also have supported Cicero.

Cicero during these next years had one end only in view, the consulship, and to that end all else was subordinated. He must continue to build up a background of support and goodwill, for since he was a *novus homo*, he must depend upon himself. It was a difficult task; for though he must depend on the goodwill of Equites and people, his own ambitions drew him towards the Senate and nobles, among whom he wished to be numbered. He could not therefore wholly identify himself with the interests of the Populares, since this would incur the hostility of those he wished to join; he must proceed with care, winning the confidence of the one side without forfeiting the goodwill of the other. In this he was successful; he broadened the basis of his support, not least among the *municipia*, by his choice of persons to defend in court; the country towns tended to look with sympathetic interest on his career; to them he was one of themselves, and they gladly urged his interests where they could.

The year 67 was important for Cicero, for in this year he was intending to seek the praetorship, the first of the major offices; and the year was for his purposes perversely difficult, requiring considerable adroitness not to commit himself too heavily on one or the other side. One of the tribunes of the year, A. Gabinius, an able soldier and Pompeian supporter, was promoting legislation in Pompey's interest, and since Pompey was unpopular with the nobles by reason of his conduct as consul, support of Gabinius would engage the hostility of these persons. Gabinius had already in this year passed a law by which Bithynia and Pontus were given to M'. Acilius Glabrio, one of the consuls; this was in Pompey's interests, for Lucullus, a Senatorian, was thus stripped of part of his Eastern command against Mithridates; the significance of this will be seen in the next year. He was therefore already hated by the nobles, but for that reason and for his support of Pompey was a popular figure. He now proposed a law to deal with the pirates who infested the Mediterranean, against whom Senatorial generals had proved themselves incompetent.

The Roman state maintained no navy, and for many years there had been no other power in the eastern Mediterranean to supply the deficiency. The result was that piracy, previously kept in check by the fleet of Rhodes, had flourished undisturbed; in 100 B.C. a law had been passed giving considerable powers to some general to deal with the menace; M. Antonius had as praetor in 102 been sent out with a special command, but had achieved little; in 74 his son was given a similar command and had achieved as little as his father; he had in 68 been followed by Q. Metellus, who had captured Crete but not significantly reduced piracy. By now they had complete control of the sea; the corn fleets were in constant danger, every ship that sailed feared the appearance of a pirate sail; nor had they any respect for Romans or the majesty of Rome. Even the coasts of Italy were attacked and citizens kidnapped in Italy itself; the situation had become intolerable, the corn supply was endangered, and the Senatorial officers charged with the duty of suppressing them had failed in their task. Gabinius now proposed a law by which yet again a special command against the pirates should be instituted, that one man should be given supreme command for three years throughout the Mediterranean and for 50 miles inland of all the provinces with a coastline, and that he should have twenty-four *legati* of his own choosing to help him in this task. No name was mentioned, but every one knew that, if the law was passed, Pompey would be chosen.

Statesmanship and politics were inextricably confused in this measure, and this it was that complicated Cicero's position. The reality of the menace and the cost to individuals and state of the pirates' activities were not to be gainsaid; it is the duty of government to assure the safety of its citizens and protect the commerce of its nationals; Rome was under a particular obligation in this respect, since she had refused to allow any of her subjects to carry out the task which she was so obviously reluctant to do herself.

She had failed abysmally in her responsibility, and the persons she had nominated to deal with the pirates had been wholly inadequate for a task that required a first-class commander; to propose a measure by which this running sore could be eradicated was a piece of statesmanship; and Pompey might well be the man best suited to the task. Pompey had since his consulship been in Rome, having refused a province after his year of office; his prestige and influence were at this time as great probably as at any period of his life, and he was hankering for some extraordinary command in keeping with his hitherto extraordinary career, a command worthy not merely of a *consularis* but of Pompeius Magnus. He had his eye on the command against Mithridates, but this plum was not quite ripe for plucking; for the moment the command against the pirates would suffice, provided it were defined in large enough terms.

It is certain that Gabinius' proposal was the result of previous discussion with Pompey, who made clear the scope of his requirements. Were he given all that was laid down in the bill, he would be in a very strong position, once he had dealt with the pirates, to 'request' some further command if he should see fit; and this must have been abundantly clear to the nobles. On the other hand Pompey was a very able strategist and soldier; he would have sized up the extent of the problem of extirpating piracy, and have realised that less than what was asked for would be insufficient to achieve the object; and certainly its opponents could hardly, in view of their own failures, argue that such powers and forces were unnecessary.

The line that Cicero should take was therefore tantalisingly difficult. He enjoyed the friendship of Pompey, a friendship based on admiration of his qualities and his power against the nobles, a friendship destined to be of great importance for Cicero. Pompey was also high in favour with the people by reason both of his military reputation and his consulship, and also because he was opposed to the nobles; support, therefore, of Pompey would win him votes among the mass of Pompeian supporters. But this would antagonise those noble families and their supporters. some of whom he hoped would look with favour on his candidature; and, moreover, he saw his future among them, not as a Popularis whose career was to lie in opposition to the Senate. He seems therefore to have followed the path of prudence; he did not openly commit himself on the bill. That he favoured it, both because of his friendship with Pompey and because he saw that it was in the interests of the state and in particular of his friends the Equites, whose commercial activities the pirates seriously hampered, seems clear from his attitude towards it in the next year when he spoke in favour of the Lex Manilia; his refusal to commit himself openly was probably accompanied by *sotto voce* coos of approval, since he was top of the polls in the praetorian elections; and this indicates that he still enjoyed the favour of people and Equites.

By the time of the elections, therefore, Pompey had received an important commission with considerable forces and great power, against the nobles' wishes; Catulus and Hortensius had vainly tried to argue against granting such powers to any single man, as contrary to Roman tradition; they had been forced to accept the will of the people and, we may suspect, a considerable part of the Senators. The atmosphere had been further tainted by the proposal of another tribune, C. Cornelius, to deal with bribery by candidates for office, particularly the consulship, since this was a much-sought prize. The Senate thereupon instructed the consuls to produce a bill of their own on the same subject, whose terms were to be milder than those laid down in Cornelius' bill. Meanwhile canvassing for the elections was at its height, and rough and rowdy scenes, leading even to death, occurred; the Senate therefore ordered the consuls to proceed with their bill before the elections were held, a procedure normally forbidden. Further trouble now ensued, during which the consul C. Piso was in danger of his life and was rescued by Cornelius himself. The law was passed and the two consuls-designate, P. Autronius and P. Sulla, were accused of bribery and declared to have forfeited their election. During all this commotion and wrangling between Senate and tribune and all the hectic hooliganism of the elections, the praetorian elections were held; twice for some reason, almost certainly connected with these disturbances, they were not formally completed or were declared void; and three times Cicero emerged at the top of the polls. It was a great victory for Cicero, of which he was justifiably proud; it was a measure of his popularity with all classes at Rome, an indication of the respect felt for his political attitude and of the support which this countryman and *novus homo* could command.

As praetor he had charge of the *quaestio de repetundis*; amongst the cases that came before him was that of C. Licinius Macer, who as tribune in 73 had made himself particularly distasteful to the nobles by his violent agitation for the restoration of the tribunician powers; he had also written a history of Rome during the Sullan régime from his own political point of view. He had, it seems, been praetor in the early 60s and then proceeded to a province, where he was now accused of having practised extortion. M. Crassus, an important personage in the politics of this time and no friend of the nobles, was defending him. The conviction of Macer in spite of Crassus' great efforts to procure his acquittal had therefore a certain political significance, and Cicero's impartial conduct, when he might have won friends by acquiescing in an acquittal, heightened his reputation among the people; as he himself says, his conduct was received *incredibili ac singulari populi voluntate*; and this would be of future help. As he wrote to his friend Atticus, he reaped *multo maiorem fructum ex populi existimatione* than he could have done by winning Macer's support through favouring him.[1]

The most important event during his praetorship was his speech in favour of the Lex Manilia, by which C. Manilius, a tribune, proposed to transfer the command against Mithridates to Pompey. Something certainly needed to be done about this. Lucullus, an able soldier and a friend of the Senate, had in 74 been the first

---

[1] *ad Att.* 1, 4, 2.

commander. At first successful, he had driven Mithridates out of Asia, and was preparing to deal with his father-in-law Tigranes, king of Armenia. But here his troubles began. He was an able administrator, who saw the misery to which Rome's Asiatic subjects had been reduced by the dishonesty and greed of the tax collectors, as a result of which they had been reduced to near-bankruptcy before Mithridates had launched his war. He therefore made strict regulations to prevent their further exploitation at the hands of the Equites. This action won the gratitude of the provincials and the hostility of the Equites, who set about compassing his downfall.

The protracted nature of the war was their ally; two of the legions in particular had a record of mischievous disloyalty, dating from the time when they had first gone to Asia with Flaccus and Fimbria during the first Mithridatic war; they were ready to cause mischief once again, if by doing so they might effect some personal gain. The campaigning during the years 69–67 was undoubtedly severe, and the conditions of snow and mountainous terrain increased the rigours of what was in any case a long and tiring ordeal. Lucullus, himself an aristocrat, had little patience with indiscipline; he enforced a stricter discipline than the soldiers were prepared to accept for so long and arduous a stretch of time. Lucullus was in truth out of touch and sympathy with the sort of persons who composed these armies; they were no longer the conscripts of the second century, but in large part men who had volunteered for military service; if more was asked of them than they felt fair or proper, they were ready enough to show their displeasure, and had on earlier occasions already done so. The troops of Pompeius Strabo in 88, who murdered the general sent to take over command, the troops of Cinna in 84, these selfsame two legions who first murdered their commander, L. Valerius Flaccus, and then deserted Fimbria, in whose interest they had murdered Flaccus; all these armies had shown the different spirit and temper of the first-century army. Not only were the men different; the political atmosphere too was different; armies tended to become instruments in the hands of ambitious men who with an army became invincible. The armies therefore acquired an improper importance in the calculations of the politicians; and the bad behaviour of an army was liable to go unpunished or even to find active encouragement at Rome from persons opposed to its general. This had happened on this occasion; the Lex Gabinia which had given Glabrio Bithynia and Pontus had also terminated the services of these two legions, thus deliberately depriving Lucullus of much-needed troops at a critical juncture; the province of Cilicia had already in 68 been given to Q. Marcius Rex, and Asia had been withdrawn in 69; Lucullus had therefore at this moment no province and an inadequate army, while Glabrio was quite incapable of conducting the war.

The two legions which had been ordered discharged under the Lex Gabinia were, as has been said, a mischievous crowd of men; but their propensity for mischief had been encouraged by the disgraceful conduct of Lucullus' own brother-in-law P. Clodius, the future tribune, a member of Lucullus' staff, who took the opportunity to ingratiate himself with Pompey by tampering with the soldiers' loyalty; the discontent in these two legions, which erupted finally into mutiny, was partly at least the result of seditious speeches made by Clodius, in which he contrasted their miserable lot with the happy condition of Pompey's veterans of the Spanish War, who were now, he suggested, settled in colonies in the full enjoyment of their families and farms, while these men fought interminably to satisfy Lucullus' greed and ambition. The result had been disastrous for Lucullus, who was now reduced to complete inactivity, while Mithridates recovered many of his losses and punished those who had supported the Romans; but it provided just the situation that Pompey could turn to his advantage. Someone must be sent to bring this war to a successful conclusion; none of the commanders on the spot were competent to accomplish this; and of those not on the spot none could compete with Pompey's claims both by reason of his past successes, most particularly his spectacular achievement against the pirates, and because he was at this moment handily situated to assume the command. He was most probably at this moment in Cilicia with a large part of the forces he had used against the pirates; it would therefore anyhow be not unreasonable, and might well be thought prudent and proper, to appoint him to the command. Since this was the command which he had for some time been coveting and for which he had been making agitation, now that the time was come, obviously one of his supporters would take action, since the Senate would not humiliate further their own commander, whose present failure was partly due to Pompey's machinations. The tribune Manilius it was who proposed direct to the people the legislation which gave Pompey the command.

Although there was a political content to the bill, it could not be denied that the proposal was statesmanlike and in Rome's best interests, a fact recognised by some of the most distinguished consulars. None the less Catulus and Hortensius, who had so bitterly opposed the Lex Gabinia, were equally hostile to this further extension of Pompey's power; and Cicero, who had remained officially silent the previous year about the Lex Gabinia, decided to address the people in support of the present law, in the speech known as the *de Imperio Cn. Pompei*. Several considerations will have conspired to persuade him to a course which could bring difficulties for his future ambitions; he would certainly incur unpopularity with those sections of the nobles who supported Catulus and Hortensius, and this could prove awkward when he came to seek the consulship. On the other hand, there were many who agreed with the proposal; either course therefore would offend some group and forfeit their support. But support of Pompey would win him far more friends in other quarters than would opposition; particularly would he strengthen his alliance with the Equites, whose interests had suffered cruelly from the war and from Lucullus' measures in Asia, and who were wholehearted in their support of Pompey in the hope of getting the war ended. Further, he would show the enemies of Senatorial dominance that, even though he would not openly declare war on the Senate, yet he was prepared to embrace their policies when they were in the state's interest, however desperately the 'pauci' might seek to thwart them. He might also expect that Pompey's vast influence would be thrown in the balance in his favour; and friendship and support of Pompey were cardinal principles of his life. Nor is there any reason to doubt his asseverations that his chief concern was the interests of the state; he must have seen that this was the only possible solution in the circumstances for a situation that was at once grave, humiliating and urgent.

The law was passed and Pompey proceeded upon his task. The end of his year of office confronted Cicero with an embarrassing dilemma, from which he was aided by luck in extricating himself. During his last days of office Manilius, whose tribunate ended on 9 December, was prosecuted for extortion, and would thus be tried before Cicero. The prosecution was launched in revenge for his laws: and Cicero had pledged himself in his speech in favour of the law to defend Manilius, were he attacked. Hence Cicero's embarrassment; to have supported the law was possibly permissible, and did not of itself mark him out as a Popularis, a risk which his studied moderation in that speech had carefully avoided. But to defend the man responsible not only for this law but for another one, dealing with the distribution of freedmen in the tribes, which had antagonised the majority of the nobles, this would surely indicate an interest that went deeper than the single law in favour of Pompey. It was most important that Cicero should not thus commit himself, and thus alienate many influential nobles; yet the pledge had been given. He could avoid the embarrassment only by hearing the case himself; for then he could not defend. But he had only a few days left, and Manilius had asked for time to prepare his defence, a request which it was customary to grant. Cicero, however, gave him only a few days, setting the last day of his praetorship for the trial. Manilius' friends were outraged, Cicero was compelled by the tribunes to address a *contio*, in which he defended his action by saying that he wished Manilius to enjoy Cicero's friendly oversight of the court; the people, while accepting the explanation, made him promise to undertake the defence. This he found himself compelled to do; he was extricated from this embarrassment, which could have had serious consequences for his future, by the civil disturbances of the following year, in the midst of which the prosecution seems to have lapsed. Manilius, then prosecuted for *maiestas*, on the first occasion forcibly broke up the court, then, when it met under the consuls' presidency, condemned himself by failing to turn up.

His praetorship was now ended, and he could look back on a successful year as far as his hopes of the consulship were concerned. His conduct in the *quaestio de repetundis* had been just and impartial; his speech on behalf of Pompey had cemented his friendship with the Equites and added fresh strength to his supporters; the cases he had assumed in the law courts had won him additional support, and further helped the Equites; and in his defence of Cluentius he had made his first open statement of the ideal that was to become the mainspring of his political aims, namely the unity of Senate and Equites (*ei equites ordini senatorio dignitate proximos concordia coniunctissimos esse cupiunt*). He emphasised the main obstacle to the consummation of this ideal, the 'pauci', who had tried to deny justice to the Sicilians, who despised Cicero himself and all others like him, and who were the chief obstruction to the harmony of Italy, by their contemptuous and exclusive behaviour towards those countrymen who could contribute so much to running the empire (*sed ei, qui sese volunt posse omnia neque praeterea quicquam esse aut in homine ullo aut in ordine*). During the next two years he must, if he wished to be consul *suo anno*, win sufficient support to be able to counter the influence of these 'pauci'—and it was very great—who would resent his candidature and would do all in their power to keep the highest magistracy within the hands of the noble families.

CHAPTER 6

THE RISE TO THE CONSULSHIP

DURING the next year and a half Cicero had to consolidate his position and win sufficient support from whatever quarters he could to be able to present himself successfully for the consulship for 63, the elections for which would take place in the middle of 64. The times were far from calm; and the readiness to behave mischievously, to conceive plans for the subversion of government or for the personal advancement of those who were prepared to despise the constitution, made every situation potentially inflammable. A comparatively small group of nobles had an influence out of all proportion to their numbers; the mass of the Senators were comparatively impotent except as appendages to one or other of the powerful nobles, whose great concern was to hold on to the considerable power that still remained to them from Sulla's constitution in spite of the restoration of the tribunes' powers, and to run the state in their own interests. The Equites were a powerful and unscrupulous group, determined that whoever governed the state and in whatever way, it should be possible for them to pursue unimpeded their business and their money-making in Italy and the provinces. Then there were the persons who saw no political future as acolytes of the nobles, and whose ambitions either for personal power or the destruction of that of the nobles led them to seek their fortunes through the people and largely through tribunician legislation, some of them men of high hopes, matched by a commensurate ability. The people themselves seem to have been antagonistic to the nobles, largely as a result of the political propaganda of the previous seventy years, and because the tribunes, through whom so much of the legislation was effected, were peculiarly the people's officers, and were constantly making plain that this or that piece of legislation was designed to help the people against the nobles' high-handed behaviour, or to bring to pass what the nobles for selfish reasons were frustrating. Above all hung the sombre shadow of the absent Pompey, powerful politically, the people's hero, Rome's greatest soldier, now in process of completing the Mithridatic War. Soon the task would be accomplished; then would come the return, and what then? It was assumed by most people that he would return with his army, and like Sulla would claim some position of supreme authority and would wreak his vengeance on those who had tried to thwart his ambitions or had shown him hostility. In this atmosphere Cicero had to build up his position to become a candidate for the consulship.

His task was particularly hard, for he had no wish to give himself completely to either side. His ideals and ambitions directed him towards the Senate and orderly government; yet the hard core of nobles continued to despise his *novitas*, and would be particularly alert to prevent the upstart from joining their ranks. But to seek his end through the people by becoming an open enemy of Senatorial prerogative went completely contrary to all his ideals; the Scipionic order was his dream, and this could not be achieved through tribunician legislation. Yet Cicero was by now an important figure; his powers of oratory and his political career had won him considerable respect and powerful support in many quarters; by all but those wholly committed to one or other of the extremes he was deemed a man of courage and sincerity; he had topped the polls for the praetorship, not by the nobles' willing; the people liked him just because he was no noble, and because he did not fear to attack the 'pauci'; humbler members of the Senate will have blessed his courage. With the Equites he had always been on good terms; he anxiously reminded them that he was one of them and understood their interests; while they, perennially hostile to the nobles, were his ready supporters. Although he was at all times careful not to identify himself with the extreme policies of those who were called Populares, yet he had been ready not only to attack the prerogatives of the 'pauci', but to support such measures of the Populares as seemed to him in the interests of the state; he had put his oratory at the disposal of men who could exercise influence in his interest, but he had also promised support to Manilius, and was in this year (65) to defend another ex-tribune, Cornelius, who had earned the nobles' hostility by legislation which had not seemed extreme to Cicero.

There was in the general tenor of his political life a consistency of outlook and purpose which is often underrated; he showed a readiness to oppose the excesses of both extremes, and had made himself the spokesman and the leader of those who were ready for reform without the mischief of the Populares or the self-interested opposition to all change which characterised many of the Optimates. His remarkable success both in the aedilician and praetorian elections is the measure of the support which he had enlisted for himself and his policy of controlled reform; he must now strengthen and add to this support in order to counteract the opposition which would be roused by the nobles against his entry into their ranks. For his ideals did not meet with their approval; he was prepared to trust Pompey and support his cause, and had publicly done so; they hated and feared Pompey, and would have prevented either of his commands, had they been able. To Cicero Pompey was the man whose pre-eminence fitted him to be the chief personage in Roman politics, putting an end to the fierce antagonisms between the two extremes, making possible the Scipionic order in which Cicero's talents would have full play and influence; to the nobles he was a pernicious war-lord, whose whole career had been a flouting of the constitution, whose armies had compelled from a reluctant Senate concessions which they had bitterly resented, who now through tribunician legislation had become Rome's greatest and most powerful figure, the popular hero of the people, contemptuous of themselves and their pretensions. During the next eighteen months Cicero re-mained constant to his policy; he showed himself ready to support what he thought proper from both extremes; he did not, to commend himself to the nobles, attack everything of which they disapproved; nor did he so conduct himself as to become identified with the extremists. He looked for additional support, and was ready to assume the defence in cases where he might add to it, though not at the expense of his political conscience.

The year 65 was full of political commotion. The two men elected as consuls for this year, P. Autronius Paetus and P. Cornelius Sulla, had won their election by such flagrant bribery that they were prosecuted, though consuls-designate, by L. Aurelius Cotta, one of the unsuccessful candidates, and L. Torquatus, the son of the other unsuccessful candidate, also L. Torquatus. The prosecution was successful, the elections were annulled, and Cotta and Torquatus elected in their place. The two frustrated candidates, who had spent so much to win the consulship, with the province that would then follow and allow them to recoup their extravagant expenditure, were not minded to accept the disastrous consequence of their conviction; they formed a conspiracy by which they were to murder the two consuls and substitute themselves. They found a few ready adherents, among them a young man, Cn. Piso, and L. Sergius Catilina. Crassus and Caesar were alleged to be privy to the plot; according to one version they were the leading lights; Crassus was to assume the dictatorship with Caesar as his Master of Horse. While both men were restrained neither by scruple nor respect for the constitution from such a move, and were both ready to join an enterprise where their interests so demanded, it is most unlikely that they had involved themselves in this wretched plot; for while both of them were ready to bend the constitution to their ends, Crassus in particular was always careful not to put himself at the front; he intrigued in his own interest, content to let others run the risks. Caesar, ready also to intrigue, was also ready to take the lead; but it is unlikely that he would have involved himself in a revolutionary *coup d'état* of doubtful value and most uncertain of success, when he still hoped to be able to advance his career by using the constitution for his purposes; and while both were ever ready to fish in troubled waters, and this conspiracy might conceivably create conditions from which they might extract some profit, the risks were in the circumstances too great for the possible rewards; they could still hope to gain their ends by legal means.

Catiline was a member of the plot. A patrician with a dismal record of selfish cruelty and greed, he had been responsible for many deaths during the Sullan tyranny, had held the praetorship and then the governorship of Africa, where his conduct had been the cause of complaint by the province in 66 to the Senate by reason of his extortionate practices. As a result of this complaint and the prosecution which would necessarily follow, Catiline had been forbidden to be a candidate for the consulship for 65, and, since the prosecution was still impending, would not be eligible to sue for 64. He therefore had a motive, and his record showed that he had the readiness, to join in a conspiracy from which he might extract some personal gain. Owing to the conspiracy which he organised in the year of Cicero's consulship, 63, the suppressing of which represented the highest moment of Cicero's life, Catiline has been given a greater prominence in this first conspiracy than he merited. To Cicero, faced with the serious conspiracy of 63, it seemed that this was merely the climax of three years' plotting and scheming, which had begun with this abortive conspiracy, of which Catiline was therefore the leader and instigator. The truth was rather that this so-called first conspiracy of Catiline was a conspiracy by two disgruntled men, cheated of the consulship and the consequential chance of profit, to snatch forcibly what the law had denied them; and round them gathered a small number of persons, who saw in the plot a possible chance of self-interest or whose similar displeasure at failure to attain office urged them to join the malcontents.

The conspiracy failed through the failure of nerve and organisation on the part of the conspirators, and made little outward impact on the life of Rome. But if Crassus and Caesar had no part in this affair, they were certainly the initiators of an attempt to find for themselves some counterweight to Pompey's great power. Crassus was censor, Caesar curule aedile this year. Caesar, a younger man than Crassus, slightly younger than Cicero, had been independent in his outlook and behaviour from his early years during the Sullan régime. Connected to Marius through his aunt, he had refused to renounce the dangerous affiliation when Sulla tried to bring him to the other side, and had preferred a self-imposed exile from the dangerous vicinity of Rome. He had then served in the army and made his first acquaintance with military affairs; when he returned to Rome and entered the political arena, he left no doubt that he had no intention of disowning the Marian connexion; he entered politics as the opponent of the Senate and the Sullan constitution. In this very year, 65, he made a public gesture of his attitude by replacing the trophies of Marius' victories over Jugurtha and the Cimbri, which had been torn down by Sulla. This defiant gesture, together with the *laudatio* he spoke two years earlier over his aunt, Marius' widow, mark with unambiguous clarity the line he had adopted in politics; for to stand forth as champion of Marius was to declare war on the Sullan order, of which the Senate was the chief beneficiary and guardian; he showed courage in his challenging action at this time, when his career was yet to make, and consistency in pursuing this policy throughout his career. Ambitious and without scruple in his determination to destroy the supremacy of the Senatorial nobles, he lent himself during this decade to a number of schemes whose object it was in one way or another to wrest power from the Senate, and to make it possible for individuals not within the charmed circle to pursue a policy other than that followed by the Senate. Realising that the people were devoted to Pompey and that he could best enhance his own popularity by supporting measures that were in Pompey's interest, he had been one of those who had spoken in favour of the Lex Gabinia, and had also supported the Lex Manilia; but he realised as clearly as any one the threat that Pompey now posed to the constitution and to his own career; he was hardly less anxious than Crassus to be in a posture to reach an accommodation with Rome's most powerful citizen on terms of something like equality.

Crassus and Caesar would have known how to use the conspiracy in their own interests, but since it had fizzled out, they must look for some other means of attaining their end. Crassus therefore suggested that Egypt should become a tributary to Rome, in other words, that it should become a province. The only pretext for such immoral behaviour was an untrue story that the king, Alexander II, had bequeathed the kingdom to the Roman people; no one in authority believed the story, certainly not Crassus. Caesar, meanwhile, was trying to organise a tribunician bill by which he should be entrusted with this task, a task which he would see to it would need both money and troops. He would then be installed with armed forces in a highly strategical position to threaten Pompey.

The scheme was naturally opposed by those nobles who had unsuccessfully opposed Pompey's great commands; Catulus could well appreciate that whatever the danger posed by Pompey's present power, it could not be lessened by calling into being a second force, controlled by other enemies; this would merely double their danger. On this issue Cicero was with the nobles; he was never ready to support the wild schemes of the left any more than the reactionary policies of the right; a central course was his ideal, progressive, so he believed, but neither revolutionary nor reactionary. Further, support of Pompey was his established policy, and this was, he thought, designed against Pompey; he was therefore as firmly opposed to the measure as were Catulus and his friends, and he was able to join their opposition and at the same time to do Pompey a service.

The nobles were determined to reassert their position and to serve warning on those who might think it a profitable political exercise to attack what was left to them of their entrenched position in the state. Tribunician legislation was the instrument of attack; the tribunes therefore, who wielded the instrument, were the persons in need of a lesson. Two such persons, Manilius and Cornelius, had in particular aroused their anger by their legislation, and the small group of nobles who saw their own position threatened by such behaviour, if it were allowed to go unpunished, determined to strike. Manilius had incurred their wrath by sponsoring the law which gave Pompey command against Mithridates; not merely did this give power and added glory to a man hated by these nobles, but it had humiliated their own general, Lucullus, who was superseded. The fact that however unfortunate Lucullus was and however unmerited the treatment of which he had been the victim, his position was now quite impossible, and that in Rome's interests a general able to inspire confidence must be sent out, did not for these men diminish the heinousness of Manilius' action. They had first arraigned him at the end of Cicero's praetorship for extortion; and Cicero, it will be remembered, had been compelled to promise his aid in defence. He was, however, relieved from what might have been an embarrassment to his consular prospects; for Manilius seems to have avoided coming to trial on this charge; he was then prosecuted for *maiestas*, and Cicero was careful not to involve himself a second time. Manilius was convicted *in absentia* and withdrew into exile. Thus did the nobles take vengeance on the first of their enemies; with the second, Cornelius, they had less success.

Cornelius had been tribune in 67, and had been responsible for legislation which, while not in any way radical, was aimed at the small clique of nobles who wielded undue power in the Senate. He had proposed a bill to impose heavier penalties on those convicted of corruption at elections; so flagrant was the corruption in that year (67) that no one could object to a move that might reduce its incidence. So obvious was the need for such a bill that the nobles' only alternative to Cornelius' bill was one of their own, imposing less severe penalties, and this they enjoined the consul, Piso, to present. But by now it was strictly not permissible to submit it, since the elections were under way, and legislation connected with the conduct of elections was not allowed during the course of elections. The Senate therefore gave Piso permission to present his bill, thus dispensing him from the law. This the Senate had usurped the right to do and not infrequently did without protest; but strictly such dispensation required the assent of the people, and this the Senate had grown accustomed to ignoring, as they had done on this occasion. Cornelius therefore, foiled of his original purpose to take away this power, had proposed that the Senate should be empowered to grant such dispensation only when there were at least 200 Senators present; but that such a dispensation might not be vetoed when submitted for ratification to the people.

There was nothing either revolutionary or demagogic in the bill; yet it provoked the antagonism of the small group of nobles at whom it was aimed. For this clique depended for their influence largely on the fact that the meetings of the Senate were very frequently only sparsely attended, and they were able on these occasions to command a sufficient number of votes to win their way; but this would be much less likely in a House in which 200 members were present. For, as Cicero frequently pointed out, they were 'pauci', and were imposing their will in spite of their small numbers; had they commanded the support of a majority in the Senate, the strictures would have had less justification. They saw the threat involved in Cornelius' bill, and procured a tribune's veto; Cornelius prevented the tribune from exercising his veto, and this was the pretext on which he was now arraigned a second time before the court. He had been summoned in 66, but the prosecutors had, owing to threats, not dared to appear; the success against Manilius emboldened them to make a second attempt; and Cicero accepted the defence.

His reason was clear; he too was opposed to the improper influence which the 'pauci' exercised, the pressure they exerted in their own interests both against what he believed to be Rome's proper policy and against persons such as himself. He had attacked them at the time of Verres' prosecution, and had continued to do so; he knew that he would not enjoy their support for his candidature; but a show of his own power and influence would be no bad thing both for them and for himself. To defend Cornelius would chime in both with his interests and his political sentiments; it would gain him valuable support from all those within and without the Senate who resented the improper influence exercised by these 'pauci', and would also allow him to pursue his policy of moderation and cautious broadening of the basis of government by the admission of able persons from whatever origin. He therefore accepted the defence, attacked those responsible for the prosecution, jibing at their seeming concern for the tribunes' rights, when they had fought so pertinaciously to prevent their restoration, criticising their narrow selfishness; and he was completely successful. Almost all the jury, including the greater part of the Senatorial section, voted for acquittal, a fact which showed that many of the undistinguished Senators felt as did Cicero, but had not the oratorical genius or the courage to take an independent line. They looked now to Cicero's lead, as they had looked to others in the 70s, when the tribunes' rights were the centre of controversy. He had won valuable support for himself, and roused the goodwill of many who admired both his courage and his parts. The fact that Cornelius had been Pompey's quaestor, and his successful defence a matter of pleasure to the great man, was a further source of satisfaction to Cicero, to whom support of Pompey was so important an element of his policy.

Cicero had worked intensively on behalf of his candidacy and continued to do so. He had written to his great friend Atticus asking him to come to Rome to use his influence with his aristocratic friends on Cicero's behalf, and he seems to have come at the turn of the year 65/64. His younger brother Quintus wrote him a pamphlet, in which he sized up the chances and gave advice how to win over the different groups whose support he would need for success. It is a most interesting document, which throws valuable light on what was involved in suing for the consulship; three most important points to remember, he stresses, are that he is a *novus homo*, is seeking the consulship, and that it is in Rome that the election takes place. He indicates the opposition he may expect from certain groups, and how best to charm it to his side; the advantages he has won from his previous career, his high reputation as an orator, the men he has defended; and he sounds a confident note that his brother, whose talents he clearly admires, will be successful, if he proceeds with care and circumspection.

Cicero did in fact command considerable support, both as a result of his successful activity in the law courts, and because of the attitude he had adopted towards the 'pauci' on the one hand and to Pompey and to the tribunate on the other. To most persons except those of the extreme right or left—the 'pauci' and Crassus, Caesar and their followers—Cicero represented a policy of moderate reform, neither reactionary nor revolutionary; he had shown undoubted courage in attacking the 'pauci', and equally in opposing Crassus' Egyptian scheme; there was in him a sincerity of conduct stemming from his beliefs and ideals, which attracted people to him. The country votes would be largely for him, because he was one of them; the Equites supported him; and some noble families and many less influential Senators approved of what he sought to do and the courage with which he did it, as they had done ever since in Sulla's time they had looked to this young countryman to attack Chrysogonus.

His ideal was to restore to the state that harmony which seemed to him to have existed in the days of the younger Scipio, before the schisms created by the Gracchi had split the state into contending factions. Since then Equites and Senate had been at loggerheads, and the Equites had given constant encouragement to those persons who had determined to oppose Senatorial policy and implement their own schemes through legislation by means of the tribunate; yet the Equites' interest was for strong and peaceful government, and this, so Cicero thought, only the Senate could provide. If only the points of friction between the two Orders could be removed, their common interests should bring them together in a harmonious relationship which would ensure the orderly government of the Roman world. This was what he called the 'concordia ordinum'; and if this were to be achieved, then the Senate's hostile attitude towards the Equites, bred of decades of political and judicial hostility, must make way for a policy of understanding and accommodation; and for this high purpose Cicero regarded himself as peculiarly well qualified. Himself an *eques* he appreciated their point of view, and felt himself admirably fitted to interpret that point of view to the Senate; as a Senator he thought that he sympathised with the feelings and the apprehensions of all but the entrenched 'pauci', on whom he had in any case declared war; and his line of conduct hitherto seemed to him to confirm his hopes and beliefs. For he had consistently shown concern for the interests of the Equites, and had in general won their confidence; he had also made clear his respect for the Senate as Rome's governing body, and had criticised only to help and to protect its interests; all but a small minority must realise his good intentions towards that body.

At this stage his ideas hardly extended further; as his brother had pointed out, the election was held at Rome, and it was the affairs and issues of Rome rather than of Italy which at the moment occupied his thoughts. The districts of Italy could not be ignored; in fact Cicero, like other candidates, was careful to make himself known to different parts of Italy and to woo their support. But except occasionally and exceptionally their interests did not become the basis of a politician's programme; in this as in so much else Caesar's outlook was far broader than that of most of his contemporaries. Cicero's thoughts and ideas were centred on the Senate and Senatorial government, and it was its inadequacies, weaknesses and failures that he sought to remedy by effecting an agreement between the two Orders which would remove from the Populares and add to the Senate a large and powerful body of persons whose financial interests gave them vast influence throughout the Roman world. The conspiracy of Catiline, fated to explode during Cicero's consulship, forced him to look beyond Rome itself; faced with a conspiracy which aimed to raise parts of Italy in revolt he realised that he must expand his ideal to include the 'boni', loyal persons, throughout all Italy within his plan for a harmonious state; but not just yet; for the moment 'concordia ordinum', his personality and his country origin and *novitas* were his weapons.

His two chief opponents were Catiline and C. Antonius, son of the famous orator. Catiline we have already met; having been acquitted of the charge of extortion he was at last eligible to sue for the consulship, even though a second prosecution, arising out of his conduct during the Sullan terror, hung over him. Antonius had an equally disreputable career behind him, which included the plundering of allies, near-bankruptcy and the threat to arm his slaves in his own interest; but they were both nobles, of old families, who could hope for the support of the 'pauci' against the *novus homo*. They had other and more important supporters, Caesar and Crassus; together they had formed a compact whose object it was to win the consulship for these two men in return, we need not doubt, for political advantage to be given when they were elected. Crassus and Caesar were a formidable pair, having between them both money and experience in political intrigue. Money was spent lavishly in the cause; so much so that the Senate tried to promote a bill adding further penalties for corruption and bribery at elections. The coalition, however, without difficulty found a tribune to exercise his veto; and in the course of a speech seeking to justify his conduct he made some insulting references to Cicero, the chief intended victim of the coalition; for the other candidates offered no cause for worry. Cicero was the man they feared, whose success must spell failure for one of their two candidates; and his success would jeopardise, if not completely frustrate, any plans they might have for the following year.

The Senate was indignant at this rebuff, and on the next day Cicero took the opportunity to state his views about his two rivals, the compact, and the insulting tribune. It was a forthright speech, in which he again showed his courage, attacking Catiline and Antonius for their past conduct and their present mischievous intentions; now for the first time Cicero regarded Catiline, almost certainly wrongly, as one of the leaders of the so-called first Catilinarian conspiracy. He also attacked, without naming, Caesar and Crassus. It was a bold speech, of such effect that its chief victims felt compelled to answer back; but their only counter-attack lay in taunts at Cicero's provincial background and lack of family, precisely the points which were winning him so many supporters.

The elections duly came and Cicero was triumphantly elected at the top of the polls; Antonius, far behind, narrowly beat Catiline, who was thus once again cheated of his ambition. His success represented in Cicero's eyes the high point of his career, and rightly so; he had come from his country town of Arpinum, had embarked on a political career in which he had headed the polls both for the aedileship and the praetorship, and now, in the first year in which he was eligible to be a candidate, had by his own genius and character completely defeated his noble opponents. It was an achievement of which he might well be proud, and was a testimony to the rightness of his political instinct; for, as was now shown, it was not merely what he, but what an overwhelming majority of the citizens thought best for Rome. With truth he regarded it as a victory for the *municipia* and the whole of Italy; the voters had ignored the skullduggery of the nobles and Crassus and Caesar; their money was wasted when a candidate who could command the support of so many groups presented himself; it gave a blessing to his policy, if he could persevere to bring it to fruition.

In later times Sallust, looking back on the events of these years and striving to understand and to interpret their significance, was impressed particularly by the social and moral failure of the Republic, the result of the Senate's and the nobles' refusal to think in any other terms but those of their own advantage, and their determination to prevent new blood from playing its proper part in government. How, then, had Cicero achieved his success at the elections? Sallust was sure that without the nobles he must have failed; the nobles, therefore, must have given their support.

But why? Because they were fearful of the threats of revolution which in fact came to a head in the next year, 63. Fearful of what they might lose and suffer if Catiline were to become consul, since he was the revolutionary leader, they decided to support Cicero, whom they despised but did not fear, knowing that he would be utterly opposed to revolution, and that he commanded an allegiance among groups that disliked and mistrusted the nobles.

Such is Sallust's explanation of Cicero's success; but it is wrong. In the first place it seems clear from Cicero's speeches that the 'pauci' did not support him; some nobles did support him, as they had done earlier, because they respected his talents and found no fault with the general tenor of his policy; but the group that had constantly opposed Cicero and his claims, those whom in the Senate just before the election he had once again castigated for their attempts to keep power within the hands of a few, will have opposed him on the day of the election, preferring Antonius and Catiline, whom they certainly favoured up to that moment; and this explains why Antonius was second and Catiline third. Had they really been afraid of revolution, there were other candidates to whom they could have given their suffrage, thus ensuring the elimination of the revolutionaries. And, more important, at the time of the elections (July 64) there was no cause to fear any revolutionary movement. Catiline began to plot violence only after yet further defeat for the consulship in 63; what Catiline had conspired with Caesar and Crassus to do, if he were elected consul, must have been known to those persons, since the compact was an open secret, and they must have been informed of some at least of its aims.

Cicero's success was their defeat; it remained to see whether he could give the required leadership to those many groups who were no less anxious than himself for harmonious progress; for if he failed, then events would necessarily continue along the path of faction and hostility, a path that had already led through one civil war, and would as certainly end in a second one. His first concern, even before he assumed office, must be to reach some sort of accommodation with his future colleague, Antonius, for if Cicero could hope to frustrate him, so too could he frustrate Cicero. Antonius was in close league with Catiline, Caesar and Crassus, three men whose readiness and aptitude for mischief would be whetted by their discomfiture at the elections; if he failed to win him over, or at least to reduce him to a complaisant silence, he must expect his year of office to be one of frustration and possible conflict. Fortunately the means were ready to hand; by the Sempronian law the provinces to be allotted to the consuls were named before the elections; Macedonia and Cisalpine Gaul were the consular provinces, and the lot had given Macedonia to Cicero. Macedonia was far the more attractive to an ambitious or unscrupulous governor; the ambitious could engage in war with the neighbouring peoples and thus win a triumph; the unscrupulous could use the excuse of war to enrich himself with booty. Antonius wanted money, and money could be got from Macedonia, though not from Gaul, where conditions were different; Cicero longed to complete the honour of his family by the signal addition of a triumph, but at this stage of his career he had no wish to leave Rome, the centre of political activity; he had learnt his lesson when he served his quaestorship in Sicily. He therefore offered Antonius to exchange provinces, thus giving Antonius the opportunity the lot had denied him, and by this simple expedient won him over to an acquiescence which was to prove of inestimable value.

It is true that Cicero preferred politics to war and the prospect of a triumph, and in the event he declined to go to Gaul; none the less his action revealed a quality of character and an ambition to serve his country. Few there were in Rome who would have rejected the chance of a province with prospects of fame and wealth; and Cicero was not a wealthy man. It also revealed a political shrewdness of a high order, which marked him out from the common run of would-be consuls. By his character and personality he had triumphed over a powerful combination that had aimed to put two men into the highest office for their own political purposes; with one of these he was saddled as partner; by this shrewd move he outmanoeuvred his opponents, and at the same time made himself the dominant consul-designate, soon to be the dominant consul. Crassus and Caesar had been beaten by Cicero in a political struggle of which we see only a few surface ripples; already he had shown himself as an outstanding senior politician, to be regarded seriously by any intending opponent.

Even before he entered upon his consulship, Crassus and Caesar were scheming to give themselves popularity and the power to oppose, if necessary, Pompey, whose return would not be much longer delayed, and whose power and prestige would be such that he could, if he chose, be the arbiter of their and Rome's destiny. They had persuaded an incoming tribune, Servilius Rullus, to sponsor a land law by which land was to be given to the landless proletariat of the city. Cicero heard of the intention, and sought information from Rullus on the details of the plan, in order, so he said, to lend his consular aid to the bill; he was, however, rebuffed, and had to wait until the bill was proposed.

As soon as the tribunes entered office (10 December), Rullus made a speech, which threw little light on his proposals; then he published his bill, and Cicero heard for the first time what was planned. It then became clear that the measure was designed to put great power into the hands of a body of decemvirs, by which they would control large sums of money and, if necessary, troops, and that this, rather than the distribution of land, was its main object. The decemvirs were to be chosen by a minority of the tribes, they were to have control of considerable state funds with which to purchase land both in Italy and in the provinces; Egypt was to be regarded as Roman in virtue of the alleged will of Ptolemy XI, and thus taken over and its resources dedicated to the decemvirs' task. Crassus and Caesar had in 65 unsuccessfully tried to give themselves military and financial resources by means of Egypt; now they made a second attempt in a somewhat different context.

7-2

If the bill were passed, Caesar and Crassus would certainly be among the decemvirs, and would be the leading members; thus provided with money and an army they would be able to oppose and if necessary dictate to Pompey, who would be reduced to comparative impotence. Cicero on his first day of office spoke in the Senate, attacking the provisions of the bill; very soon after he addressed the people in his first *contio*, in which after thanking them for his election to the consulship he turned to criticise the Rullan bill; and when Rullus replied in his absence, Cicero in a second address persuaded them to oppose the bill. We need not consider the details of his arguments; his shrewd insight showed him the implications and hidden intentions of the bill, and these he revealed; and even though much of what he claimed to be the dangerous threat to the people was a gross exaggeration, almost a bogy conjured up to frighten them, this was because only bogies would frighten them; the true sources of apprehension, namely the quasi-dictatorial power which Crassus and Caesar would wield, and the way in which they would probably wield it, were not likely to have any great effect on the Roman populace; somehow they must, in the interests of peace and good government, be persuaded that a bill which was proposing to give them something was not in their interest and should be rejected. This he succeeded in doing; it represented a political victory for himself and for his policy, and won him the support of many in the Senate who had hitherto opposed him. It also represented a further victory for Cicero over Crassus and Caesar, the third such victory.

He emphasised that he, not those who were making speciously 'popular' proposals, was the 'popularis'; the objects of his 'popular' policy were *pax, concordia, otium*.[1] These were endangered by a proposal which threatened to provoke commotion and discord between powerful persons in the state; the tribunes

---

[1] In his speech to the people *libertas* was substituted for *concordia*, since *concordia* did not strictly include the plebs, who were something of a necessary evil to be placated and kept in good temper. At the end of the speech *tranquillitas* replaces *libertas*.

should join with the 'boni' to maintain orderly government; and orderly government, so he believed, was to be found only in the *auctoritas* of the Senate, which he hoped it would be his achievement to restore after its long eclipse. He appealed to the tribunes to abandon those by whom they will themselves, unless they are careful, be abandoned, to join with him, harmonise their plans with those of the loyal 'boni', and with a common love and enthusiasm to defend the country which belongs to all of them.[1] Aware that the distempers of the state came from within, not without, he knew that they were serious; to prevent this intestinal discord required the support and co-operation of all loyal men and harmony between the two chief Orders, the Senatorial and Equestrian. But the social discontent which produced this disorder within the state Cicero did not fully recognise, nor did he properly realise that so long as there was a fertile soil for revolutionary movements, there would continue to be threats of such upheavals; the harmony that he so sincerely and desperately sought could not be won by political alliances alone; it could be achieved only by removing the causes. There is justice in the criticism that Cicero failed to appreciate the social and economic distress and injustice which underlay the discontent at this time; that he saw the problem only in political terms, and that he supposed that if government could but be restored to the orderly harmony of early days, Rome's problems would be solved; that he was seeking to cure the symptom, not the malady. It is none the less true that without the harmony of the two leading Orders and the support of the substantial middle class throughout Italy, the economic problems would be solved by violent and disorderly means, which could only end in chaos and possible civil war; from this point of view harmony was the first essential; if concord could be attained, the problems could be attacked. To

---

[1] '...conspirate nobiscum, consentite cum bonis, communem rem publicam communi studio atque amore defendite.' Note the reiterated 'con-', emphasising the unity and harmony which he is anxious to create instead of the existing divisions.

Cicero the attainment of concord was the first, most pressing need; whether he realised what must then be done we cannot know for certain; for the first end was not achieved, and he never ceased to lament its failure; he was thus unable to address himself to the next problem, even if he was aware of it; his first ideals remained predominant in the consul and ex-consul.

A second attack was now made by Caesar, this time on the Senate's claim by means of its *senatus consultum ultimum* to empower the consuls to treat citizens as enemies, to suspend, in fact, the constitution in time of crisis. Since the disappearance of the original dictatorship there had been no constitutional means by which the Senate could handle an internal crisis; and in the storm and stress of C. Gracchus' last days the Senate had passed what came to be known as the 'last decree', by which the consuls were empowered to take whatever action they thought fit to deal with the emergency. Strictly the Senate could only give advice, and the consuls were not empowered to act unconstitutionally, but they knew that they had the support of the Senate for whatever action they might deem necessary; and since the decisions of the Senate had for many years been accepted on many issues as equivalent to a constitutional decision, the consuls might well feel a reasonable confidence. In fact in this first case their action was subsequently upheld and by implication the Senate's right to issue its 'last decree'. When in 100 the 'last decree' empowered Marius to deal with the commotions occasioned by Saturninus, no objection had been raised, and the procedure was now regarded as part of the constitution.

Caesar, however, was not of this mind. He regarded it as an instrument devised by the nobles to prevent their opponents from successfully vindicating their policy against the interests of the nobles; it had been invoked against tribunes whose policies had incurred Senatorial opposition to the point where serious civil disturbance had resulted; in Caesar's eyes it was merely an instrument whereby the Senate successfully blocked unpleasant legislation, and as such it should be destroyed.

His attack took the form of an attack on a man, now old, who had been involved in the murder of Saturninus, which had occurred in 100 under the aegis of the 'last decree'; if the 'last decree' was sufficient authority, then Saturninus' death followed naturally, since he opposed the consul, Marius, and was struck down. But if it did not authorise such treatment of citizens, then those responsible for his death were guilty of putting a citizen to death without a trial; and this was the point on which Caesar instigated the prosecution of C. Rabirius Postumus, who was alleged to have shared in the death of Saturninus. A tribune, C. Labienus, later one of Caesar's most able legates in Gaul, prosecuted Rabirius for the murder of Saturninus during the crisis of 100, and by a plebiscite procured that it should be tried as a case of *perduellio*. The details are by no means clear nor are they here important; it seems that Rabirius would, in spite of Cicero's pleading, have been convicted, had not the trial, itself an outmoded procedure at this time, been ended by the equally outmoded procedure of hoisting a red flag on the Janiculum.

Cicero was able to convince the Senate that a trial for *perduellio*, with the possible penalty, if convicted, of crucifixion, was contrary to the spirit of the age; the Senate would in any case need no persuasion on the point, since the issue was not obscure; and Labienus did not renew the prosecution in the same form. He now instituted proceedings before the people to fine Rabirius for his action in 100; if he were convicted, Caesar's point would equally be established, though in a less dramatic form. On this occasion Hortensius and Cicero spoke for the defence, and although Labienus restricted their speeches to half an hour, Rabirius was acquitted by a large majority. Caesar had thus suffered further discomfiture, the Senate had received confirmation of its action in the use of the 'last decree', and Cicero's standing in the Senate among the nobles was enhanced. The trial had in view of later events a significance unperceived at the time; for Caesar had defined his opposition to the principle of the 'last decree', and the Senate and Cicero were now certain that it was permissible under its aegis even to put citizens to death should the emergency warrant such extreme action. Cicero was to act on that assumption, and in consequence to give a handle to his enemies, led by Caesar, by which they were able to procure his banishment and effectively to silence him during the last desperate throes of the Republic. But for the moment Cicero had led his forces to victory, worsted the mischief-makers, and made further progress in establishing his *concordia*.

CHAPTER 7

THE CATILINARIAN CONSPIRACY
AND CICERO'S ACHIEVEMENT

THE consular elections for 62 would take place in July, and Cicero had cause to be worried about the possible outcome, since Catiline was once again a candidate; and with the backing, perhaps, of Caesar and Crassus and the goodwill of Cicero's fellow-consul he might well succeed. Cicero had with the Senate's support been responsible for a law to increase the penalties for corrupt and improper practices at the elections; but this in itself was slight protection, and in so far as it was allowed to operate, imposed equal limitations and disabilities on all the candidates. It was clear that for Catiline this was the last attempt to win the supreme magistracy by legal means; if this venture failed as had his previous one, he would turn to more direct methods to achieve his aim. He had already boasted, when Cato threatened him with prosecution, that if his future were set fire to, he would extinguish the blaze not with water but by pulling down the whole house. He had at a meeting in his own house put himself forward as the defender of the 'unfortunate', with dark suggestions of the proper way to disentangle oneself from one's pecuniary misfortunes, and expressed himself ready to lead in the revolutionary enterprise at which he was hinting. It will be well at this juncture briefly to consider his aims and intentions, in order to evaluate the extent of the danger which he represented to the state.

There was at this time in Italy great wealth and great poverty; the wars of this century continued the influx of wealth which had begun in the second century and had first unbalanced the structure of society. Opulence had led to extravagance; wealth which was seized from others was often lightly spent, with the easy reflexion that, when that was gone, there was plenty more to take. The readiness with which men volunteered for campaigns where the prospects of booty were good, the eagerness with which magistrates sought lucrative provinces, indicate this tendency at both the lower and the higher levels. Cicero had won over Antonius by ceding to him the province of Macedonia; Caesar would shortly go to Spain and disencumber himself of a staggering load of debt.

Extravagance in high places had reached alarming proportions. Cicero himself, who would never enrich himself by what he felt to be dishonourable means, was in chronic debt through living above his means in order to maintain the standard proper to his station. Others, less scrupulous, having run through their patrimony or loaded it with mortgages, had only two resources left, to acquire a fresh fortune by provincial plunder, or to borrow in Rome. To meet the second alternative there was always Crassus, ready for a consideration to help someone who could help him; and many Senators were beholden to him, their indebtedness no great burden, provided they supported Crassus by their vote when that was asked for. Those who had no value in Crassus' eyes must find some other solution; there were many such, who could hope for neither a loan from Crassus nor a provincial command, since they were unlikely to reach the senior magistracies.

At lower levels debt was no less common. During this century the army provided a livelihood with a good prospect of acquiring property in the form of booty, and a piece of land at the end of service; since 100 there had been many thousands thus settled in Italy and elsewhere; Sulla had himself settled many thousands of his veterans in colonies on land confiscated for the purpose. Many of these men had lived the lives of country gentlemen while their resources lasted, but now their money was exhausted, their farms either mortgaged or sold; for such persons the future must seem bleak, with little hope of any amelioration of the depressing circumstances into which their feckless improvidence had plunged them, except through a revolution which would at once cancel their debts and offer them a chance to acquire a fresh fortune. There were men whose debts were large but whose estates were larger, but who could not endure to clear their debts by the sale of their estates. There were debtors who hoped for a revolution and the chance to win the powerful position for themselves which they seemed otherwise unable to achieve. There were debtors who were prepared to join with Catiline as a final, hopeless gesture; there were murderers and criminals, to whom violence and the chance of easy spoil at the expense of others seemed natural; and finally there were younger persons, whom Catiline had seduced to his influence by providing the means for the debauched and disreputable life which he had encouraged them to enjoy; instructed by him in evil ways, they were eager to join him in his present infamous adventure.

All these persons—and they amounted to many thousands—were ready to join in any desperate venture which could relieve them of their burden of debt and pander to their sense of mischief and excitement; and Catiline was at hand to provide the leadership. Himself unscrupulous, in debt, and unrestrained by sense of patriotism, he had twice been prevented from suing and thus failed to be elected consul, and his feeling of frustration, his hatred of those who frustrated him, and his determination to wreak his vengeance had increased. Had he been elected consul for 63, he would probably have been content to pass some popular and mischievous legislation, to award himself a lucrative province, if the lot failed in its task, and then to build up his fortunes as a dishonest and rapacious governor. He would have been a disgrace, but not a danger, to Rome. But when he had despaired of the consulship, chagrin, desperation and vindictiveness conspired to make him dangerous and his schemes a threat to peace and order in Italy. What he failed to attain by proper means, he would attain by force, and would create turmoil throughout Italy; when his second candidature failed, he set himself seriously to organising these diverse elements into a cohesive body for the purpose of overthrowing the government and establishing himself as Rome's ruler.

Catiline's meeting with his followers, to which we have referred, became known to Cicero through a certain Fulvia, whose young admirer, Q. Curius, a follower of Catiline, being without funds to maintain his mistress as she expected, excused his present poverty by the promise of untold wealth soon to be his. Fulvia's persistent inquiry revealed how this transformation was to come about: by some desperate enterprise which Catiline was then organising, which would involve war and its attendant chances for enrichment. Fulvia at once reported the story to Cicero; and throughout this critical year Cicero's source of information never failed him, thus enabling him to know what was planned as soon as the plan was formed. Cicero procured from the Senate a short postponement of the elections while the matter was investigated, and on the following day revealed in the Senate what he knew. Catiline brazened it out, remarking that the state consisted of two bodies, one decrepit with a feeble head, the other strong but headless; and that he would become its head. In spite of this intemperate language the Senate would take no action against Catiline; some disbelieved the story, others were friends of Catiline.

Catiline was therefore a candidate for the consulship, the elections for which were held soon after, in late July or early August. On that day Cicero, the presiding magistrate, melodramatically entered the Campus Martius protected by a bodyguard and a breastplate, which he was careful to let be seen by everyone, in order to emphasise his danger. If there was any such danger, it did not materialise; the elections proceeded smoothly and L. Murena and D. Junius Silanus were elected consuls. Catiline's last hopes of achieving his object through the consulship were now shattered; he therefore gave himself wholly to his alternative means, namely revolution; and Cicero's worries began in earnest.

Catiline needed time to complete his preparations, and although

Cicero was apprised through Fulvia of what was afoot, he still had no evidence with which to convince a disbelieving Senate. A meeting of the Senate on 22 September reached no decision on the matter, since, apart from the small number of Senators involved with Catiline, no one was prepared to believe the consul, who was suspected of puffing a matter of no significance in his own interest. His colleague, Antonius, was still at this time secretly in favour of Catiline, and his attitude and influence did not help Cicero. And so matters continued until the night of 20 and 21 October.

On that night Crassus, accompanied by M. Marcellus and Metellus Scipio, called on Cicero and handed him some letters which had been delivered at his house, addressed to various persons; he had opened only the one addressed to himself, which had proved to contain an anonymous warning of an intended massacre instigated by Catiline, and urged him to escape secretly at once. Cicero summoned the Senate the next day, the letters were read, and a certain Q. Arrius added the further information that troops were being levied in Etruria. The intention, so Cicero himself reported, was that a certain Manlius should raise the standard of revolt in Etruria on 27 October, and that on the 28th there should be a massacre of the nobles in Rome. The letters, together with this menacing information, at last persuaded the Senate to take some action to deal with the situation whose reality they had hitherto refused to accept; they passed the *senatus consultum ultimum*, by which the consuls were instructed to take whatever steps they saw fit for the protection of the state; it gave Cicero, in fact, well-nigh dictatorial powers with which to handle Catiline. He at once raised a body of volunteers to be in readiness against sudden disturbance in the city, thus preventing any attempt at massacre on the 21st; the day passed uneventfully, the only result of Cicero's vigilant activity being that he was once again believed by some to have exaggerated the danger in his own interest.

However, at the end of the month L. Saenius read in the Senate a letter he had received from Faesulae, to the effect that on the 17th Manlius had taken up arms; others reported slave revolts in Capua and Apulia. The Senate took immediate steps; the proconsuls Q. Marcius Rex and Q. Metellus Creticus, who were still waiting outside Rome in the hope of being awarded a triumph, were sent to Faesulae and Capua respectively, and Q. Metellus Celer, a praetor, who had been allotted the province which Cicero had declined, was sent to Cisalpine Gaul; all were empowered to raise troops for their purpose. Rewards were offered for information, and the gladiators at Capua were distributed in small numbers in the surrounding municipalities.

A certain L. Aemilius Paullus now announced his intention of prosecuting Catiline for violence; Catiline, secure in the knowledge of influential support within the Senate, and in the expectation that Manlius' rising was close at hand, preferred to remain for the present in Rome; as a pledge of his innocence and a token of his *sang froid* he offered to place himself in free custody with Cicero himself, and when he declined, with other Senators, who also refused, until M. Metellus was found to accept the responsibility, possibly because he was, according to Cicero, himself involved in the conspiracy. It was hardly therefore cause for surprise that Catiline contrived without great difficulty to hold a meeting of his fellow-conspirators on the night of 5 November at the house of M. Porcius Laeca in the Sickle Makers' Lane, where he unfolded his plans and gave his instructions; he himself would join Manlius, others were to proceed to Etruria, Picenum and Cisalpine Gaul, while others, including Lentulus and Cethegus, were to remain in charge of affairs in Rome and to prepare for the rising there. At the moment the most important thing was to dispose of Cicero; this mission C. Cornelius and L. Vargunteius undertook for the next night; but Cicero was as usual informed through Fulvia of the intention, and when the two gentlemen arrived to pay their respects, they found his house guarded and barricaded against their entry, and the attempt perforce miscarried.

Cicero at once summoned the Senate to meet in the temple of Jupiter Stator, thinking that Catiline would by now have left Rome, as seemed to have been agreed at the meeting at Laeca's house, and that he would, in view of the new situation, be able to rouse the Senate to more active and drastic measures. Imagine, then, his surprise when Catiline himself brazenly took his place in the Senate! No one would sit next to him; but his very presence made it impossible for Cicero to shock the minds of his audience to the imminent danger; for Catiline was not with Manlius at Faesulae, but here in Rome. Catiline's friends in the Senate were in a strong position; and those both within and without the Senate in favour of some sort of social reform would not be willing to take strong action against Catiline, unless they were convinced of the danger of an uprising and civil war; and Cicero, certain as he might be of the rightness of his information, had as yet no proof. He must proceed cautiously, if he did not want to find himself discredited and Catiline's position dangerously strengthened; there were still too many doubters for firm action.

Cicero therefore delivered a speech, which we know as the First Catilinarian, which he published three years later; whether therefore it precisely corresponds with his actual words on this occasion we cannot be certain; its general tenor was certainly closely akin, but slight changes in view of the later political situation may have been made in any or all of these Catilinarian speeches. Feeling unable to use his constitutional powers to take positive action against him, he aimed to shame Catiline into revealing his hand by forcing him to leave Rome and join his confederates; only when he was at the head of his forces and had begun to set his plans in motion, could Cicero feel confident to react firmly. He revealed the details of Catiline's recent activities and his future intentions, thus showing that his every move was known to him; in this way might he be panicked into action; and he appealed to him in his country's interests to take himself out of Rome either to his forces or into exile. Catiline was stung;

he was hated by many in the Senate, and his friends dare not declare themselves; except for some futile interruptions he had been unable to reply to or to counter the charges; angry and humiliated he did what Cicero wanted: he left Rome.

Cicero had won an important victory; without incurring enmity and unpopularity by using his powers against a man whose guilt was not yet proven, he had contrived to force Catiline's hand and provoke him to do exactly what he wanted him to do. But since there was yet no evidence of Catiline's guilt, and since much of his revolutionary programme found favour with certain sections of the plebs, whose unhappy situation could only be improved by what Catiline seemed to promise, Cicero felt it important to justify his behaviour in the Senate and to inform the people of the position. The following day therefore he addressed them in a *contio*, explaining the previous day's proceedings in the Senate, and justifying both what he had and had not done. As it was there were murmurs of his high-handed behaviour in hounding an innocent man into exile; on the other hand, if he was guilty, as Cicero claimed, why had he not taken drastic action in defence of the state? Cicero explained his dilemma, and warned the people that since Catiline's accomplices were still in Rome, and Catiline would have gone, not into exile, but to his army, there was still considerable danger to be apprehended; but that he would as consul take whatever action was necessary, and would not flinch through fear of unpopularity from acting as firmly as the situation demanded.

About a week later Q. Catulus read aloud in the Senate a letter he had received from Catiline, in which Catiline attempted to justify what he was doing, namely to defend the injury done to his *dignitas* by espousing the cause of the classes oppressed like himself by cliques and unworthy persons. This left no doubt of his intention to use force against the state; the Senate at once declared both Catiline and Manlius *hostes*, and stipulated a time within which his followers should lay down their arms without fear of punishment. At the same time they ordered the consuls to hold a levy, Antonius to pursue Catiline, and Cicero to protect Rome. None the less, since there was no open commotion in Rome, Cicero was still held by many to have exaggerated the danger, and in fact by his untimely behaviour to have provoked the war. His embarrassment was increased by the behaviour of one of the tribunes-elect, Q. Metellus, a friend and supporter of Pompey, who had recently returned from Pompey's army to seek the tribunate, probably in Pompey's interests. In view of Cicero's attitude to Pompey and the great importance of not offending him at this juncture, the mischievous Metellus was indeed a thorny opponent which a harassed consul should have been spared.

But there was more to add to his tribulation. Even the Optimates seem to have believed that with Catiline's departure the urgency was past, and Cato and Sulpicius chose this inauspicious moment to settle a political score by prosecuting L. Licinius Murena, one of the consuls-designate, for bribery at the election. A more ill-timed gesture could scarcely be conceived; if they succeeded, the new year would open with one consul only, just when the crisis might be expected to break. Further, a split in the ranks of the *boni* at this moment could advantage only Catiline, and would disrupt the *concordia* which was so important. To complete his embarrassment, the law under which he was to be prosecuted had been passed by Cicero himself, by which the then existing law relating to bribery had been made stricter and sterner penalties imposed. Clearly Cicero must, amid all his more anxious worries, accept the defence.

Hortensius and Crassus had also offered their services for the defence, thus showing a greater sense of responsibility than did Cato, whose obstinate spirit and narrow conception of statesmanship now as on future occasions brought to jeopardy that which he fondly supposed he was defending. On this occasion the ability of Hortensius and Crassus and Cicero's felicity in the final speech saved Murena and, possibly, the state. He poked fun both at Sulpicius' profession of the law and at Cato's rather stubborn stoicism and won the jury to his side by his humorous pleasantries, so that the question of bribery seemed almost trivial; then he drew attention to the gravity of the present time and the disaster to the state if there were not two consuls on 1 January, particularly if the one with an impressive military record were not in office. Murena was acquitted and Cicero could return to his more important duties.

Within the next few days events moved swiftly. Q. Fabius Sanga, who was the patron of a Gallic tribe, the Allobroges, reported to Cicero that an Allobrogian embassy, which was at this moment on business at Rome, had informed him that they had been approached by certain persons with a view to lending armed aid to Catiline's enterprise; and although their people were in a desperate situation through the activities of Roman moneylenders, they had thought it right to inform their patron of what had been suggested to them. This gave Cicero his opportunity to acquire the evidence he so far lacked. The Allobroges were to pretend to agree to the suggestion, but to ask the leaders in Rome for written statements of their requests and promises, in order that they might have clear written proposals to put before their people. Lentulus, Cethegus, and Statilius all provided such letters, and a certain T. Volturcius, armed with a letter to Catiline, was charged to accompany them to Catiline's presence on their way home.

All was now ready, and the embassy was due to leave Rome in the early hours of 3 December. Cicero instructed two praetors, L. Valerius Flaccus and C. Pomptinus, to be at hand with an armed escort to intercept them on the Milvian bridge, to arrest everyone and to seize the letters. This was successfully accomplished, the letters, unopened, were brought to Cicero, together with the prisoners; and Cicero further invited Lentulus, Cethegus, Statilius, P. Gabinius Capito and M. Caeparius to his house. The first four, knowing nothing of what had transpired at the Milvian bridge, walked unsuspectingly into the trap; Caeparius, who had heard of the night's events, escaped, but was caught soon after.

Cicero at once consulted with leading members of the Senate who, still not convinced of the magnitude of the plot, wanted Cicero to open the letters at once rather than bring them to the Senate unopened, in case there should be nothing particularly incriminating in them; Cicero, however, confident of what he would find, preferred to bring them to the Senate untampered with in any way.

The Senate was immediately convoked to meet in the temple of Concord, whither Cicero personally conducted Lentulus, since he was praetor; the others were brought under guard. While the Senate was in session, Cethegus' house was, on the information of the Allobroges, searched and a vast quantity of weapons discovered and brought to the Senate. Volturcius was given an assurance of safety and asked to reveal what he knew; this was to the effect that he had a letter from Lentulus to Catiline asking him to increase his forces by including slaves, and to advance on Rome at the earliest opportunity, in order that when they had started fires in different quarters of Rome and begun a general massacre, Catiline's forces should be at hand to intercept would-be fugitives. The Allobroges then told what they knew of the affair; then came the letters. Each in turn admitted that the seal and the handwriting were his; they were then read. Lentulus at first tried to deny his complicity, but after a short time suddenly broke down and admitted everything. Further corroborative evidence was then produced by the consul-designate, Silanus, and the Senate decided what should be done. A vote of thanks to Cicero was passed, 'quod virtute, consilio, providentia mea res publica maximis periculis sit liberata'. The two praetors who had been in charge at the Milvian bridge were congratulated on their courageous and loyal conduct; and Antonius, Cicero's colleague, was congratulated on having severed his earlier alliance with the conspirators! The four conspirators brought to the Senate were to be guarded in custody, as also were five others, yet to be caught, whose complicity was proved by the evidence that day. Finally a *supplicatio* was decreed 'quod urbem incendiis, caede civis,

Italiam bello liberassem'; the first occasion, as Cicero presently pointed out, on which a *supplicatio* had been granted for what a *togatus* had done; it had always hitherto been for military success. Q. Catulus referred to him as 'parens patriae'; in the following year Cato would refer to him as 'pater patriae'.

Cicero had now, after months of suspicion and incredulity on the part of Senate and people, been proved right; by his courage and tenacity in continuing in spite of disbelief to maintain a close watch on Catiline and his followers, he had triumphantly proved his point in time to save Rome and Italy from civil war and bloodshed. The Senate was lavish in its appreciation, balm enough for a *novus homo* yearning to be accepted by the nobles; but, more important, it might seem to strengthen if not to consummate the *concordia ordinum*. For the Equites, ever averse to civil commotion, would certainly co-operate with the Senate in whatever action might be deemed necessary to handle a crisis whose reality could no longer be denied. But in fact Cicero was far from free of worry; Catiline was still at large with his army, and in spite of what Cicero might say, there could still be considerable support for him from those whose situation was desperate or depressed. Further, he might seem in the conspirators he had arrested to have a wolf by the ears; what was he to do with them? He must proceed with great circumspection, for the nobles, grateful though they might be for what he had done, had not forgotten that he was a *novus homo*, and would be ready to resent any overstrong action against one of themselves, even a traitor; three of them were nobles, and Lentulus was a Cornelius and had been praetor until forced to resign after the disclosure. However justified any action might be, his personal hopes and ambitions were too closely involved in his relations with the aristocrats for his course of action to be easy.

For the moment they were held in custody by five senators, among them Caesar and Crassus. The same evening Cicero addressed the people in a *contio*, to explain what had transpired and to justify his actions to persons, many of whom would have sympathy for some at least of Catiline's intentions. He pointed out the rightness of his action in hounding Catiline out of Rome, since he had earlier been criticised for his supposed harsh attitude towards one whose guilt had not been proven; now everyone could see his guilt, and Cicero's wisdom in disencumbering Rome of so mischievous a person. He concluded with an appeal to the people to protect him and his reputation against those who would, when the whole affair was dead, attempt to bring him into disrepute because of what he was now doing. This appeal was probably added when he worked over the speech for publication in 60; for by then he had been attacked for his high-handed behaviour.

He spent the night with friends, as his own house was being used for the celebration of the Bona Dea, from which men were excluded. With them he discussed what should be the next step; severity and mildness were alike open to criticism, severity because of the possible reaction of the nobles, mildness because of the danger of sparing the prisoners while Catiline was still at large; it might also be construed as cowardice. In the midst of their deliberations his wife Terentia appeared to report an omen from the sacrifice at the celebration of the Bona Dea, which was interpreted as a sign of Heaven's blessing and an encouragement to firm action; his brother and Nigidius Figulus, who had a reputation for divination, who were with him, supported the interpretation. It would seem that in the discussion Cicero had been leaning towards clemency; the awful responsibility of taking the harsher decision, together with his natural concern to give no offence to the nobles, had probably weighed him down; to have succeeded so far from his country equestrian birth, to have reached the consulship and hence nobility, and then to risk throwing away the fruits by taking too strong action now was to ask a bitter price; we may sympathise with his inclination to reason himself out of such a course.

The Senate met again on 4 December. The main business concerned a certain L. Tarquinius, who had been arrested on his way to Catiline, and who under questioning claimed to have been sent by Crassus to Catiline to urge him to hasten his march on Rome. Nothing could have been more embarrassing than this, if it were true; many Senators, beholden financially to Crassus, did not wish to find themselves concerned in voting him guilty; to Cicero the suggestion of Crassus' complicity in the plot could be disastrous for his *concordia*; and such was his power and influence that it would certainly have undesirable and possibly serious repercussions. In view of the fact that Crassus had in October provided Cicero with information, and had joined in the defence of Murena, it is unlikely that he had anything to do at this stage with the matter. Crassus later complained that Cicero had himself rigged the affair to compromise him; that, too, is at this juncture unthinkable. Another view was that Autronius had tried to involve the name of so powerful a figure in order to induce the Senate to act more leniently towards the prisoners. Whatever the reason, the Senate decided that Tarquinius' evidence was untrue, and that he should be kept in custody until he revealed the authors of the plot.

Meanwhile two disgruntled nobles, Q. Catulus and C. Piso, tried to drag in Caesar's name; his general behaviour made it a possible charge, and this would therefore be an opportunity to end Caesar's career. Cicero would have none of this; as things were, he had at last reduced the problem to Catiline and his armed forces; to drag in so powerful and popular a figure as Caesar must inevitably introduce a political element which was at the moment absent, and the attempt to take political revenge by dragging in one's opponents could only inflame the situation and might go far to provoke the civil war that Cicero was so anxious to prevent. The attempts to implicate Crassus and Caesar were not therefore allowed to succeed.

During this meeting of the Senate Cicero received information that the freedmen and dependents of Lentulus and Cethegus were organising shopkeepers and others in the vicinity of the Forum for an attempt to release the prisoners; he therefore posted guards in the Forum and on the Capitol, a large part of whom on the Capitol consisted of Equites.

On the following day, 5 December, the Senate again met, and Cicero asked what should be done with the prisoners. Silanus, a consul-elect, was first asked his opinion, which he gave to the effect that the prisoners had deserved the extreme penalty. In this view Murena, his fellow consul-designate, and fourteen consulars concurred. Then Caesar spoke. After pointing out that the Porcian and Sempronian laws protected citizens from the death penalty by a court not established by the people's authority, and also allowed the alternative of exile, he suggested that their property should be confiscated, and that they should be kept in detention for life in different *municipia* throughout Italy; that anyone who tried to release them should be severely punished, and that any future magistrate who should attempt to re-open their case should be regarded as an enemy of the state. This, he maintained, was a punishment worse than death, and did not force them to ignore the established laws.

Caesar, as a leader of the Populares, was in a difficult and embarrassing position: so embarrassing that his fellow-leader, Crassus, found it prudent to absent himself from this meeting. The Populares did not recognise the *senatus consultum ultimum* as a valid justification for putting citizens to death; and Caesar himself had called its validity in question only a little earlier in the case of Rabirius. Yet the present occasion was different from those of C. Gracchus and Saturninus, as Caesar himself recognised. It was not a question of the disposing of a popular leader by doubtfully legal means; Catiline was the head of a conspiracy to seize power by force, impose a revolutionary policy upon the state, and to use external forces, the Allobroges, in pursuit of his ends. The prisoners whose fate was under discussion were self-admitted partners in the conspiracy, and had been cast for a leading part in the mischief. Caesar was known to have had close relations with many of the extreme Populares, and was suspected by some of involvement in both the previous and the present conspiracy. In these circumstances his speech must be considered a *tour de force*; for by emphasising the protection which the laws gave to a Roman citizen he maintained the position and claims of the Populares; while by advocating a penalty which he described as worse than death he showed that he had no wish to plead on behalf of these particular enemies of the state, that they were not his friends, and by implication that he had no part in the conspiracy.

But in fact it resolved nothing but his own standing with his supporters. The penalty he advocated was, as Cicero pointed out, impossible to impose in all its rigour for all time; it was hardly less contrary to Roman law and practice than would be their execution; and the confiscation of their property involved the visiting of the sins of the fathers upon the wives and children. Such a suggestion was a tacit admission of the Senate's right to take strong and unprecedented action in a crisis under the S.C.U.; and once that was admitted, the question whether the Senate might in certain circumstances take the lives of citizens assumed a rather different complexion, and could not depend entirely on existing legislation. The position certainly needed to be defined and clarified; but it was by no means as clear and obvious as Caesar claimed; and the Senate could maintain that the right to take this extreme action had been recognised in the aftermath of C. Gracchus' death, when Opimius had been held justified in his action.

The question does arise why Cicero and the Senate did not submit the matter to the Comitia; for this was nowhere suggested, even by Caesar, who used the point only to argue against the death sentence. The answer must probably be that Cicero was satisfied as to the legality of action under the S.C.U., and that to submit these cases to the Comitia would imply a tacit admission that the deaths of C. Gracchus and Saturninus were illegal, exactly the opposite of what he had maintained in the trial of Rabirius. Further, in the present critical situation, when unity and action were essential, to submit the case to the Comitia was to bring the matter into the political arena, where the whole question would be argued with partisan passion; division, not unity, would ensue, with the argument centring upon the legality or otherwise of the S.C.U. rather than on what to do with six self-confessed conspirators whose leader stood at that moment not many miles from Rome at the head of an army. And Caesar in his compromised position could have wished for nothing less than to be compelled to give a lead in the Comitia on this thorny topic, where he must, unless he wished to abdicate his leading position with the Populares, associate himself with the views he had earlier enunciated, though this would seem to associate himself also with Catiline and his projects.

Caesar's speech had a profound impression on his audience, in many of whom the seeds of doubt were now sown. Ti. Claudius Nero, a former praetor, proposed that consideration of the penalty be deferred until Catiline had been defeated; this rather weak escape from the dilemma was seized upon by others, and Cicero decided to speak himself in order to clarify the issue, in the speech known as the Fourth Catilinarian. After pointing out the danger of postponement, which would encourage Catiline and the others, he emphasised that the decision must lie between Silanus' and Caesar's motions; and while the sterner measure had much to commend it, he would, if the Senate thought fit, carry out the milder punishment advocated by Caesar. He then argued the legal points made by Caesar, and the feasibility of his alternative. On the legal issue whether traitors were covered by the Lex Sempronia, he maintained that a traitor was a 'hostis' and had therefore forfeited his rights as a citizen; and the Senate's right to take what action it thought fit under the S.C.U. had been accepted in the earlier cases, even though they were not guilty of plotting against their country. As for the feasibility of Caesar's punishment, it would impose a most invidious task on the *municipia* concerned, which in any case Rome had not the power to enforce. He then expatiated upon the uniqueness and heinousness of Catiline's intended crime, the only redeeming feature of which was that it had brought together the two Orders and the people of Rome; and the *concordia* was the ultimate guarantee of the safety of the state, if proper measures were taken at this moment. He himself was ready to accept the odium for whatever measures the Senate should ask him to carry out.

The great value of this speech was that it clearly defined the two choices before the Senate, and showed the inconsistencies in Caesar's alternative. The first reactions to Caesar's speech had shown the need for this; Cicero had now reminded them that there were good grounds and precedents for proceeding to the death penalty, and little to be said in favour of Caesar's alternative; nor could there be in the minds of the Senate any doubt as to Cicero's own preference. By exposing the weakness of Caesar's arguments, by emphasising the danger to the state and his own readiness to carry out either sentence even at the risk of personal danger and unpopularity, he had left no doubt as to his own preference for the death penalty.

If Cicero had defined the choice and had indicated where his own inclination lay, he had also by that very fact turned Silanus' bowels to water. Oppressed by the doubts Caesar had cast on the legitimacy of the death penalty, and no doubt fearing the possible revenge which the Populares might choose to wreak on him, now that he saw his motion as the only alternative to Caesar's, he was fearful to find himself its author; if Cicero wanted the death penalty, let someone else propose it. For his part he proceeded to explain that by 'utmost penalty' he had meant the severest penalty *prescribed by law*, i.e. imprisonment, and many of his former supporters, including Cicero's own brother, agreed that this was their intention; only Catulus demurred. Someone was now needed to give a forthright lead along the lines suggested by Cicero; if the Senate would find the courage to vote for death, Cicero had shown that there was constitutional and legal justification for it.

At this critical juncture Cato rose to speak. Never fearful, always a strong advocate of Senatorial government and an opponent of the Populares, he was quite ready to oppose Caesar and what he regarded as Caesar's effort to soften the Senate's anger in favour of his friends. In a forceful speech he emphasised, as Cicero had done, the mischievous nature of what the prisoners and Catiline intended, which compelled the Senate in the interests of the state to take the strongest possible action, if it were to prevent the horrors of a bloody revolution. Like Cicero he showed the impracticability of Caesar's suggested punishment, and like Cicero he argued that the prisoners were confessed *hostes* who should be treated accordingly. He ended by moving that they be put to death 'more maiorum'.

This speech had the desired effect of stiffening the Senators' resolution; its firm and courageous tone in unflinchingly advocating the death penalty was successful in rallying everyone. But it was the character of the man and what he said that was the deciding factor; the constitutional dilemma posed by Caesar was not touched upon. The precedent which he quoted was hardly relevant, because the Lex Sempronia had not then been passed; if the 'mos maiorum' to which he appealed belonged to a time before the passage of that law, it no longer had a bearing or indeed a meaning. Herein lay the importance of Cicero's speech; he had argued the constitutional points, had shown the precedents for capital punishment since the Lex Sempronia; and by emphasising the point that a traitor was a *hostis*, he had given some sort of ground for regarding them as no longer citizens. Cato accepted the points made by Cicero, and was thus able to talk of *mos maiorum* without seeming irrelevant, as his example certainly was. Had Cicero not made what was, in spite of Sallust's silence, a most effective chairman's speech, it must remain doubtful whether Cato would have made so direct an appeal for the death sentence; and had he done so, there must have been a considerable hesitation amongst his hearers as to its legality; and judging from his speech one may doubt whether he would have handled that theme convincingly to his audience. The speeches were complementary to each other; together they dissipated the doubts sowed by Caesar.

Cato's motion was put to the House, and was passed by an overwhelming majority, including all the ex-consuls. The confiscation of their property was, it seems, involved in Cato's motion, for Caesar objected to this on the ground that, having rejected the milder part of his resolution, they retained the sterner element in conjunction with an even harsher alternative; but by now the Senate's courage was restored, and they would make no concession; and Caesar turned for aid to the tribunes. But the tribunes would not or dare not help, and it was left to Cicero to exclude that part of the resolution by ignoring it. Such was now the strength of feeling against Caesar that he stood in danger of his life from the Equites drawn up outside the Temple, and for his safety had to be escorted by Cicero, aided by Curio.

The prisoners were then led from their different places of confinement to the Tullianum, where the *tresviri capitales* had been instructed to put them to death forthwith, Lentulus escorted by Cicero himself, the others by four praetors, through a vast crowd that had collected, followed by the Senators in procession. The executions were carried out by strangling by the public executioner; it was now evening, and Cicero, to leave no doubt of their fate among Catiline's supporters, solemnly and euphemistically announced that their lives were ended: 'Vixerunt'. He then returned home, escorted by a large crowd, including Senators, through cheering throngs of people acclaiming him as their saviour, while torches were set before many of the houses to create a bright and gay scene on this auspicious occasion.

It must have been for Cicero a moment of exaltation, of high achievement and satisfaction; the *novus homo* was supported by Senators and acclaimed as Rome's saviour; could one ask for more? True, Catiline was in the field; but thanks to Cicero his plans were unmasked, the armies stood ready, and the Senate was strong in its resolution to grapple with him. His beloved *concordia* had come to pass, and seemed so firm that statesmanship should not be hard pressed to maintain it; and if it did continue, then, so it seemed to Cicero, the vexatious quarrels which had embarrassed and embittered political life would be ended. He might, he thought, be justly compared with the great names of the past, Scipios and Fabii; among his contemporaries he might take his place beside great Pompey, and so he had suggested.

To the end of his life he was to talk of this great achievement, and everyone was to become heartily sick of all his self-praise. Yet while the note of a self-blown trumpet tires, it was none the less true that Rome owed him a debt of gratitude for preventing a revolution of doubtful outcome and limited success at best, but which would none the less have required much bloodshed for its quenching. And how would its end have come? Probably at Pompey's hand, when he returned with his army; what had happened on Sulla's return could have found a repetition; for the cleavage in Rome and Italy was great, and this could have been the chance to fight it out; last time the Populares had been worsted; but where did Pompey stand? It could have been as bitter and as unproductive of a true solution as Sulla's war had been. And but for Cicero this might have been. The Senate had been incredulous and loath to act; even at the last firmness had not come willingly to their reluctant hands; and Cicero's task had been that much made heavier. Unwilling to follow his leadership, they had had a sneaking sympathy for the rotten sprig of nobility that was Catiline, because he was a noble; to Cato's lead they could submit, because he was of themselves; his speech, made by some less distinguished man, would not have had the same effect. Yet Cicero had somehow done it, and here they were all cheering him!

But elated though Cicero might be, he knew that he had given grave offence to the Populares; not all the people's cheers could drown the words of Caesar's speech and its warning that he held the death penalty to be illegal; sooner or later they would take their revenge, when they felt they safely could. Aware of these dangers he had had the prisoners' evidence taken down and circulated to the towns of Italy and the provinces; so too was Cato's speech publicised, that all might know that Cicero had not acted on his own, and that the penalty of death had been urged by no less a man than Cato. He also wrote to Pompey an elaborate account of the whole affair, for Pompey's attitude was vital, since he was known to be no friend of the nobles, as they were not of him. But this attempt to woo Pompey to the Senate's side alas! miscarried; Pompey, enamoured of himself and his achievements, took umbrage that Cicero should claim to be his equal, and replied in frigid terms which took no note of Cicero's achievement; Pompey was not, regrettably, the man that Cicero continued to believe he was.

Q. Metellus Nepos, one of the new tribunes, a lieutenant of Pompey's who had come to Rome to seek the tribunate and to look after Pompey's interests now that the end of the Eastern War was near, at once made clear his hostility to Cicero and what he had done; he jeered at him as a *novus homo*, accused him of being power-drunk, and compared him to Sulla; such expressions, contemptible though they were, augured ill for the future, coming so soon after the event when Cicero's popularity was in its blaze. Cicero's position was complicated by the two facts that Nepos was a friend of Pompey and the brother of Metellus Celer, the praetor in charge of the army in Cisalpine Gaul; and though Cicero asked him to use his influence with his brother, considerations of family prevailed and he refused his aid. Nepos imposed the final indignity at the end of the year; at the ceremony at which Cicero laid down his office, Nepos forbade him to address the people, as was the normal custom; a man, he argued, who had put citizens to death and denied them the chance to speak in their defence, should not himself be given opportunity to address the people; he therefore vetoed Cicero's attempt to speak. But on this occasion Cicero won the final round; for while taking the oath that he had respected the laws during his year of office, he swore that he alone had saved the city and the state; the assembled people swore that he spoke the truth, and conducted him with cheers and torches home.

Here we may briefly reflect upon the conspiracy and its importance. That it was serious cannot be in doubt, and might have been much more so, had Cicero almost unaided not robbed it of most of its threat and made it appear an ill-conceived plot hatched by a desperado. He had had to fight not only the Populares but the suspicions and contempt of those who should have been his chief supporters, the Senatorial nobles; some secretly sympathised with Catiline, few were alive to the realities of the political situation, the danger of such a conspiracy, and the keenness of the hostility towards their selfish form of government. The Senate's reluctance to act on the information he provided testifies to the difficulties with which his own side hampered him; the people had to be persuaded that a conspiracy whose ostensible ends were the relief of their poverty and distress was in fact designed to subject them to the rule of tyranny. The Equites, ever the shrewdest group of all, took least persuasion; but they had to be lured to support the Senate, to whose government they had been for years opposed.

All this Cicero successfully accomplished; and it was no mean accomplishment. Particularly was he proud to have brought Senate and Equites together, his own two halves united, as it were; a schism which had begun with C. Gracchus, become deeper in Sullan times, was now, he thought, repaired; if this new-found *concordia ordinum* could be maintained, then Rome's problems could be solved; for stability would be assured and the chance for responsible government. But the prospects of its maintenance beyond the present crisis were bleak; Rome's history had brought about the schism, and made its removal impossible. The attitudes, the ambitions and the outlooks of both groups were now the product of the past; and they could not be sloughed; either they dominated or were dominated by a greater force. For a brief moment there had been unity in the face of danger; but once the danger was removed, the interests of the group again broke forth. Herein lay Cicero's fallacy.

Yet he had achieved a temporary harmony and thus been able

to handle the crisis with the least of bloodshed and of passion, so that his enemies could claim that but for him there would have been no crisis, a tribute to the efficacy of his control. And this harmony had included a third element, of which Cicero had hardly before taken account, namely the supporters of constitutional government throughout Italy. This third element now became an integral part of his political ideal; Senate, Equites, and the support of 'loyalists' throughout Italy, 'consensus omnium bonorum' or 'Italiae'. By 'loyalists' he had in mind the substantial equestrian middle class which were the backbone of the *municipia* of Italy, families like his own, dedicated to peace and order, averse from war and bloodshed, conservative in their views and supporters of solid government. He had, of course, been aware of these people before and recognised their worth and merit, for of such were his family and many others that he knew; but his political ideals had hitherto been focused on Rome and her tensions; he had not yet thought in terms of Italy and her possible contribution to Rome's stability; nor, with very few exceptions, had others. Government was at Rome; the Senate and the Comitia made the laws, the people of Rome voted at elections for the magistrates; everything was done at Rome, Italy's task since the Social War had seemed to consist in remaining quiet and providing soldiers.

But the events of this year had opened Cicero's eyes to the importance of Italy; Catiline had plotted a revolution which involved uprisings in different parts of the peninsula; he and the Senate had dispatched armies to parts of Italy to anticipate and prevent uprisings; and if the danger was not even graver than it was, this was because of the solid support that Cicero had found throughout Italy for peace and the suppression of the danger. Had these substantial burghers chosen to join their lot to Catiline, Rome would have been confronted with a second Social War; instead, slaves only helped him from these areas. The need to think in terms of Italy and the behaviour of the Italians in this year convinced Cicero both that Rome must now include Italy, and that the stability of government which he sought to effect through the *concordia* must for its success include the support of all these loyal country gentlemen throughout the towns of Italy. The three elements were now fused together in his thinking, and the third element became increasingly important in his ideas as the failures of the other two became ever more transparent and dangerous. His ideal had become an appeal to loyalists in Rome and Italy to combine in the interests of law and stable government against the factious and destructive strife of groups.

But the conspiracy was a symptom of something deeper. Roman society and Roman government had been sick for decades now; civil war had blazed with Sulla, and Sulla, his enemies defeated, had applied a remedy of sorts; the Senate's supremacy, established beyond all doubt, should end this bitter fight. This might have seemed to end the Roman crisis; but civil wars solve nothing, unless the defeated are suppressed until the memory of the past is dead; for defeat in war does not convince the vanquished that their cause was wrong. Sulla's system seemed to his defeated enemies unjust; the Senate made no effort to heal the wounds and win the vanquished to its side; luxuriating in their inviolable strength they ate the lotus for a decade, until Pompey restored the tribunes' powers. Things were now much as they were before, except that hostility was deeper set; the causes for hostility remained, but the determination to take revenge for their former impotence was now too strong to be denied.

This dissatisfaction had a cause. The Gracchi had revolted against the Senate's domination because they believed that their government was fundamentally selfish and not prepared to come to grips with the social and economic problems of the state, and that only by overriding Senatorial opposition and presenting their legislation direct to the people could they procure action. Their behaviour, however commendable their motives, was irresponsible; for it made responsible government difficult and, it might be, impossible. The next years showed the crisis to which they had brought the government of Rome; and the Senatorial leaders began to protect their own interests rather than those of the state.

The attack on noble privilege continued; the fiercer the attacks the more determined became the governing class to retain their primacy and as much of their privileges as they could. In consequence the problems which the years of expansion had created tended to become matters of narrow political quarrel, in which neither side could claim disinterested virtue. The Italians, driven to despair, had won the citizenship by open war; the provinces were victims of Senatorial and Equestrian injustice and rapacity; most of them hated hopelessly the cruel power that held and wounded them, taking no thought for their prosperity and well-being. All these deep consequences of imperial expansion required an effort of sustained statesmanship for their successful resolution; yet energy was concentrated on the fight for power at Rome. There was large discontent in Rome and Italy, a restless uncertainty, unhappiness, and lack of leadership, and all this sickness needed remedy; to suppress the conspiracy was a profitable achievement only if suppression was the first step to a combined attack on the causes which had made the conspiracy attractive to so many. How far did Cicero appreciate this point? Did he perhaps feel that the suppression was the climax, not the first step? His criticisms of the conspiracy's aims and of the Rullan bill which had preceded it hardly suggest this deeper understanding; rather did he see it as the mischievous behaviour of a few; and his appeal to the people not to surrender the joys of idleness at Rome for the hard drudgery of work on the land, even though its aim was to defeat Caesar's land bill, indicates perhaps an ignorance of the underlying causes. Did he ask himself why Caesar chose this bait with which to lure the people? Probably not, one feels.

But when all is said about the limitation of his views, it cannot detract from what he did; nor should it blind us to the fact that only he and Caesar thought the problem worth consideration; most men were content to let things carry drifting on, so long as there was something good for them; Pompey had no ideas except for his own primacy; Cato could only defend a Senate not deserving of defence. All credit then, to Cicero, who glimpsed at least the depth and danger of the problem and proposed a solution which, even if imperfect, could have made a contribution to its solution. And for that he was admired in Italy and respected; he became one of Rome's most influential men, his *novitas* notwithstanding, because so many thousands saw in him and his ideals their own aspirations for a society at peace.

CHAPTER 8

THE RISE OF THE FIRST
TRIUMVIRATE

CICERO had known full well the implications and possible consequences to himself of what had happened, and had taken what steps he could to make clear that the decisions belonged to the Senate, not himself, and to publicise Cato's fighting speech in the Senate on the fateful day. None the less it was he who had goaded the Senate into taking any action, it was he who had pursued remorselessly the conspirators, and forced them to bungle their plans; he it was who had led the opposition to Caesar's and Crassus' attempts to create for themselves a countervailing power to that of Pompey; and as a *novus homo* he would be more susceptible than many to attacks; for though he had proved useful to the nobles in a crisis, they still did not accept him as of themselves. Much would depend on Pompey's attitude; if Pompey would acknowledge his services and agree to help maintain the *concordia*, Cicero would be strong and influential. But Pompey's allegiance had been hitherto with the Senate's enemies, and everyone knew that Pompey on his return would have it in his power to dictate Rome's future; if only Pompey would listen to Cicero's advice, Pompey's power and Cicero's wisdom would, he was certain, restore harmony and responsibility in government and bring back the steady days of which he dreamt.

He therefore wrote a full account to Pompey of his achievements, hoping to win him to his point of view; for he must win Pompey to the side of his *concordia* and end his union with the Populares. But Pompey was too uncertain of his own affairs and prospects to be ready to help Cicero with his; the Senate had never been his friend, the Populares and the tribunes had. Thanks to Cicero he had been cheated of his hope of crushing the conspiracy with his army, and without his army he knew not how to enforce his wishes. He wanted power and influence, but hoped to attain these delectable ends by constitutional means and with the blessing of the government; unlike Caesar, he did not relish the dirt and grime of the political arena, nor wish to involve himself in all its degradation. He could not therefore at this moment commit himself to Cicero's policy, and as yet he ostentatiously declined to comment on Cicero's achievements or to ally himself with Senate or *concordia*.

The new year began stormily, with the tribune Metellus Nepos and Caesar, now praetor, in mischievous mood. Metellus at once attacked Cicero, and Caesar tried to curry favour with Pompey at Catulus' expense. In fact both of them were determined, if it were possible, to bring Pompey back to Italy in arms, Nepos because this was the object of his having come to Rome, Caesar because he had no choice. Since he had failed with Crassus to provide himself with the means to bargain with or against great Pompey, he knew that he must now support him whom he could not equal yet; so far he had not been conspicuously successful on his own, and he must therefore keep his place in popular favour by showing zeal for the interests of the people's friend. Metellus therefore with the support of Caesar set about the moving of a bill whereby Pompey should be elected to the consulship *in absentia* and given the command against Catiline, who was still in arms; at the same time he renewed his threats against Cicero. But knowing that there would be opposition to such a bill, particularly as Cato was a fellow-tribune, he and Caesar had made their dispositions; they would use force to prevent any interference with their scheme. They organised a gang of roughs to threaten violence and, if need be, to use it against any would-be interrupter or opponent; and all worked well until Cato, refusing to be intimidated, forced his way to the platform and prevented the voting on the bill. Rowdy scenes ensued in which Cato stood in danger of his life, until the Senate passed the S.C.U., suspended both Caesar and Metellus from their offices and declared that anyone demanding the punishment of those responsible for the deaths of the Catilinarians should be regarded as an enemy of the state. Caesar had once more failed.

This final scheme to bring Pompey back in arms had foundered and Metellus at once betook himself to Pompey's camp; Caesar after a display of proper contrition was allowed to resume the duties of his office. Cicero was embarrassed by the attitude of Metellus' brother, Metellus Celer, one of the praetors of 63, commander now in Cisalpine Gaul, who insisted that the Senate's anger against his brother had been fomented by Cicero; this led to an acrimonious correspondence in which Cicero, though anxious not further to antagonise Metellus, would none the less not be unjustly attacked as the instigator when in truth he was the victim. Fortunately in February Catiline was defeated and himself killed; this ended the tension of the internal danger, and prevented further manoeuvres for Pompey's recall in arms. The next months saw those suspected of complicity with Catiline haled before the courts, some to be convicted and put to death, and one, P. Sulla, actually defended by Hortensius and Cicero.

At the year's end Pompey landed in Italy, his eastern task completed and no further task in contemplation for his army or himself. Cicero had earlier proposed a *supplicatio* of twelve days in honour of his victories, and Pompey had at last consented to murmur a few laudatory remarks on Cicero. For years this moment had been in all men's minds; some were full of hope, some of trepidation, the Senate was apprehensive but determined to prevent, if possible, his renewed dictation of his affairs through tribunes. During these last five years they had not been idle; they had revenged themselves on those who had earlier sponsored Pompey's cause against the pirates and Mithridates; and now they were firmly in the saddle. And here was Pompey back in person, the object alike of Caesar's and Cicero's blandishments, with a large army, huge popularity and an enigmatic purpose.

If Pompey chose to march on Rome, a second Sulla, nothing could prevent him; if he shrank from such a course, then he might be kept in some restraint.

But Pompey was no revolutionary to march thus on Rome; always he hoped to gain his ends without the distasteful task of asking or demanding, for he much preferred to have power thrust upon him. On this occasion he had failed of his hope to be recalled to deal with Catiline, as he had been to deal with Spartacus; for this would have sanctioned the retention of his army in Italy. But Metellus' efforts had gone awry, because the Senate was resolved he should not succeed, and because Catiline was defeated before catastrophe could force the Senate's hand. He therefore no longer had excuse to retain his army, which the law required to be discharged as soon as he reached Italian soil. He had kept it hopefully together, but now, deprived of hope and excuse, he discharged it at Brundisium.

To us this decision conforms to the pattern of his character; to his contemporaries it was as surprising as it was gratifying. Caesar and Crassus had assumed the opposite, and had unsuccessfully struggled to create a force with which to countervail and, if need be, oppose him; Crassus had ostentatiously withdrawn to Macedonia and Asia Minor with his family, claiming that he was fearful for his life. Pompey hoped that his popularity with the masses would ensure his continued influence in politics, and that popular pressure would carry him along in the direction in which he wished to go. He had asked that the consular elections be postponed until his arrival, that he might canvass on behalf of M. Pupius Piso, but on Cato's persuasion the Senate had declined. Piso was none the less elected, a promising augury for Pompey.

The next months were critical for Cicero's political plans, for in this time would be decided whether his *concordia* was to continue and be strengthened, or whether it would be shattered by the greater forces of disruption which had been brought under temporary control. If Pompey were to join the Populares and throw into the scales against the Senate all his power and popularity, then all that Cicero had worked for would be destroyed; but if he could be induced to work in harmony with the Senate, then Cicero might properly be sanguine for the future. He had tried to woo him before his return; he continued his courtship now, and not without success. For Pompey would prefer to march to future greatness with the Senate's blessing rather than in its despite; and Cicero was an influential figure. During this year relations between the two grew very close, and Cicero could flatter himself that he had won Pompey to his side and was influencing him in the right direction; men were referring to Pompey as Cnaeus Cicero.

But a series of events prevented this alliance from achieving Cicero's cherished aim. He himself was entangled in the trial of Clodius for profaning the sacred rites of the Bona Dea. Of Clodius we shall hear more; an unscrupulous aristocrat of the Claudian *gens*, whose mischievous career had begun much earlier, when he helped incite Lucullus' troops to mutiny, he sought fame and power as a Popularis. He had in 62, disguised as a woman, profaned the rites of Bona Dea, which were being celebrated in Caesar's house, and he had been discovered. A fierce political battle ensued over the composition of the court that was to try him, in which animosities were inflamed; and although, thanks largely to Crassus' gold, he was acquitted, Cicero had given evidence which utterly destroyed the alibi on which Clodius' defence depended, and thereby roused an enmity which was one day to cost him dear.

Pompey had celebrated his triumph in September, and splendid though it was, he had carefully refrained from making it as popular as he might have done, and had tactfully omitted all reference to Crete to assuage the hostility of Metellus Creticus. He had also by free use of money and influence procured the election of his former legate, L. Afranius, to the consulship for 60, and Afranius, he hoped, would help the accomplishment of his two main aims, the ratification of the arrangements he had made in the East, and the provision of land for his veterans. To these aims he hoped the Senate would at least give blessing; hence his alliance with Cicero. But if Pompey had a friend in Cicero, he had enemies among the nobles, men whom he had insulted or humiliated, and who saw now the chance of evening the score, men who were so certain of their dominating position and contemptuous of Cicero's attempts to found an alliance of Senators and Equites that they preferred to humiliate and antagonise the man whose support could have given strength and security to themselves and Rome.

Lucullus had cause to feel aggrieved by Pompey's behaviour in the East; after scheming to supplant him in the command, on arrival he had treated him insultingly, and had upset the dispositions of himself and the Senatorial commission. Metellus Creticus, too, had suffered what he regarded as insults from Pompey during his campaign against the pirates; Crassus had never been his friend and had feared—or pretended to fear—for his life; jealousy spurred Crassus to enmity and opposition. Finally Cato, determined to maintain the Senate's dominance and to cut Pompey down to size, certain that only opposition, now that he had no army, could prevent a repetition of his earlier behaviour, was ranged among his opponents. Nor might their calculations seem so wildly wrong; during his absence they had shown what opposition to the Senate's wishes might expect; now that the Populares once more had their leader, it seemed important to prevent him leading. They had not realised that Pompey did not wish to be their leader; much rather would he seek his future through and with the Senate, and Cicero might have been successful. But Lucullus and the others willed otherwise; they would not give wholesale recognition to his arrangements in the East; each clause of each agreement must be examined and lengthily debated, until Pompey by the year's end was feeling embarrassment, and Cicero despondency for his great design.

But Pompey was hopeful that 60 would be more fruitful for his purposes. Afranius was consul, and a friendly tribune, L. Flavius, was to sponsor a bill to provide land for his veterans. But the land bill, introduced at the year's beginning, at once ran into trouble. The Senate, the landlords' stronghold, opposed it both in their own imagined interests, and also because its prime object seemed to be to provide Pompey with some new power; and they were not minded to raise him from the helplessness to which they had reduced him. Cicero, though he did not think highly of the bill, for the sake of his coalition did his best; but in vain. The other consul, Metellus Celer, was implacably opposed to it and to Pompey; and Flavius had him put in prison. But the situation then became absurd, for Flavius with his tribune's bench banned entry to the prison, while Metellus had the prison walls knocked down; Pompey in desperate shame told Flavius to release him, and before the end of May the bill was dead. Pompey had suffered humiliation and defeat, and his embarrassment was such that to Cicero's disgust he had said nothing openly; his alliance with Cicero had proved unequal to the task.

During May and June of this year Atticus was cautioning Cicero against too great friendship with Pompey, since he was giving the impression of joining the Populares rather than winning Pompey to the Senate's side. Cicero explained the position to Atticus; thanks to the behaviour of a small number of nobles either in their own interest or because they resented Cicero's leadership, the *concordia* was for the moment shattered. The Equites were estranged both because as a result of the scandal of the trial of Clodius the immunity of Equestrian jurymen from prosecution for taking bribes was being threatened, and because the Senate was proving obdurate to a request from the company that had bought the right to collect the Asian taxes for a reduction of the purchase price. On both issues there was really nothing to be said in favour of the Equites; clearly they should be liable to punishment for improper conduct on the jury equally with their Senatorial colleagues, and it was only a historical accident that they were not. Similarly the company was bound by the bid it had made to win the contract; otherwise the whole contract was null and void. But, argued Cicero, the interests of political harmony were better served by keeping equestrian friendship through concession on these points than by turning them to seek support elsewhere. Their treatment of Pompey, too, was calculated to drive him once again to demagogues to satisfy his needs; whereas co-operation by the Senate would deny their leader to the Populares and win for the Senate his great name and power; and so the *concordia* would find both guarantee and safeguard. In sum, his present line of policy was, he contended, in the best interests of the Optimates and Senatorial government.

He did not appreciate that the *concordia* of 63 was the exceptional consequence of a serious threat to stability and peace, and that once the cause had been removed, the political tensions had returned to plague affairs. Nobody's heart had changed; the animosities of groups remained as fierce as ever. If the Equites could be retained only by condoning flagrant injustice, what was the worth of their support? However Cicero might rightly feel about the 'boni' throughout Italy, their impact on politics was normally indiscernible; it was the wealthy business men at Rome who counted among the Equites, and they were concerned for profit, and not fastidious about the means; the nobles saw no cause to fawn in friendship on those they socially despised and politically cursed. For Pompey they had hate, contempt and fear; they did not want his leadership, and since he had put himself in their hands, let him take a mauling such as some of them had received from him. Unless therefore Cicero could communicate to the Senators his sense of urgency, his plans were destined to shipwreck; and this he could not do. The terms in which he thought were not those of the nobles, Optimate though he sought to be. Even though he could not see the end of this political disarray, he knew how much worse things were now from what they had been, and was sure that, unless Rome pulled herself together, they would grow worse still. It is improbable that he could have remedied them; he might woo Pompey; but to impose Pompey's leadership upon the Senate was beyond his powers.

Caesar, recently returned from his Spanish province, was a candidate for the consulship for 59; and his unpopularity with the nobles needed strong antidote to overcome their still great influence with the Centuries. Crassus could be relied on to help his former colleague; and Crassus' money could make many friends; L. Lucceius, a fellow-candidate and friend of Pompey, also helped his cause; and Caesar's own popularity was great. The Senate, dismayed at the success his campaign was enjoying, exerted all their strength to procure the election of at least the second consul, that thus whatever designs he had in mind might be frustrated; and to this laudable end a fund was opened to bribe the electorate, on whose subscription list stood Cato's name. Both candidates were elected, Caesar and the nobles' candidate, M. Bibulus.

The Senate might therefore anticipate the coming year with some complacency; Bibulus could block whatever they did not like of Caesar's; and in precaution lest Caesar's candidature should succeed, they had named for the consuls' provinces a duty in Italy insulting and insignificant, which would effectively exclude Caesar from a province and an army. Cato and the nobles might well be wrapped in euphoria; they had shown the Equites their strength, they had brought humiliation on Pompey, and Caesar was checked before he could begin; the Senate was supreme, the *concordia* unnecessary.

But the nobles had reckoned without Caesar, whose hour of decision was almost come. His career hitherto had hardly matched his ambitions; having entered politics as Marius' champion, the enemy of the nobles and the Sullan settlement, as a Popularis he had achieved popularity. He had supported Pompey's ambitions, and sought unsuccessfully to satisfy his own. During Pompey's absence in the East he had with Crassus made two unsuccessful bids to arm himself with something more substantial than his influence with the people against the realities of Pompey's power; and twice he had been foiled, in no small degree by Cicero, before the very people who should have been with him. Having failed to become Pompey's equal or opponent he must needs remain his supporter. He had therefore begun his praetorship by insulting Catulus on behalf of Pompey, and by joining with Nepos to compel a law in Pompey's interest. Their attempt to force its passage by means of arms and bullying had foundered on Cato's stubborn courage; and Caesar had suffered deserved humiliation and defeat. Now he was consul-designate, his prospect bleak indeed; a hostile colleague, an insulting *provincia*, and then retirement as a *consularis*. Could all his ambitions have been still-born, his greatest moments his election to the chief priesthood and his governorship in Spain? Either he must break the chain that held him tight, or accept defeat and failure.

Caesar knew well the strength of the opposing forces, and knew that alone he could not match them. But the Senate had provided the means to recruit his strength; Pompey, embarrassed and in despair at the posture of his affairs, Crassus indignant at the refusal to reduce the Asian contract, stood ready to receive the help that only a determined magistrate could give, the only obstacle their mutual antagonism. Caesar's charm and their own exigencies smoothed the path to reconciliation and an agreement between the three that they should use all their influence—and it was very great indeed—to support Caesar, and that Caesar would see that nothing in the following year was done that conflicted with the interests of any of them; the corollary was that Caesar would promote the interests of all three. This political alliance, known as the first Triumvirate, ushered in the end of the Republic; for Caesar was committed to take action on the affairs of all of them which it was known the Senate could and would oppose; they had in this very year prevented Flavius' bill becoming law; the constitution could prevent the passage of the laws; yet Caesar must act, and knew he must; he had it all planned, whatever the cost might be.

At the year's end Cornelius Balbus, a former officer of Pompey's and now on Caesar's staff, approached Cicero with a proposal to join the alliance; his close relations with Pompey would suggest this course, and Caesar well knew what Cicero's influence could be, for twice already he had upset his schemes. Tempted though Cicero was, he had misgivings that alliance with Caesar spelt the abandonment of his ideals and policy:

For I must either firmly oppose the agrarian law...or I must remain altogether passive, which is about equivalent to retiring to Solonium or Antium; or lastly, I must actually assist the bill, which I am told Caesar fully expects from me without any doubt. For Cornelius (Balbus) has been with me...and solemnly assured me that he (Caesar) meant to avail himself of my advice and Pompey's in everything... In this last course there are the following advantages...But the conclusion of the third book of my poem has a strong hold on me...and I cannot doubt that I shall always hold that 'the best of omens is our country's cause'.[1]

He would not therefore at this moment join their number; and the events of 59 quickly confirmed his instinct.

This was for Cicero a decision full of fate, though he could not know it at the time. For the consequence of his refusal was his enforced silence and withdrawal from independence in politics for fifteen years with one brief exception, connected also with the Triumvirate. Yet had he known the consequences, he could hardly have chosen differently; for to join with Caesar was to abandon his political ideals. His evaluation to Atticus shows that he realised that he might find himself committed to policies and bills with which he must disagree, and therefore he preferred his independence, so that he could, if necessary, oppose in what he called 'his country's cause'. Independence to do what he thought right was his reason for refusing; in fact his refusal took just that away from him. He could not divine the extremes to which Caesar was prepared to go; no one appreciated Caesar's desperation and his necessity to act. He could not know that Caesar would, if he must, use force and compulsion to impose his will upon the Senate, and that he would without hesitation force those who would otherwise oppose him into silence or sub-

[1] *ad Att.* II, 3, 3.

servience to himself. Nor, had he joined with Caesar, would he
have had the power or eloquence to persuade him; Caesar was
never open to advice, and neither Pompey could deflect or turn
him nor would Cicero; Caesar took his own decisions on these
matters. If the nobles had proved a worthier set and followed
Cicero's lead, his decision would have justified itself; in the event
only his conscience gained.

Caesar had certain pledges to redeem; he must satisfy his
associates' immediate needs, land for Pompey's veterans and the
ratification of his Eastern *acta*, for Crassus the reduction of the
price bid for the Asian taxes; then he must give himself some
province other than the one at present named, and an army too,
for his proconsulship. Whatever else he might be planning, these
were the first essentials; all of them would rouse the nobles'
hostility, particularly as Caesar was their author; clash there must
be, the only point in doubt, who would prove stronger. The land
bill was the first he chose to handle, on which he had been at work
since his election; it was most suitable for his purpose, since it
could be made to satisfy not only Pompey but the landless plebs
of Rome, and hence win a popularity impossible for the other
bills.

He began the year on his best behaviour, deferential to his
colleague and ostentatiously ready to work in harmony with the
Senate. Shrewdly he brought his bill before the Senate for their
views; land was to be distributed to Pompey's veterans and to
some of the city landless; public land in Italy except the Campanian, whose income to the state was so important, would be
used, and further land bought at a fair price with the owners'
consent; a commission of twenty was to have charge of the
distribution, of whom Caesar would not be one. In itself there
was nothing exceptionable in the bill; Pompey's veterans were
by custom entitled to a grant of land, the inclusion of the urban
mass was socially justified and handled a problem that should
have been dealt with long ago; and the means of acquiring the
necessary land were reasonable and fair. The nobles should not

have been provoked to anger—except that Caesar was the author; it was not surprising that they opposed such a proposal, however sweetly reasonable, when it came from the man who had identified himself with Marius, tried to snatch power in his own interests, and had tried forcibly to bring Pompey back in arms. The irrational fear of all land laws and their sponsors, which made all such proposals suspect and their authors regarded as would-be Gracchi, was in the present instance magnified; and there was the very real fact that Caesar's *clientela* would be considerably increased in many parts of Italy if the bill became law; and these considerations determined them to oppose it. They therefore set about frustrating it, and when Cato had by filibustering exhausted Caesar's patience, he brusquely told the Senate that he would take it to the people without their approval. And here Caesar showed his hand.

He must have foreseen the likelihood of what had happened, realised too that the opposition could pursue him to the Comitia; and he must have laid his plans accordingly. His past experiences had taught him much; at least twice he had failed to persuade the people in his interest, Flavius had failed this very year in Pompey's. In 62 he had failed humiliatingly to use a bully's tactics, and nearly lost his praetorship; this time the price of failure was his political demise. But all these failures showed the only way by which he might succeed; he must ignore all constitutional vetoes that could be used against him; the people must be, if necessary, compelled to do his bidding, and he must so intimidate Senate and magistrates that no one would dare to act against him; he must be ready to bring all Rome by force to heel. That moment now was come; compelled to ignore the Senate he would reveal the weapons he had kept concealed.

After his setback in the Senate he went directly to the people, and at a meeting at which Pompey and Crassus were present, he invited them to state their views upon the bill; when Pompey expressed agreement with the legislation, he was asked whether he would help the people, if resistance were offered to it; to which he replied that he would come against those threatening swords, bringing sword and shield. This was the crisis; through Pompey's mouth he was giving notice that he would tolerate no opposition, and would use force without compunction. When Bibulus, aided by Lucullus and Cato, tried to suspend proceedings on the bill, he was handled forcibly, insulted, driven from the Forum, and two supporting tribunes were wounded. Such was the treatment meted out that Bibulus made no further intervention, but remained in his house, depending on edicts for his obstruction. Nor dared the Senate heed his protests on the following day; fearful they let this insult to their consul pass, though lesser breaches of the peace had incurred their censure and, if need be, their punishment.

This deliberate use of force had the desired effect; neither Bibulus nor anyone else attempted further direct opposition. Planned from the outset the compulsion was to depend chiefly on Pompey's veterans and the elaborately staged dialogue between the two was the signal: Pompey then, in Plutarch's words, 'filled the city with his soldiers and carried everything by force (βίᾳ)'; the treatment of Bibulus was the first incident, whose meaning was so clear that nothing more was needed. Senators were often fearful to attend the Senate in terror of the soldiers, a sombre indication of the atmosphere that now surrounded all. When a young man, C. Cato, frustrated in his attempt to bring a prosecution against Gabinius for bribery at the consular elections, dared in a public meeting to call Pompey 'privatus dictator', the soldiers so mauled him that he was almost killed. Caesar had surely taken over Roman government.

The Triumvirs at least initially enjoyed the goodwill of the people, for they were joint beneficiaries in the land allotment; and here the shrewdness in making this bill his first was seen. But by May the first flush of their popularity had worn off, and by July they were hated, but no less determined; nothing was done this year against their will. At the Ludi Apollinares in July Curio, a young man as yet of no great consequence, who had been critical of the Triumvirs, was given an ovation when he entered the theatre; Caesar was received in frigid silence, while Pompey, the supposed arch-villain since he provided the force, was the target of the actor's innuendoes. But Pompey was in fact a broken man, haggard and desperate at his unpopularity, tortured in mind at having to behave against his nature, but unable to extricate himself; he had made a treaty with the Devil which he must honour. Without opposition Caesar carried out his undertakings, ratified Pompey's *acta* and reduced the Asian contract price by a third; he then turned to his own concerns.

The Senate had decreed as *provincia* for the consuls of 59 'silvae callesque Italiae', an insulting sphere of duty offering no scope, no opportunity for wealth or military fame, and destined to leave Caesar powerless against the machinations of his enemies. He had ignored already laws, obstructions, vetoes; his legislation, thanks chiefly to Bibulus, was in law invalid, and would undoubtedly be challenged in the next year; and, his proconsulship over, he would be prosecuted and politically ruined. This was certain; but Caesar did not include among his ambitions political death at the age of 40; having taken control by force, he would use that force to order his own destiny, and that required a change of province.

The situation in Gaul gave him his chance. There had been uneasy movements among the southern Gauls since 62, involving tribes who were allied with Rome. The Sequani and Arverni had then enlisted the aid of the Suebian leader, Ariovistus, who crossed the Rhine, helped the Sequani and then demanded a part of their territory as recompense. The Romans, always apprehensive of Gallic restlessness in these parts, were naturally concerned at these events, and had ordered the consuls of 60 at once to draw lots for the two Gallic provinces, and to raise additional armies with a view to military action. A seeming improvement in the situation forestalled the immediate need for arms; Metellus Celer, to whom Transalpine fell, died early in 59 while still in Rome; Afranius was probably at this moment governing Cisalpine. If Caesar could make these provinces his own, he would have exactly what he wanted, a province with an army and the chance to indulge in war to the great benefit of his purse and his military renown, while at the same time keeping in touch with politics at Rome; thus could he avoid the embarrassing troubles that had befallen Pompey through being too long too far from Rome. Gaul therefore it should be.

To lay hands on it presented now no problems; with all who might oppose intimidated and himself sole master of Rome, he could himself or through a tribune have the necessary legislation passed. A tribune, P. Vatinius, one of Caesar's men, stood ready; in May by a plebiscite Cisalpine Gaul, with the addition of Illyricum, was given at once to Caesar, together with three legions; no question of his successor might be raised before 1 March 54; he had therefore taken a province and an army for the next six years.[1] A little later the Senate on Pompey's proposal (should we say, rather, instruction?) added Transalpine Gaul with an additional legion, though this province, since it was given by the Senate, could equally be taken back by the Senate at its discretion.

One may wonder what turned Caesar's choice first to Cisalpine Gaul, though Transalpine might seem to offer greater scope. Probably he intended from the first to have them both, but since there was a governor of Cisalpine Gaul, his removal was best effected through a tribunician bill; further, Cisalpine of the two had greater value for his purpose since it commanded Italy, and its proximity to Rome allowed him to exercise control of sorts over the political manoeuvres of the city. To take Transalpine was simple; the intended governor was dead, Pompey had but to propose for those few Senators who still had courage to attend to agree without demur, knowing that Caesar would accept no other disposition. There was nothing strange in the Senate's

---

[1] Since it would only be named in 54 as a consular province for the consuls of 53, to be elected in 54, who would not normally take up their province until 52. If it were made praetorian, it could be vetoed.

apparent generosity to their enemy; it was fear and the knowledge that government was in other hands; the wise course was to concur, lest worse befall.

Caesar had now satisfied the needs of all the Triumvirs, and he set about raising additional troops for his Gallic legions. Other legislation there was this year, but these were laws that would have passed in normal times; the others were the ones that drove Caesar to the use of force and all its consequences; for the consequences were of necessity grave. Since all his legislation was by the constitution invalid, what would become of it when his year of office ended? From Caesar's point of view 58 was no less important than 59; Livius Drusus and Sulpicius had had their legislation swept aside for less convincing grounds than could be adduced for undoing Caesar's; and after this year of domination he knew that this must be the fate of his. Two things he must therefore do: assure that next year's consuls would not allow the dismantling of his work, and prevent his chief opponents from initiating an attack. In spite of Bibulus, who postponed the consular elections until October, the Triumvirs, not surprisingly, contrived that their two candidates were elected, Gabinius, a Pompeian, and Piso, a Caesarian; this would assure control within the Senate. But what about his opponents in the Senate and the possibility of a tribune's independent legislation? Here we must turn back to Cicero.

In March the Populares had put C. Antonius, Cicero's partner of 63, on trial *de maiestate*, as punishment for his defection from their ranks; Caesar for this very reason would not help him; but Cicero felt obliged to assume the defence of his former colleague. During his speech he made some bitter reflexions on the present situation, and this proved fatal to him. Within three hours of his speech Caesar as *pontifex maximus* with the help of Pompey as augur had arranged the adoption of Clodius into a plebeian *gens*, a translation which he had been unsuccessfully seeking for the past year, since it opened the door to the tribunate. Clodius had never forgiven Cicero for his damning evidence at his trial

148

for profanation; but he needed the tribunate to wreak revenge, since he could not otherwise initiate legislation. It was a harsh warning to Cicero not to dare to criticise the Triumvirs; since he had refused to join them, he must keep silence. Caesar had little love for Clodius, whose name was not among the land commissioners; and Pompey, still on close terms with Cicero, claimed to have forbidden him to take action against Cicero. But having deliberately let the genie out of the bottle it was idle to pretend either that they had not or that it was no genie. Clodius claimed at first to be incensed with the Triumvirs; whether he really was is immaterial; he was unscrupulous and unreliable, and if anger at Caesar had taken temporary possession of his mind, it had not killed his hate of Cicero, even though Cicero professed to suck consolation from the fact.

This brutal warning of his loss of independence drove him to his house at Antium, and thence to Formiae and Arpinum, whence he returned to Rome in June. He told Atticus that he had left Rome because he was no longer allowed to play the statesman there; he referred to 'the unconstitutional behaviour of the triumvirs who have ignored the auspices, the Aelian, Julian, Licinian, and the Caecilian and Didian laws, who have handed over kingdoms as though they were private estates to tetrarchs, and immense sums of money to a small coterie'.[1] No one was able to gainsay or oppose them; they held everything by force. For this degrading situation Cicero, as most others, held Pompey chiefly responsible, since it was his veterans, organised by Pompey, that provided the force, and it was the ruthless use of force that had silenced Bibulus and government. He could speak to Atticus of a 'regnum', but add that he preferred the present despotism with absence of fighting to any attempt to struggle with them, because Pompey might grow really violent. By May both he and Atticus were certain that Pompey was planning a despotism. Criticism alone was tolerated; 'people now speak openly and groan aloud, yet no remedy is applied; for we do not think

[1] *ad Att.* II, 9, 1.

resistance possible without a general slaughter, nor see what the end of concession is to be except ruin'.[1] But action was forbidden, as Bibulus and Cicero himself could prove, and later C. Cato.

Cicero, therefore, was in no doubt what was afoot: they had lost their political freedom; 'the upshot is that there is no hope, I don't say of private persons, but even of magistrates being ever free again';[2] and in the event this pessimistic forecast proved the truth. And with the loss of freedom had gone, of course, all hope of recalling the *concordia*; he realised that Rome had fallen under the heels of compulsive force which made nonsense of the concept of Senatorial government; this realisation is explicit in all of his letters in this sad year, and probably was just as manifest in his conversation. His dream of winning Pompey to the Senatorial cause was destroyed; if he had nourished still some lingering hope, Pompey's marriage to Julia in this year convinced him that the alliance was intended to outlast the year. Yet he continued on close terms with Pompey, regretting his loss of popularity and the embarrassment fallen upon a good man turned enemy against his will; for Pompey suffered the greatest unpopularity, and he never recovered that popular touch which had characterised his earlier career.

In view of his understanding and criticism of affairs he was greatly worried by what Clodius might do, if—as now seemed certain—he became tribune in 58. Clodius himself was claiming friendship with the Senate and hostility to the Triumvirs; but even if chagrin with Caesar might make him fleetingly vexed, he had certainly not transferred his rabid hate of Cicero to Caesar; his nature was well able to embrace two enmities, and his hatred of Cicero was a deep thing. Pompey assured Cicero that only over his dead body would Clodius harm him, that he had forced from him guarantees for Cicero's safety, given, if at all, as lightly as broken, and that his ill-famed sister, Clodia, had assured him that she was guiding him along the right path. Sometimes Cicero would write with confidence to Atticus, confident

[1] *ad Att.* II, 20, 3.   [2] *Ibid.* II, 18, 2.

that the 'boni' would not desert their hero, anxious, he claimed, to come to grips; at other times he did not conceal his worry. In truth neither he nor Pompey understood truly what was happening; neither had plumbed the depths of Caesar's will; Clodius and he were merely deceiving Pompey, in order not to offend or embarrass his dignity. But Caesar had no intention of allowing Cicero to upset all that he had done; whether Clodius was allowed to strike his victim down depended on the victim, not on Pompey, as both of them would soon discover; but whatever was or was not done, it would be done by Caesar's will.

Cicero was uneasily aware of his unpopularity with the Populares; they had attacked Antonius for ratting on them; they also prosecuted Flaccus, a praetor in 63, ostensibly for impropriety in his province of Asia, in reality for his part in the events of 63; and Cicero in his defence referred to the motives of the prosecutors of both these men, describing the pleasure Antonius' conviction had given to Catiline's supporters, and their hopes of a similar fate for Flaccus. Flaccus was acquitted, but the temper of the Populares was revealed.

Caesar still hoped to win him to his side, or at least to neutralise his power to overturn his edifice; he had offered him a place on the land commission; now he offered him a post on his staff in Gaul; either would have taken him into honourable retirement from Rome, and thus accomplished Caesar's purpose to prevent him taking the initiative when Caesar had left for Gaul. For Caesar respected Cicero's influence with the people; twice he had swayed that selfsame people against Caesar, and he had shown the will and power to lead which only Cato besides had shown; this very year he had criticised the behaviour of the Triumvirs, and he would certainly not rest content until he had undone this mischievous year's work. He was one of the two men Caesar consented to fear, the other Cato; if Cicero would not choose to leave the city, Clodius must have free run to wreak his vengeance; this was the plan throughout, whatever Pompey's simplicity supposed.

But for Cicero the choice did not exist; Caesar's consulship had shattered his ideal and that Senatorial leadership in government which was the basis of his political beliefs. Acceptance of Caesar's offer would have been a betrayal of his faith and a severance from the Senatorial cause which was his own; his future would have been ruined, had he supped thus with the Devil, and he could never have consented to follow Caesar's path. His refusal was therefore certain; his life was in Rome, as he had sworn after his quaestorship; yet his refusal to escape from this possibly dangerous and certainly ugly predicament must rouse our admiration for his courage. And Caesar's determination to silence or hound him out is the greatest tribute to his influence and standing at this time.

CHAPTER 9

CICERO'S EXILE AND RETURN

THE Triumvirs had won the two consulships, but they could not keep all the magistracies within their influence; two praetors in particular and some of the tribunes were their enemies. But attempts which the praetors made to attack Caesar and the validity of his legislation came to nothing; even though Caesar was no longer consul, his methods still prevented free decisions being taken. He was still making his preparations for his departure to Gaul and high among these preparations were arrangements to prevent attacks upon his legislation; and the instrument for this purpose was Clodius.

There can be little doubt of the close relations between Caesar and Clodius at this time; for Caesar's plans required that someone there should be to do what Clodius did, and Caesar did not leave such matters to chance; he had opened up the possibility of the tribunate to him, and now he gave him his directions. It was essential that Clodius did not fail; he must therefore use Caesar's methods, and be ready to compel, if persuasion failed; and for that purpose he must have the means of using force; a ready pupil, with his master still at the gates of Rome to give counsel and instruction, he quickly organised an army of persons ready to do his will and compel others to do likewise; Caesar's rule of force had apt continuator. Caesar had but two demands to make, to rid Rome of Cicero and of Cato; with these two gone, however done, and Clodius in control of legislation, no one would dare to call in question the events of 59, and Caesar could proceed in confidence to his province, leaving Pompey to guard their mutual interests.

Clodius had wasted no time from the moment his tribunate began in taking the centre of the political stage. He prevented

153

Bibulus from making his farewell speech as consul, as Metellus had prevented Cicero. He then began to pour forth bills, the first ones designed to win the mob's support and to prevent the religious interference with his laws that Bibulus had used against Caesar. He removed the small charge for public corn still remaining after Cato's reduction in 62; this free distribution, as it now was, imposed on the treasury a heavy burden which absorbed a considerable part of its resources. He then modified the rules by which proceedings in the assembly might be stopped or invalidated by the religious obstruction of 'observing the heavens', the means by which Bibulus had invalidated most of Caesar's legislation. This was, in fact, to restrict the use of a means of vetoing what might be selfish or irresponsible legislation; and in view of the machinery of legislation at Rome, with an irresponsible mob of persons able, if suitably bribed or rewarded, to pass legislation of a pernicious kind whose effect might be felt in any or every part of the Roman world, it was a valuable safeguard; Bibulus' use of it in the previous year was no argument against its continued use, for he was using the only method still open to him to check Caesar, when Caesar was trampling on the constitution. But Clodius was determined not to be checked himself by a device which had imperilled and, strictly, nullified Caesar's programme.

In order to simplify the recruiting of toughs to serve him as Pompey's veterans had served Caesar, he once again made lawful *collegia* or political associations, banned since 64 as being mischievous and dangerous; and such they were to prove again. Finally he restricted the powers of censors to remove and exclude men from the Senate, thus protecting himself and his supporters from this penalty for their present behaviour. One thing only remained, to ensure the co-operation of the two consuls, as had probably been agreed with Caesar, for the consuls had a large part to play; this was easily effected by arranging for them to have lucrative provinces from which they might expect by provoking war to acquire wealth and prestige. He was now ready to attack Cicero.

At the end of January he promulgated a bill the purport of which was that anyone who had put a citizen to death without the consent of the people should be banished. It was in itself no more than a restatement of that Lex Sempronia to which Caesar in 63 had drawn attention during the debate on the fate of the Catilinarians, and no names were mentioned; but everyone knew that Clodius was aiming at Cicero, who as consul had ordered the executions at that time. Cicero had, however, been most careful to act on the advice of the Senate, and the decision which he had carried out was the Senate's, not his alone; he had taken the further precaution of having notes of all the proceedings made and circulated, that all Italy might know the truth of what had happened.

None the less Cicero, knowing that he was Clodius' target, chose to regard the bill as an attack on himself, a course which he later regretted, and which was indeed a serious mistake, since, had he not chosen thus to simplify Clodius' task, Clodius would have found it difficult to dissociate Cicero from the Senate, and an issue of some magnitude would have been raised, namely, the authority and powers of the Senate in the post-Sullan world. But Cicero laid aside his Senatorial dress, let his hair grow long, and made himself the scapegoat for the decision taken in 63. He solicited the aid of his many friends both within and without the Senate, who showed their sympathy and tried to help; the Knights, ever his friends, resolved to wear mourning, and a deputation of their number, led by two Senators, was introduced to the Senate to plead on his behalf, but Gabinius would not receive them. Clodius' armed guard badly mauled the two Senators when they tried to address the people, and a third one was so badly hurt that he died; truly Caesar's pupil had learnt his lesson. Ninnius, a tribune friendly to Cicero's cause, was prevented by Clodius from taking any action on Cicero's behalf, and we need not doubt that the prevention was brought about by violence or its threat. Gabinius went so far as to banish by edict Aelius Lamia, a leading Knight, *pour encourager les autres*;

and when the Senate resolved to put on mourning, he again forbade it.

Senate, Equites and people were thus forced into acquiescence, and the importance of the consul's part can now be recognised. Clodius with his armed force could compel the Concilium to pass his bills and forbid his fellow-tribunes to legislate against his wishes; he could also use his force against both Senators and Equites; all this he had in Caesar's pattern done. But if the consuls had not been privy to the plot, Clodius must have suffered Saturninus' fate in 100; the Senate could have passed its S.C.U. as it did as recently as 62, and Clodius' reign of force would have had short shrift; as it was, neither Equites nor Senate could do anything but submit and Caesar's foresight in controlling the consular elections was manifest; Caesar's technique required the consulship; the tribunate alone would not suffice. Caesar and Vatinius, Gabinius and Clodius, with the consulship the more important instrument.

Clodius boasted that his actions enjoyed the Triumvirs' support; and this we may well believe. Pompey's position was humiliating; he had been closely allied to Cicero in the past, and owed much to Cicero's support; he had encouraged Cicero to have no fear of Clodius, had assured him of pledges extracted from Clodius, and had sworn that only over his dead body would he harm Cicero; Cicero now turned to him to redeem his pledges. But Pompey was not his own master. He had bound himself to Caesar, and had enjoyed the fruits of that alliance; in his own interests he must continue his support of Caesar, since the benefits he had reaped from Caesar's acts equally depended on the maintenance of Caesar's legislation. Cicero had shown himself opposed to the events of 59 and was, with good reason, regarded as one of the two men most capable of organising an attack on Caesar's consulship. It was impossible, therefore, for Pompey, in spite of all his promises and pledges, to raise a finger at this moment in Cicero's behalf; he betook himself in shame to his Alban villa, and when Cicero there visited him beseeching his aid with tears, he could only reply with truth that without Caesar's consent he could do nothing. Cicero later spoke with some bitterness of Pompey's sudden betrayal, his double-faced behaviour and his unfriendly replies.

It was now the beginning of March; Clodius had, like Caesar last year, reduced to silence all opponents; Cicero, having allowed himself to become the target of the bill, was without resource. Clodius invited the consuls to express their views on Cicero's consulship; Piso concealed his commitment to Caesar beneath a cloak of negative advice, for which Cicero never forgave him; Gabinius replied in cryptic but unfavourable terms, being likewise determined not to help. Clodius then held a meeting in the Circus Flaminius, in order that Caesar might be able to attend, and asked him his opinion on the contemplated legislation. He replied that he had at the time disapproved of what was done in 63, but he none the less did not approve of a law whose effect was retrospective; thus did he again make clear his position on this issue, and also, it may be, gave Cicero a final chance to accept his offer of an honourable retreat. If that was his object, it failed, for such an escape never occurred to Cicero. Since it was certain that the bill would pass, Cicero must decide whether to await its passage or to withdraw at once. He consulted all his friends, and almost to a man, including Atticus and Cato, they urged withdrawal now until the turn of the wheel should make possible his return. There was no other course open to him; Clodius had with Caesar's tools and tactics taken his revenge; and his friends on whom he had set such store were powerless to save him. Force had once more triumphed; not all his influence with the Equites and in Italy, nor all his influence in the Senate, could confront the force and threat of violence that Caesar's pupil threatened.

Opposition was hopeless; the previous year and all that had happened in this year made that much clear. The only counter to Clodius was organised force, and at this moment the only possibility of organised force lay with Clodius, Caesar and Pompey; no one else had forces to draw upon, and the consuls refused to act. Resistance, as Cicero saw, could only have one end, bloodshed, and this he wished to avoid; and so deep was the feeling in Rome that Cicero could believe that resistance might touch off a civil war. Exaggeration perhaps, but sombre evidence of the bitterness that Caesar had introduced to Roman politics. Cicero chose to anticipate the law; dedicating an image of Minerva in the temple of Jupiter Capitolinus, that same night he left Rome. Next day the bill became law, and Clodius without delay burnt to the ground his house on the Palatine and destroyed his Tusculan villa. A few days later he passed a second law outlawing Cicero by name for having put Roman citizens to death without an appeal to the people, and forbidding the rescinding of the law; it also required Cicero to remove himself to a distance of at least 400 miles from Rome; within that area no one might help or harbour him on pain of severe penalties.

We need not follow in detail Cicero's wanderings. He had at first had it in mind to go to Sicily, but was warned by its governor, C. Vergilius, not to approach, since he feared the consequences to himself in view of the penalties laid down by Clodius. He decided therefore to go East. From Vibo, where his friend Sicca had courageously provided hospitality, he moved up to Brundisium, where he reached his friend M. Laenius Flaccus' house on 17 April, and remained there until the 29th, Flaccus paying no attention to the punishments prescribed in Clodius' law. From there he sailed to Dyrrachium; Greece and Athens he did not wish to traverse, much though he would have liked to visit Athens; for Autronius and many other Catilinarians were there and he had no mind to encounter them at this moment. He therefore proceeded by way of the Via Egnatia to Thessalonica, in the province of Macedonia. There he was most kindly and hospitably received by Cn. Plancius, the quaestor of the province, and there he remained until the end of November.

During this time Cicero continued in a state of exquisite unhappiness and self-recrimination, and in his letters to Atticus both criticised his own tactics and actions at the time the law was passing, and was bitterly critical both of Atticus and his Senatorial friends for their weak counsels in persuading him to yield to the storm in the assurance that he would soon be back in Rome. From the self-assured confidence of early 59, when he claimed to be spoiling for a fight, in the certain assurance that Senate, Equites and all Italy would support him, he was plunged into the most abject grief and despair; he should never have trusted his false counsellors; since he was doomed to eke out an existence far away from Rome, he should have committed suicide and ended a life that had ceased to be useful and could only now be irksome and humiliating. Because movements initiated for his restoration were not instantly successful, he became impatient and assumed that all such movements were destined to failure. So deeply were his emotions stirred that he avoided meeting his brother, to whom he was deeply attached, because he felt unable to bear the strain of such a meeting; and his letters to his wife reveal the same weakness and excess of grief.

It is easy to criticise Cicero on the evidence of intimate letters never intended for our eyes, and to argue that they reveal a mercurial quality of character which must be considered a weakness in one who sought to be a leader. But we should remember how little we know of the innermost feelings of so many whose leadership we admire; the stories we have heard of Sir Winston Churchill's tears on failing to win an election should give us ground to pause before denying leadership for such a cause. The opposite could well be argued; the frustration of able men, prevented through circumstances from exercising their talents in the sphere where they can achieve most good, can bring honest tears to a brave man's eyes; and as no Englishman would argue Churchill's incapacity to lead because of those early tears, so should we not too readily condemn Cicero; he knew at first hand the danger confronting the Republic, yet was he powerless to raise his voice or hand in its defence, and his angry frustration was in part at least the father of these weak-sounding dirges and complaints. As Rome would later witness, courage in leadership amid the greatest dangers was not wanting to Cicero in the Republic's final agony of death.

We must now briefly examine what was done in Rome during the rest of this year. Clodius, having ridded himself and Caesar of Cicero, turned on the other man that Caesar feared, Cato. He passed a law by which the kingdom of Cyprus, ruled by Ptolemy, brother of the Egyptian king, should be annexed, a punishment for having failed to bribe the triumvirs; Cato was then named to carry out the task of annexation. The wretched king committed suicide, but there was still much to do, and Cato would not disobey an order of the people. Thus were two objects simultaneously achieved: Cato removed from Rome, and involved in the consequences of Clodius' tribunate. If the legality of Clodius' acts should ever be called in question, Cato would have to defend them in order not to be himself involved in illegality. Caesar wrote congratulating Clodius on having thus neatly dealt with Cato.

Clodius had satisfied Caesar and was now free to satisfy himself; he respected no one, not even Pompey. For a bribe from the Armenian king he engineered his son's release from the safe keeping in which Pompey, who had brought him as a hostage from the East, had placed him. Nor was he slow to use his gangs on Pompey, to such effect that Pompey dared not move about for the rest of the year. But such behaviour, satisfying as it might be to Clodius himself, only provoked Pompey's resentment; and Pompey was still a powerful man. He began to think of Cicero, whom he had unwillingly betrayed, and whose return would salve his conscience and serve to challenge Clodius. Atticus even in June could report a rosier situation after conversations with Pompey and his friend Varro. At the beginning of June the first tentative effort was made; the tribune Ninnius moved in the Senate that Cicero be restored; it was unanimously approved, but vetoed by the tribune Aelius Ligus; Clodius himself was absent. A suggestion that the Senate should handle no other business until this matter had been dealt with was prevented by the consuls, who claimed that they were bound by the Lex Clodia. Pompey continued to use his influence in the cause; but Caesar, whose agreement was essential, was apparently sounded and not found responsive to the suggestion.

The consular elections for 57 had returned Lentulus Spinther and Metellus Nepos, Pompey's tribune of 62, who had been suspended from his office. Under Pompey's influence and Atticus' persuasion he let it be known that his feud with Cicero would not prevent his fighting on his behalf; the other consul was wholly for Cicero, and almost all the tribunes. Caesar in Gaul had almost lost control; what he had prevented for 58 had come to pass for 57, and all would then depend on Pompey as the guardian of the Triumvirs' interests. Among the tribunes was T. Annius Milo, who was to show how to handle Clodius' armed force by the simple expedient of organising counter-force; P. Sestius, a second tribune, was also indefatigable in Cicero's behalf. He it was who towards the end of 58 made a special pilgrimage to Caesar to plead Cicero's case, with what success is not clear; yet it would seem that Caesar was not wholly opposed, for Sestius began the drafting of a bill to present when he became tribune. With both consuls, most of the tribunes, Pompey and the Senate prepared to work for his return, and Clodius out of office, the year 57 seemed full of hope and promise. Even in October 58 the eight friendly tribunes had prepared a bill for his restoration, thwarted only by a tribune's veto.

In late November Cicero crossed to Dyrrachium, both to be nearer Italy, and because the consul Piso, who had shown his hostility to Cicero throughout the year, would soon be assuming the governorship of Macedonia. Clodius, now towards the end of his tribunate, vexed with the turn events were taking, tried vainly to frighten the Triumvirs with the consequences of Pompey's present behaviour towards Cicero by calling in question the validity of Caesar's acts. He convened an assembly in the Forum, to which he invited Bibulus, Caesar's fellow-consul, and the college of augurs. Having asked Bibulus whether he had not observed lightning when Caesar carried his laws, and the augurs whether this did not invalidate the legislation, when they agreed, he replied that, such being the case, all Caesar's acts including his own adoption were void, that they should be set aside by the Senate, and that he would himself bring Cicero back to Rome on his shoulders. The intention was clear; Caesar must be content with all or nothing; if he wished to tamper with the legislation affecting Cicero, Clodius would undo all Caesar's legislation. But his year was running out, and no one wanted Clodius as an ally even in a good cause; the hint was not taken up and the incident remained a further illustration of his irresponsibility.

The first act of the new consul Lentulus was to raise in the Senate, with the support of his colleague, the question of Cicero's return. L. Aurelius Cotta, who was first asked his opinion, gave it as his view that a decree of the Senate was sufficient, since Clodius' law was not valid, but Pompey thought that to prevent all possible objection a law should be passed annulling the Lex Clodia and expressly restoring Cicero to all his rights. This view was approved by the Senate, but no action could be taken owing to one tribune, who said that he wanted time to think it over, and then at subsequent meetings prevented a decision being reached.

None the less a bill was brought before the people by eight of the tribunes on 23 January; but Clodius with his armed gangs, supported by some gladiators of his brother, who was a praetor, took possession of the Forum, and on the morning of the Assembly a veritable battle occurred, in which many persons lost their lives; Q. Cicero himself came very near to death on this occasion. It put an end to this attempt; nor were his friends able for some little time to renew their efforts, until they could put themselves on something like equal terms with Clodius and his terrorist activities. To this end Milo and Sestius now directed their attention, and gradually the object was accomplished; Clodius no longer ruled the city; Milo's gangs neutralised those of Clodius, government could work again, and Cicero's friends could set about their task.

Late in May Pompey spoke openly in favour of his recall, the Senate invited everyone in Italy to come to Rome to vote in favour of a bill for his recall, Plancius and the communities who had offered Cicero hospitality were thanked for their kindness, and Cicero was commended to the protection of all Roman magistrates. Early in July the consuls raised the question in the Senate and the whole Senate with the solitary exception of Clodius voted in favour of the motion; the Senate then decreed that anyone who attempted to prevent the passage of the bill by 'observing the heavens' or in any other way should be deemed a public enemy; and that, if the matter had not been brought before the people within the next five days on which business might be handled, Cicero should be allowed to return without the passage of the law. On 4 August the law was brought before the Comitia Centuriata and passed overwhelmingly.

Cicero had crossed to Brundisium from Dyrrachium on 4 August, where he was met by his daughter, Tullia, recently become a widow. Both at Brundisium and along the whole journey to Rome he was given a hero's welcome and was met at the gates of Rome on 4 September both by his friends and by everyone of note except his known and open enemies; of his popularity and esteem among both the Roman plebs and the country folk there could be no doubt. And this triumphal welcome by all classes both in Italy and Rome makes clear the unwillingness with which they had seen him go; it was not they who had willed his exile, but Clodius and Caesar using forceful methods to compel the people's acquiescence. The smooth efficiency with which Pompey and the Senate acted when they had friendly consuls and no intimidation and the tremendous popularity of Cicero are evidence enough that Caesar needed to use force to compel his measures and prevent them being upset and that he was right to fear Cicero's influence and leadership with the people.

But the Rome to which Cicero returned was not the Rome he had led in 63; Caesar's consulship and Clodius' tribunate had changed all that. Force and one man's will now dominated the scene, with change now possible only if Pompey agreed to intercede with Caesar. It had been possible this year to undo the chief effect of 58; and the Senate was once again precariously in the saddle, with orderly government assured only by Milo's counterforce. But it needed more than this to undo the effects of Caesar, including 59; at any time Caesar through Pompey could compel once more. The depth of the crisis was hardly felt by Cicero's contemporaries; too long they thought that if they could still manipulate the machinery to their own advantage, they had no cause for worry or dismay; nothing, they felt, could take from them their perquisites and rank, and this was for many the only substance and reality.

But Cicero knew better. He had thought in 63 that the loyal support of Senators and Equites, agreed to defend the state and its institutions, would restore and guarantee the stability of the constitution. That short-lived hope had ended with the ending of the crisis that had given it birth; but Cicero had seen the vital need for its continuance, if Caesar and his like were to be thwarted. All loyalists throughout Italy must support his *concordia*; it must be a *consensus omnium bonorum*, an upper and middle class alliance in defence of the existing order; both property and constitution needed protection. His failure to bring about this *consensus* in 60 had given Caesar his chance, and he had taken it; an unscrupulous determination to use as much of force as was needed to give him what he wanted had guaranteed success. His opponents, cocooned in their haughty traditions, could not compete, and after Bibulus' failure made little effort to put themselves on equal terms; unlike Cicero they could not see what these events portended.

But Cicero knew, knew also that temporarily at least the advantage had moved to the side of law and order, and that the vulnerable point in Caesar's armour was Pompey; if Pompey could be won to the Senate's side, Caesar in Gaul would find it very difficult to control affairs and magistrates in Rome; the Gallic enemy would absorb his time and energy. In the first flush of pleasurable excitement at his return and at the manner of it, he made two speeches of thanks to the Senate and the people; his speech to the Senate particularly underlined the way in which force had taken control of events during 58 and with the aid of consuls in collusion made possible his banishment; his exile had in effect been the exile of the Republic, as his restoration had spelt the Republic's restoration. To the people he spoke in more general terms, though he did make glancing criticisms of those in high places who had betrayed or failed to help his cause; this might seem tactless in one but recently returned; but he was right. The present was precarious, the future quite unassured; the need to strengthen the present uncertain advantage was urgent and compulsive; leadership and support were needed in a cause far greater than petty personalities, and those who were ready to subordinate the Republic's cause to personal prejudices were not worth the having; those who had failed to help Cicero for personal reasons had done just that.

Although Pompey's behaviour in 59 had been so treacherous to one who had constantly supported him, and to whom he had given so many solemn pledges of protection, yet Cicero forgave him all because of his efforts to procure his recall; fulsome gratitude for one 'who has had, has and will have no rival in virtue, sagacity and renown'[1] marks both these speeches. For this there was an obvious reason; disappointed though he had been by Pompey's desertion, yet he realised that Pompey had not been master and that Caesar's influence had been paramount; and he continued to admire his achievements and qualities of character, and to repose confidence in him as the man who should be the leader, together with himself, of the forces of law and order, the man to re-establish the Senate's primacy in government. A sudden shortage of corn at Rome gave Cicero his chance to show his gratitude and also to take a lead in the Senate. Whatever the causes, Clodius was extracting the utmost from it for his purposes, assigning the blame for it in some mysterious way to Cicero.

[1] *post Red. in Sen.* 5.

Many were for handing the task to Pompey, and Cicero spoke in favour of such a step, and proposed the motion in the Senate. Pompey should have full powers for five years to organise the corn supply, helped by fifteen legates of his own naming; the first nomination was Cicero. A tribune, Messius, proposed a second bill, which would have given Pompey control of the treasury, an army, a fleet, and *imperium maius* in the provinces; it would have been a powerful command, comparable with Pompey's earlier ones and Caesar's present one. But this was rejected, Pompey having declared his preference for the Senate's bill.

Behind all this there lay a struggle between Pompey and the nobles. Only two consulars turned up to the meeting when Cicero spoke in favour of the proposition, the others claiming that Clodius' behaviour made it unsafe for them to come. This hardly suffices to cover the truth, namely, that they did not wish to support a motion in Pompey's interest, and therefore preferred to absent themselves; when the people embraced Cicero's proposals and Messius' alternative ones were known, they all turned up without difficulty, since by then their one concern was to prevent, if possible, the adoption of Messius' bill rather than the Senate's original proposals. They doubtless supposed that Pompey would choose the more powerful alternative and that the people would gladly give it, as they had done on earlier occasions. Whether Pompey wanted a command on Messius' terms no one could know; always evasive, concealing his wishes and ambitions from all but his inmost friends, it was impossible to know his true feelings. One may sense that had such a command come freely to him, he would have accepted it as counterpoise to Caesar's growing power and military prestige.

It is equally true that the nobles were blind to the true situation, and chose still to regard Pompey as the enemy to be feared and checked, instead of trying to reach an accommodation with a man becoming anxious for release from a situation which was embarrassing and humiliating. Likewise the one man with vision to see what needed to be done, who was labouring to bring together the two parties whose interest lay in combination, namely, Cicero, him they could not refrain from gently humbling and humiliating because he seemed to be assuming airs and postures which were in their opinion above his station. Cicero's own position was made difficult by the fact that the question of his house was under consideration by the pontiffs; he must therefore for the present be especially tactful. A little later they decided that Clodius' consecration of the ground was illegal, and the Senate voted him compensation, which was, so Cicero maintained, stingy, because, as he told Atticus, 'the self-same men who clipped my wings are unwilling that they should grow again. But they are growing again already, I hope.'[1] So much for the nobles' ideas of statesmanship.

The situation continued unsatisfactory with Clodius and Milo leading the rival gangs and no one able to put an end to this continuation of Caesar's methods. In December one of the new tribunes, Rutilius Lupus, in the course of a speech attacked Caesar's legislation on the Campanian land; no comment was made until the end, when Marcellinus, consul designate, said, 'Don't infer from our silence, Lupus, what we approve at the moment or disapprove. As far as I am concerned, and I think it is the same with the rest, I am silent only because I do not think it right that the case of the Campanian land should be debated in Pompey's absence.'[2]

A further incident blew up at this time which gave the nobles yet one more chance to obstruct Pompey. Ptolemy Auletes, whom the Triumvirs had recognised in his kingdom of Egypt for a huge consideration, had been shortly after expelled when he tried to collect from his subjects the debt he had incurred. He now called upon the Romans to restore him. The Senate had agreed that the governor of Cilicia should be entrusted with this task, this province having been allotted to one of the present consuls, Lentulus Spinther. But there was a widespread idea that Pompey coveted this assignment, and would welcome this pre-

[1] *ad Att.* IV, 2, 5.   [2] *ad Q.F.* II, 1, 1.

text for laying hands on an army. The nobles thereupon conveniently discovered from the Sibylline books that the king might indeed be restored, but not with the help of an army; whereupon Pompey's interest in the business flagged. If he had in truth set his heart on this pretext to come by an army, he had been once again frustrated by the nobles. Clodius had again set upon and discomfited him; and Pompey was made to look both incompetent and weak. Cicero, who felt himself under a great obligation to Lentulus for his part in his restoration, kept him informed of the whole affair; finally nothing was done until Pompey gave Gabinius private orders to effect the restoration in 55.

Pompey's position was becoming rapidly one of shameful humiliation. Crassus, induced by Caesar to drop his enmity to Pompey in their common cause, now that their interests had been served, had let his jealous hatred regain control. Bitterly jealous of Pompey's prospects of gaining yet another lucrative command, he had financed Clodius' armed efforts to turn the mob against Pompey's claims in favour of his own; in a conversation with Cicero Pompey revealed that plots were being formed against his life, and that he was aware of Crassus' part in the mischievous attacks made on him in the Senate and in the plots on his life; he knew further that these two mischief-makers had the support of the most extreme of the nobles, such as Bibulus; and he was becoming depressed at the unpopularity which seemed to be enwrapping him, the inevitable consequence of his part in the affairs of 59.

Clodius meanwhile was not inactive. Foiled and frustrated by Milo his power and influence dwindled rapidly, and he had had the mortification of seeing Cicero brought triumphantly back to Rome and become a person of substantial influence. Anger and the hope of removing his rival spurred him to attempt in early 56 to prosecute Milo for using force; an ironical but seriously intended attack. In an attempt to achieve his end he himself had no compunction in using force and insulting Pompey, who had appeared on Milo's behalf. But in spite of hooliganism, bullying, crude and insulting behaviour to Pompey, he failed to bring Milo to court; he had undertaken more than he could handle. His threats to Pompey had driven the great man to provide himself with a bodyguard substantial enough to frighten off Clodius, who in consequence abated his attacks on the two men most responsible for his present low fortunes; he turned instead against others. He now set his teeth in Sestius, who had been active in supporting measures for Cicero's recall and had joined with Milo in organising the force that had neutralised Clodius; he too was arraigned for using force, and unlike Milo came to trial. Cicero had at once offered Sestius his services, and the offer was gratefully received; and at the trial Pompey appeared on behalf of Sestius.

Cicero's speech of defence consisted of a description of the events that had led up to his banishment and the unsuccessful attempts to bring about his recall. He then proceeded to an elaborate account of the Optimates, whom he identified with the true patriots, concluding with an appeal to the younger generation to adopt the principles of the Optimates and to accept Senatorial government and the aim of 'cum dignitate otium'. The speech as it stands (it may well have been worked over before publication) is the most elaborate and explicit statement of Cicero's political ideals, and one may well ask why he should have chosen this moment and this opportunity to express himself so fully on this theme; for Sestius' unanimous acquittal indicates that the jurors thought it had a present relevance. To understand how this should be, we must consider the situation as it now stood.

Cicero considered that in 63 he had prevented revolution and civil war by bringing together Senate and Equites and winning the support of moderate men throughout Italy, *consensus omnium bonorum*. As a result of this alliance Senatorial government had worked harmoniously and armed rebellion had been stamped out without any of the bitter aftermath of Sulla's victory. As the architect and personification of this policy of unity he regarded its subsequent breakdown as a personal blow. The events of 59 had finally shattered it, when it was shown that three powerful individuals with money, substantial *clientelae*, and veterans and soldiers, could trample down the niceties of constitutional government and obtain by force and strictly unconstitutional means whatever they wanted; in such circumstances *concordia* and *consensus* had no place and were powerless to prevent such behaviour, even if the will for such alliance was present; and the selfishness of so many in both orders had desperately weakened the alliance before Caesar had broken it.

Cicero and Cato had alone showed a resolution to try to undo what Caesar had done, and Caesar had seen to it that they should both be silenced by removal before he left. The years 59 to early 57 were years of rule by force in the latter of which, as Cicero saw it, the powers of good which were striving to bring about his recall were overwhelmed by Clodius and his armed force; his exile therefore symbolised this period of failure and showed the consequences. But when Milo and Sestius brought Clodius' force to nullity and allowed the constitution to work again, the Senate and all decent people had quickly and unanimously taken the necessary steps to effect his recall. Orderly government had prevailed; Pompey and Senate had worked together, the Equites had added their support, and all Italy had lent their votes in the great cause. As he had been the architect of the *consensus* in 63, so in 57 was he its cause and focal point; his banishment had represented the banishment of the Republic, his restoration her restoration. If then he wished to drive the lesson home, if for any reason he thought the moment opportune for reviving this policy, the occasion of Sestius' defence was as apt as any he could wish.

Cicero believed that this policy could and must be revived, if the Republic were to be more than a pretence, and he had been patiently working to this end since his return. The atmosphere at the time of his return and since had made him feel that the times were not inimical to such a change; and other indications confirmed his feeling. Pompey's embarrassed unhappiness at Rome, the insults put upon him by Clodius, the hostility and jealousy of Crassus, his seeming ineffectiveness, had perhaps made him want to turn from an alliance which had never given him pleasure and now gave him positive pain owing to the enmity he incurred on its behalf for no return; Caesar had climbed to power through his support, Crassus had used him as a tool and now conspired his death; perhaps his interests lay rather with the forces of law and order, which might be induced to take him as their champion. Cicero knew the answer, that he would gladly join them; from the moment of his return, forgetting Pompey's less than honourable betrayal, he had nourished their close friendship, and supported his hungry ambition; and Pompey's appearance on behalf of Milo and Sestius betokens close agreement between the two; Pompey was almost, if not wholly, won to Cicero's great plan.

Clodius and all he stood for must be publicly disgraced and contemptuously disowned; but what of Caesar? Caesar was the architect of the Triumvirate, the dynamic power that had crushed the Senate and all opponents, who had unleashed his pupil Clodius to work his will on Cicero and Cato, who alone of all the three had really gained from the alliance; who stood now at the head of legions, power and wealth at his disposal, while his partners lived and squabbled in shabby impotence at Rome. If the *concordia* was to be revived, not only Clodius but Caesar must be disgraced and publicly disowned; 57 had redeemed 58, but 59 still stood, and that was the year of crisis. The trial of Sestius gave Cicero his chance to raise the issue above the sordid pros and cons of a trial *de vi*, to show the truth implicit in this trial, that what was in dispute was whether Caesarism was to be rewarded with success.

The real point at issue was not whether Sestius had used *vis*— for of that there was no doubt—but why; and this moulded the form of Cicero's defence. In essence his argument was this: during 58 Clodius by his use of force and his intimidation had made

constitutional government impossible; Cicero had been unconstitutionally banished because the forces of law and order had
been suppressed by Clodius with the hostile consuls' help, and
the only alternative to his departure was bloodshed, which he was
determined to avoid. In the following year Milo and Sestius
had by organising counter-force enabled government to work
once more, and with Pompey's help Senate and people had
undone the wickedness of 58; Cicero was recalled, and his recall
represented the triumph of constitutional government, as his
banishment had represented force and lawlessness. Sestius had
certainly used force, but only to re-establish constitutional
government. Behind Clodius stood Caesar and his form of
government by force, behind Sestius stood Cicero and the constitutional government he had done so much to strengthen against
lawlessness in 63 by his *concordia* and his *consensus*; the issue was
hardly therefore even between Clodius' and Sestius' use of force,
it was between Caesarism and Ciceronianism. The detailed
description of the events that led to his banishment was a description of Caesarism; the detailed definition of the Optimates was
a definition of the persons Cicero had in mind as supporters of
his policy of strong constitutionalism; hence its importance in
the speech. And Sestius' unanimous acquittal showed that all
sections of the jury, Senators, Equites and Tribuni Aerarii, were
heartily sick of Caesarism with its use of force, and unanimous
in preferring Ciceronianism.

The significance of this was clear; Caesarism had sustained
defeat at Cicero's hands; his appeal in the speech to the younger
generation to support constitutional government against the
attacks made upon it from outside was a summons to the rising
generation to eschew the ways of Caesar and embrace Cicero's
consensus and the constitution; and his call had been heard and
applauded. The result was proof to Caesar and the nobles of
Cicero's great standing and influence with all but the small committed groups; it was proof to Cicero himself that his great pro-
ject of undoing 59 and restoring 63 was not chimerical, but almost

a reality. Pompey was his close friend, and Pompey had supported Milo and Sestius, not Clodius, Caesar's tool. The next step was to challenge 59. On 5 April in a debate in the Senate on finance, at which 40,000,000 sesterces were voted to Pompey for his needs in connexion with the corn supply, there arose a bitter discussion on the poverty of the Treasury and on the Campanian lands, whose income had been wrested from the state by Caesar's law of 59; Cicero now proposed that this matter be fully discussed at a meeting of the Senate to be held on 15 May. As Cicero later said of this: 'Could I more decidedly invade the stronghold of his (Caesar's) policy, or show more clearly that I forgot my own present interests and remembered my former political career?'[1]

Let us not underestimate the importance of Cicero's action; certainly Caesar did not. It was the final step in his plan to undo 59 and Caesarism after his success against Clodius. He knew of Pompey's dissatisfaction with his alliance with Caesar, and of his hostility to Crassus; he knew him to be not unfriendly to the Senatorial cause, if he could be identified with its leadership; when on the evening of that very 5 April Cicero had called on Pompey, Pompey had made no demur about the motion; and Cicero had known that he would not disapprove. The general sentiment in Rome had been shown in the recent trial, and there was at this moment neither army nor hooligan to intimidate; just as between 66 and 63 the Senate had successfully controlled events when unthreatened by force, so now could the harm of 59 be undone; if the illegality of this law were established, the rest of Caesar's mischief would be equally destroyed; Caesar and Caesarism would be beaten and constitutionalism would once again have control. This was the one and necessary way for the Senate to regain command and suppress the rule of force.

And Caesar recognised the danger. Crassus, jealous as ever of Pompey, reported the situation to Caesar at Ravenna, where Caesar then was. The crisis was clear: Pompey prepared to lend

[1] *ad Fam.* 1, 9, 8.

his influence to Cicero's cause, sentiment in Rome strongly hostile to Caesar's policies and methods; Senatorial government, rallied under Cicero's leadership, ready to resume the initiative and to challenge his legislation—and this would include the law by which he held his province. If this succeeded, he would be stripped of province and army, politically ruined, and the half completed conquest of Gaul would be abandoned.

The crisis was clear, and so was Caesar's mind on what to do; Crassus was easily persuaded; now he must win back Pompey. Pompey, who had heard with equanimity Cicero's intention to call the Campanian law in question, and was about to visit Sardinia in connexion with the corn supply, where was Cicero's brother, one of his legates, diverted from his road and made for Luca, the southernmost point of Caesar's province, to which he had hastened from Ravenna to meet Pompey, urgently invited thither. Caesar must win back Pompey, to save himself; he knew Pompey's nature and his sensitivity, his feeling that Caesar alone had gained from 59, while he, Pompeius Magnus, had become something less than great, insulted by Clodius, Caesar's tool, mistrusted, feared, despised by the nobles, without real power, with influence diminished; and he knew that Cicero's coaxing invitation to join the Senatorial side had a seductive quality that Caesar must counteract. Pompey was the one that counted; Crassus, hyena-like, would certainly be near to pick up what he could; but even his defection would not worry Caesar.

Caesar succeeded, and won back Pompey to his cause. As events were to show, it was agreed that Pompey and Crassus should be consuls for 55, that both should then hold important provinces for a term of years, while Caesar should be confirmed in the tenure of his province for a further period; they were to dominate the Roman world with arms and armies for the next five years. Cicero was to be sharply warned and darkly threatened to leave the Campanian law alone; the Senatorial challenge was to be crushed, and Caesar's will to prevail; 59 was to be confirmed and any one who dared oppose that will was to be removed or destroyed. The incipient opposition to Caesar's rule of force was to be crushed before it had gained solidity; Caesar, divining how things would stand, promised to release some soldiers to come to Rome to compel by force the election of Pompey and Crassus to their consulship; the Nazi techniques of 59 and 58 were to be renewed.

Agreement reached, Caesar returned to his army, Pompey proceeded to Sardinia. Soon after his arrival he met Cicero's brother and greeted him thus: 'You are the very man I want to see... Unless you speak very strongly to your brother, Marcus, you will have to pay up what you guaranteed on his behalf.'[1] He grumbled about Cicero's behaviour, reminded him that Cicero's recall had been possible only because Caesar consented, and requested him to commend Caesar's policy and claims to Cicero, and to ask him not to attack, even if he could not support, them. A certain Vibullius Rufus was sent to Cicero to ask him not to commit himself on the question of the Campanian land until Pompey should return.

Here indeed was crisis for Cicero and, as it proved, for the Republic. As in 59 and 58, Caesar had seen that the great threat of organised opposition to his rule of force came from Cicero; Cicero had so successfully organised that opposition that he was in a posture to challenge the very basis of Caesarism, and this he had been about to do in May. The atmosphere at Rome was shown by the results of the recent trials and in other ways as well to be strongly in favour of Cicero and orderly government; given freedom to choose, there could scarce be doubt whose way of life and government the Roman people would prefer. Pompey's indifference when Cicero proposed discussion of the Campanian law in May is evidence enough that Pompey took no umbrage at the time; he had probably shown sympathy, for Cicero's ideas had a special niche for Pompey, who hoped to win a place of primacy and respect among the established order, such as had always been his pleasing ambition. But Crassus had pre-

[1] *ad Fam.* I, 9, 9.

cipitated events, and had provoked Caesar to instant action; Pompey had been won by a more substantial plum than Cicero could proffer. Once he had accepted, he had no choice but to turn against Cicero; once again he acted half unwillingly, because he would have preferred Cicero's way, but had not the force of character to bring his ambitions to fruition through his own initiative.

The nobles behaved throughout with that meanness of spirit and narrowness of understanding which had for so long characterised their conduct. They had thwarted Pompey's aspirations, rejoiced in his discomfiture, and been resolute only in their determination to support his enemies to his humiliation. His past had damned him in their eyes; so obsessed were they by fears of what he might do once again, that they seemed to ignore the greater threat which Caesar posed. And Cicero too it pleased them to use and to insult, to smile at his embarrassments with Pompey, and ostentatiously to show Clodius their favour in his presence; unable themselves to lead they resented that this *novus homo* should presume to be their leader; and even though they found it expedient to follow, they could none the less titter behind his back at the difficulties he encountered on their behalf. Now they had tittered once too often; for Cicero, fearful of some second disaster such as had befallen him in 58, knowing the nobles' mean and spiteful attitude towards him, decided that he must acquiesce in the Triumvirs' demands. At a blow the Triumvirs had silenced the one man whose constructive statesmanship could have organised an opposition to their domination, and the nobles had lost the one man who could have shown them how to fight this growing menace. Cato was less important; tiresome and troublesome he was to them, but filibusters and assertive personal opposition were the most that his infertile mind could contrive; and while such tactics could annoy and even sting, tactics they would remain; the times called for strategy, and the nobles had jeered their one strategist into the enemy's camp.

Cicero had heard from his brother and received Pompey's message from Vibullius before the meeting of 15 May; he did not therefore turn up to that meeting, and the question of the Campanian land was either not raised or allowed to lapse. In a letter to his brother he says that he does not quite see his way on this matter; presumably he was wondering how to conform to Pompey's 'orders' without appearing two-faced or betraying his whole political past. He had obeyed the order; he had not yet surrendered. But this step came soon after; a letter to Atticus refers to a 'palinode' which Cicero had written—probably to Pompey—of the substance of which he was somewhat ashamed.

Why, then, did I send it to anyone before you? I was pressed by the man to whom I sent it, and had no copy. And—well! I am nibbling at what I must, after all, swallow—my 'recantation' did seem to me a trifle discreditable! But goodbye to straightforward, honest, and high-minded policy! one could scarcely believe the amount of treachery there is in those leaders of the state, as they wish to be, and might be, if they had any principle of honour in them.[1]

Cicero had weighed up the new situation and his place in it, and realised that the nobles, whose interests he had striven and suffered to advance, so far from supporting his efforts in their behalf, were quite ready to betray him because they were jealous of a man who dared to put himself on equal social terms with them, when his talents gave him so great an intellectual lead. His plan to save the Republic was doomed to failure, since the nobles would not see the deadliness of their danger nor play the strong, courageous part that Cicero had cast them for; if they chose to be spitefully jealous and rejoice at the difficulties he incurred on their behalf, then why should Cicero risk political extinction and possible exile on behalf of such ingrates? Far preferable to seek the company of those who would respect his person and his talents in return for his support and acquiescence.

[1] *ad Att.* IV, 5, 1.

In his next letter to Atticus he dwells on the difficulties and regrets involved in this decision, in which he is none the less determined to persist. He cannot show his pain without appearing ungrateful, i.e. to Caesar, who having forced him to this decision was now showing every kindness. He could not bring himself to withdraw from politics, but he must be prepared to serve in the ranks, though he might have been the general, i.e. to do what he is told by Caesar, when he might have led the opposition. Yet how was he to express the rejection of his former policy? The decision had been taken, regretfully but firmly; within a few weeks he was to make a public revelation of his submission to the Triumvirs.

Caesar had friends in the Senate, some who approved of his contempt of the nobles, others who had put themselves in Caesar's debt and must repay by support. Everyone knew that something had been agreed at Luca, though they could not know precisely what; and in this uncertain atmosphere two decrees in Caesar's favour were passed: the first that the state should assume responsibility for the four additional legions which Caesar had raised; the second that he should have ten legates instead of the usual six to which as governor of two provinces he would normally be entitled. By the first decree the Senate was compelled to recognise the legality of Caesar's action in raising the additional legions; he did not need the money, but he wished to forestall possible attempts at a later date to rob him of these legions as being raised without permission. The second in a sense followed upon the first; if his army consisted legally of eight legions, he needed more senior officers; once more the Senate was compelled to give a sanction to his actions and his self-created position. Both these decrees received Cicero's support, and he spoke in favour of both; it may even be that it is to the speeches made on this occasion, written down and sent to Pompey, that his 'palinode' refers.

But the crisis which was to compel Cicero openly to declare his change of loyalty came probably in June. The Senate was bound to name the provinces to be held by the consuls of 55 before their election in July of 56; the opposition which had been blowing up against Caesar earlier in the year was not yet wholly spent, and suggestions were made that one or both of Caesar's provinces should be named for the purpose. Cisalpine Gaul presented a technical difficulty, since it was guaranteed to Caesar until 1 March 54 by the Lex Vatinia, and hence could not be given to a consul who technically should be its governor from 1 January. But Transalpine Gaul was not so hedged, and if they chose to name it, tribunician veto could not prevent them. Cicero must now declare himself; he who had sought to organise the opposition by challenging the Campanian law must now bend all his powers of oratory to prevent the Senate from achieving his earlier purpose.

He took the opportunity to work off his spleen once again against Piso and Gabinius, the consuls of 58, whom he rightly held responsible for letting Clodius' mischief work unhampered; they were still governing the provinces given them by Clodius in return for their acquiescence in his activities, Macedonia and Syria; these should be the provinces to name for the consuls of 55. He argued against removing Caesar from his province in view of his achievements hitherto, the importance of what remained to do, and Caesar's particular suitability to complete the task.

He dwelt at length upon his past relations with Caesar, Caesar's consideration towards him in 59, the offers made him to avoid Clodius' spite; his exile, he claimed, was the result of his own folly and not of Caesar's angry manoeuvres; and he ended with a frank and pathetic declaration that since those whom he had tried by his policies to help wished to pursue enmities for their purposes and readily allowed him to suffer for sharing those enmities, he felt now at liberty, after all he had suffered and was in danger of suffering a second time, to reach an honourable accommodation with the man who could save him from further danger and showed respect for his talents and personality. He had broken with the nobles; and thus ended this abortive attempt to check Caesar's seemingly irresistible advance.

It is perhaps not inopportune to reflect on what Cicero came so near to achieving, and to picture the circumstances in which these events took place. There can be no doubt from the speed with which Caesar acted at Luca that Cicero was thought to have come very close to success, and to have it in his power to challenge successfully Caesar's position and his past legislation. Had he been successful in this, it is difficult to know what would have followed; he nearly brought to pass the situation which developed after 52, when it was too late; the nobles, with Pompey on their side to provide the military leadership of which they stood in such need, issued their challenge to Caesar, and refused to allow him to manipulate the constitution to his advantage; vetoes were ignored, and Caesar compelled either to submit or openly to reveal the extent of his determination and the basis of his power. Had Caesar not recovered Pompey to his cause in 56, he would have been confronted with that same challenge in 56, when he could not have extricated himself from Gaul to threaten Rome with arms; what would have happened we can never know; certainly the challenge would have been issued at a time far more embarrassing to Caesar than it was in 50, and more advantageous to the Senate. Let us not underestimate what Cicero so nearly brought about: the challenge to the rule of force which Caesar had inaugurated in 59, the year in which, as Asinius Pollio knew, the Republic was fatally attacked.

For this is the reality. The Republic had in this century sustained many wounds: armed revolution in 88 and 87 with the murder of political opponents; semi-dictatorship during the mid-80s, while they prepared for Sulla's homecoming; then civil war and further murders. What emerged from all this blood and carnage was not and could not be the earlier Republic; Sulla's Republic might in other circumstances have done its job; but as things were, it could not expect to go unchallenged, if someone felt able to issue the challenge. Pompey did; and further, Pompey had learnt from Sulla the power an army could exercise upon the government. Pompey refined the operation; without directly using an army he achieved the same effect by its mere possession; in 77 and 71 he achieved his aims without recourse to violence—with such success that the nobles resolved to give him no further opportunity.

During his absence in the East there had been no powerful man at Rome to use armed threats to exert pressure upon the government. Caesar and Crassus had tried to arm themselves against Pompey; but having no arms they could be thwarted by the normal working of the constitution—and they were. During these years it was shown that constitutional government could still control affairs, if it were not suppressed by force; not only could the schemes of Caesar and Crassus be brought to nought, but the Catilinarian commotion showed how armies could be deployed in Italy without their commander turning on the government to extort concessions or to change the constitution. And Caesar observed all this; personal experience and his observation of these years showed him that bribery and popularity could achieve a limited purpose; but beyond that limit something more was needed. Pontifex Maximus and praetor he had become; but how much further would he go against the opposition of those who hated him and were resolved that he should go no further?

He became consul, as he had become pontifex and praetor; but to undo the limits of his *provincia*, to satisfy the colleagues to whom he owed his consulship, to equip himself with what his ambition had marked out, how was he not to fail in all these aims, if Cato and the nobles continued to oppose? There could be one way only, compulsion; they must be forced to obey, or at least to acquiesce in, his will, to such degree that his plans could not be upset. To this end he had introduced the use of force by groups of men, disciplined and organised to serve their master's purpose, which was to compel men to vote according to Caesar's wishes. Pompey's veterans were used in 59 as Pompey himself had not thought to use them, to compel from Senate and voters what they would not otherwise have given. Bibulus, his fellow-consul, was reduced to babbling ineffectiveness, the Senate to a sullen acceptance of the new position; the people in their assembly were left no choice but to vote for Caesar's and his tribune's laws; and unpopular as this made him with the voters, Caesar cared nought for this, so long as the constitution was twisted to give him what he was determined to have. Only Cicero and Cato had showed fight; and their silence was arranged for.

And thus Caesar had ushered in the organised use of force to compel the limbs of the constitution to bend to his will; to see that only those persons were elected to the senior magistracies who would support his plans and oppose his enemies. Clodius continued Caesar's work; force continued to be the deciding factor in Roman politics; if neither side had an army, then the side that had any force could impose its will. Caesar used veterans and recruits, Clodius organised louts; but both men used force to compel men to vote in certain ways and to prevent them acting against their wishes; blood flowed and men were killed, and in such an atmosphere political freedom cannot live. Milo and Sestius created a temporary illusion of freedom by organising force to combat Clodius' force, so far successfully that, granted Pompey's and Caesar's blessing, the Senate could procure Cicero's return.

But this was mere semblance; Cicero's recall was possible only because Pompey wanted it and Caesar agreed not to oppose—on condition that Cicero no longer acted freely as a statesman of consular standing, who might find himself opposed to much that he found in Rome. It was freedom only on sufferance; Caesar's determination remained that his arrangements should stand untouched; and since this was precisely the point on which opinion was so bitter, the freedom was hardly worth the having. This was the reality of these years; the free institutions of the Republic were no longer free; it was the rule of Caesar, directed by his agents, using the Republic's framework as its means. Neither elections nor legislation were free beyond what Caesar willed and wanted; Pompey was his agent; the nobles to free themselves must win to their side the only man whose military prestige was as great as Caesar's, Pompey; until then they were powerless. These harsh facts dominated and determined Cicero's life after his so nearly successful attempt to lead the nobles back to freedom and responsibility.

FROM LUCA TO THE CIVIL WAR

ICERO no longer sought to lead the 'boni'; in the first
flush of shame at what he felt to be the betrayal of his
principles he sought to justify the step he had taken and
to explain why he had turned to Caesar. The more he argued his
case, the less did he persuade himself; personal convictions, not
being born of logic, cannot be undermined by logic, and Cicero
was betraying or surrendering his principles. But his arguments
had strength enough and substance to justify to the nobles his
abandonment of their cause; for their behaviour to himself and
their feeble, selfish attitude to all the problems of the state were the
prime causes of his failure; their refusal to rally to his cause, their
blindness to the danger that confronted them, were the reasons for
Cicero's 'palinode'; he must join Caesar or suffer political death.

During the next years he took no independent part in politics;
able no longer to lead the party of law and order against its
enemies, he would not more actively associate with the wreckers
than his circumstances compelled. Involved to some extent he
was by reason of his reputation at the bar; those to whom he was
now bound requested his services in the interests of their clients;
and he found himself as a result in considerable embarrassment.
His letters show how deeply he felt his own and the Republic's
miserable fate; his own futility, the nagging unhappiness at being
forced into this frustrating degradation, the knowledge that the
name of Republic concealed a dictatorship in which one's only
freedom was to do what one was told to do, these bitter thoughts
recur in the letters of this period. Meanwhile the sham of the
Republic was monthly made more apparent; those with the
power forced themselves or their nominees into the posts where
power resided, compelled all others to obey, and by the power

they gave themselves made nonsense of the Republic. Where persuasion might fail, force was used; as in the earlier days of Nazism soldiers and organised bands were used to bully voters to give their votes in a particular way; assemblies and elections were likely to see bloodshed and murder; we may fairly wonder how many Romans turned up to cast their vote, when the penalty for casting it wrongly might be serious injury or death. This was Caesar's contribution to the smooth working of the Republic, introduced in 59, made permanent after Luca.

Cicero felt the ignominy of his new position; 'I', he writes to Atticus, 'who, if I say what I ought about the Republic, am looked on as mad, if what expediency dictates, as a slave, and if I say nothing, as utterly crushed and helpless—what must I be suffering? Suffer, indeed, I do, and all the more keenly that I cannot even show my pain without appearing ungrateful.'[1] In September he appeared on behalf of Cornelius Balbus, prefect both of Pompey and of Caesar, accused by the Triumvirs' enemies, when the alliance seemed almost broken, of being improperly possessed of the Roman citizenship. Balbus was acquitted, but Cicero's position was clear; he was on the side of the Triumvirs.

No elections had been held for the magistracies for 55, nor could they be; for Pompey was using the tribune, Caius Cato, to prevent them. He and Crassus were to seize the consulship for 55, for otherwise the schemes of Luca could not be translated into laws; but they were under no delusions; given a free choice the people would be most unlikely to choose them. It needed the Caesarian technique, and Caesar had promised soldiers for the purpose, but they had not yet arrived; their arrival was now awaited with some impatience to 'help' their candidacy. For long they would not admit their intention to be consuls; Rome knew only that Pompey through C. Cato was preventing the elections, and that Senators once again feared to attend meetings of the Senate; but most men suspected what was afoot. The year thus ended without magistrates for 55.

[1] *ad Att.* IV, 6, 2.

But now the soldiers had come, the 'canvass' could begin, and all but Domitius Aenobarbus in fear and desperation withdrew their candidature; Domitius would have liked to do the same, but Cato insisted that he stand firm. Domitius and his attendants were on the morning of the election attacked by Pompey's soldiers, his link-boy killed, himself wounded and driven from the scene; what people had turned up to vote now voted for the only two candidates, Pompey and Crassus, who took over Rome, as Caesar had in 59. They first saw to the election of the other magistrates, and by abundant use of force and bribery contrived to fill almost all the offices with their supporters; Cato was kept out of the praetorship, and all but two of the tribunes were their friends.

With both the senior magistracies in their hands and organised force at their disposal, the Senate cowed and the people apprehensive, they were now in position to repeat the tactics of 59; the Senate could not use the S.C.U. with hostile consuls, themselves responsible for the disorders and the use of force, while they could organise legislation either themselves or through a tribune, with the same assurance of acquiescence and absence of defiance that Caesar had guaranteed for himself. This had been the aim of this agreement, and the consulship was necessary for the task; they had therefore seized this office for themselves, displaying their contempt for the Republic, and confirming that the events of 57 and early 56 were but an interlude in Caesar's tyranny of force.

A tribune, Trebonius, now passed legislation by which Pompey and Crassus were given provinces for five years, with the right to make war and peace at their discretion, both Spains for Pompey, Syria for Crassus. Force and bloodshed marred the passing of this law as all else in these early months; Cato's and the people's opposition was in vain; with or without bloodshed they must accept. The consuls themselves then passed a law continuing Caesar's provinces for five years further. These two laws, the purpose and the outcome of Luca, expressed the determination of these three men to rule by force the Roman world; that world should be in their control for the next five years, clamped in the iron grip of three dynasts with three armies, answerable only to each other. The most important areas of the Roman world, with all their resources of men and money, were to be theirs to do with as they would, to involve, if they chose, the Roman people in war and conquest—and, it might be, defeat—without the chance to indicate their wishes. The government had become the instrument of the dynasts, who, since they had the armies, had also the means of compelling obedience to their will. And Caesar was the creator of this plan; when Cicero's challenge came, too heavily involved in Gaul to risk its consequences, he had brought his two colleagues once again together, determined on two things, one to re-enforce the rule of force at Rome, controlled through Pompey by himself; secondly, to safeguard his position until his work in Gaul was done. He had achieved his end by conceding equal power to his partners, who for this great consideration would support his use of force.

Cicero had realised the truth at once. In January he wrote to Lentulus Spinther: '(Public affairs) are all, it is true, in the power of our friends, and to such an extent that it does not seem probable that the present generation will see a change.'[1] He had, in fact, witnessed the death of the Republic. Later in the same letter:

For those objects which I had at one time in view, after having held the highest offices and endured the greatest fatigues—the power of intervening with dignity in the debates of the Senate, and a free hand in dealing with public affairs—these have been entirely abolished, and not more for me than for all. For we all have to assent to a small clique, to the utter loss of our dignity, or to dissent to no purpose...The most we can hope for is tranquillity (*otium*): and this the men now in supreme power seem likely to give us, if certain persons show more tolerance of their despotism. The old consular prestige, indeed, of a courageous and consistent senator we must no longer think of; that has been lost by the fault of those who have alienated from the Senate both an order once very closely allied to it, and an individual of the most illustrious character.[2]

[1] *ad Fam.* I, 8, 1.   [2] *Ibid.* 3 f.

As in 59, so now, Cicero's perspicacity saw the truth with clarity; in 59 he had doubted whether his generation would ever again see the magistrates exercising their proper powers; and except for that brief moment in 56 he was right. Now again he doubted whether his generation would see the release of the stranglehold upon the government, and was under no delusion as to the powerlessness of all except the Triumvirs; for consulars and senators there was no longer place in government. Of his ideal of *cum dignitate otium* half had perforce to be abandoned; *dignitas* was surely gone, for there could be no *dignitas* for senators and nobles, when they were nothing more than dynasts' lackeys. *Otium* at least might be guaranteed, though so far it had not; but if the despotism were accepted, the need for force and bloodshed in Rome's daily life would be gone; it demanded abject surrender, which Cato would have to learn. Cicero at least had learnt through suffering realism; he fully understood the meaning of the present and knew there was no escape.

The consuls' unpopularity was not in doubt; Cato, defeated for the praetorship, yet won the plaudits of the crowd; and the death and bloodshed which had stalked in their armed company had sickened and frightened everyone. The levies for their respective armies were resented, and Crassus departed to the accompaniment of curses from the tribune, Ateius Capito, who thus registered his protest that Rome should provoke a war with a nation with whom she had no quarrel, merely to satisfy the jealous ambitions of a Triumvir. But beyond a gesture interference was forbidden.

The next years, 54 and 53, saw the beginnings of the split between Pompey and Caesar. Their original 'marriage' had been only of convenience, wherein Pompey had quickly found uneasiness in his role of gang-captain, and in the next two years had drawn ever closer to the side of law and order; so much so that Caesar, fearing for himself, had arranged the conference at Luca, from which the present situation had derived. Crassus had hurried off to Syria and death, Caesar was still tied down in Gaul; Pompey had chosen to govern the two Spains by legates, appointed by himself, while he himself kept watch on events in Rome. Whether this was part of the agreement we cannot know; it was certainly important that the control they had seized in 55 should not be wrested from them, and this could best be assured by Pompey's continued presence. But this gave Pompey an advantage over Caesar, which Caesar realising took steps to counteract; and this tension, together with the jealous suspicion with which two great men are like to view each other, gave the colour to these years.

The rule of force continued; both 53 and 52 opened without consuls, their election prevented by opposing gangs, who were allowed to control the scene; the government were now no less the victims of a greater force than they had been in 59 and 55; and behind this parade of force and bloodshed lay the contention between the two dynasts. Caesar had from his first setting out for Gaul continued to keep in touch with politics; each year he held court in Cisalpine Gaul, established or re-established contacts, planned his strategy, and by profuse employment of the vast resources now at his command bought useful men and exercised an influence by no means hidden on the election of the magistrates. He had built up an intricate network of power at Rome destined for use in his own interests; if those interests clashed with Pompey's, then would the trouble start. The greater became absent Caesar's influence on affairs, the more uneasily suspicious did Pompey grow; and though he was on the spot, the difficulty of countering Caesar's power increased; the theme of these two years is the intensifying struggle between these two, whose trend at this remove of time we see, though many of the details must escape our scrutiny.

The struggle for the consulship for 53 epitomised the tensions of the scene and the extremes to which both sides would go. Even in June of 54 Cicero could tell his brother that while elections might be held, yet rumours of dictatorship were current, revealing thus how little the situation was in the consuls' control, whose early responsibility it should have been to ensure the elections at the proper time; but what could they do against Pompey's and Caesar's force, with Pompey working for dictatorship? All the candidates were guilty of bribery on a stupendous scale, which had forced up the rate of interest at Rome; in July it became known that two of them, Memmius and Domitius, had made an infamous pact with the consuls whereby they would lie in the interests of the outgoing consuls in exchange for their improper influence at the election. The pact itself was strange,[1] suggesting that the consuls had been threatened with vetoes in connexion with their provinces, unless they helped; for otherwise why bargain to have given them what should in any case be theirs? Memmius was induced by Pompey to make the revelation, and Memmius was one of Caesar's candidates; the revelation cost him Caesar's support and the consulship, though he still hoped that Caesar, when he came down to Cisalpine Gaul, would continue his support, and it was thought that a tribune would hold up the elections until his arrival. Behind this squalid story lie intrigue and tension as the two dynasts struggled to place their men in power and office, the details obscure, the fact undoubted.

The rumours of dictatorship continued, and the only candidate for such a post could be Pompey. The dictatorship would give Pompey what he needed and this he knew; but how to lay hands upon it? The rumours continued but could not be translated into fact. Milo and Clodius were playing parts, not easy to divine; but by a metamorphosis strange and ironic, Clodius, now on bad terms with Caesar, was supporting Pompey, while Milo had incurred his anger. Clodius' change of front need raise no query, but what had Milo done? Obviously used his force to the detriment of one of Pompey's candidates, or somehow else frustrated

[1] In return for the consuls' help in procuring their election, the successful candidates were to produce three augurs to depose to having been present when the *lex curiata* conferring *imperium* had been passed, which had in fact not been passed, and two consulars to depose to having helped draft a decree by which their provinces were furnished, though there had been no meeting of the Senate.

him; and as Milo was beginning his canvass for the consulship in 52, Pompey had already declared his opposition. Milo's dilemma was that, if he supported a veto of Pompey's dictatorship, Pompey would destroy his chances; if he allowed it to go through, Pompey would not help him. From these depressing calculations we may infer that Milo had used his force against Pompey's interests; and how affairs were managed at this time is clear to see.

Cicero found that the exigencies of his new alliance brought bitterness and pain. His letters to his brother in this year lay stress upon Caesar's friendship, which he was resolved not to forfeit by wrong or independent action; 'I have made up my mind not to attempt any cure of the political situation without powerful protection.'[1] But since his 'powerful protection' was bent on the destruction of the Republic, he preferred to withdraw himself from active politics.

But you must see that the Republic, the Senate, and the law courts are mere ciphers, and that not one of us has any constitutional position at all.[2]

We have lost not only all the healthy sap and blood of our constitution, but even its colour and outward show. There is no Republic to give a moment's pleasure or a feeling of security. 'And is that, then,' you will say, 'a satisfaction to you?' Precisely that. For I recall what a fair course the state had for a short time, while I was at the helm, and what a return has been made to me! It does not give me a pang that one man absorbs all the power. The men to burst with envy are those who were indignant at my having had some power.[3]

It cuts me to the heart...to think that there is no Republic, no law courts, and that my present time of life, which ought to have been in the full bloom of senatorial dignity, is distracted with the labours of the forum or eked out by private studies, and that the object on which from boyhood I had set my heart,

'Far to excel, and tower above the crowd,'

is entirely gone: that my opponents have in some cases been left un-

[1] Q.F. II, 15, 2.   [2] Q.F. III, 4, 1.   [3] ad Att. IV, 18, 2.

attacked by me, in others even defended: that not only my sympathies, but my very dislikes, are not free, and that Caesar is the one man in the world who has been found to love me to my heart's content, or even, as others think, the only one who was inclined to do so.[1]

The pathos of his position was revealed, as he truly remarked, in the law courts, where he was not allowed to attack, and on occasions was required to defend his enemies. Vatinius, the mouthpiece of so much of Caesar's legislation, was prosecuted in this year—not for the first time—and Caesar, concerned to prevent his enemies' victory and his own discomfiture, asked Cicero to assume his defence. Loath to defend one whom he hated, he yet had little choice; since Caesar was his only friend in politics, he accepted the unwelcome task, and was successful. But this was an admission of his change of friends so unambiguous and so surprising even to those whose behaviour had driven him to take the step, that it shocked others as much as it disgusted himself; and in a letter written to Lentulus Spinther he was at pains to explain how this had come about.

Later this year Gabinius returned from Syria, where he had been since 57, until now replaced by Crassus. Fierce was Cicero's hatred of this man for having countenanced Clodius and deserted Cicero during that fatal 58. He was unpopular at Rome for what he had been in 58, disliked by many nobles for what he had done in Syria under Pompey's aegis and instructions, and now exposed to their anger through the courts. It had been typical of the Triumvirs' contempt for government that, in order to redeem their pledge to Ptolemy, king of Egypt, who had paid them handsomely, Pompey himself had given Gabinius orders to restore this trashy monarch to his throne, involving a Roman army in a war without the Senate's or the people's knowledge or consent; Gabinius' prosecution was therefore also Pompey's.

But Gabinius was wrapped around by Pompey's mantle, whose man he was, and Cicero, keen though he was to square accounts, felt that he could not move.

[1] Q.F. III, 5 and 6, 4.

Some people...say that I ought to have been the prosecuting counsel. Was I to have exposed myself to such a jury as this?...But there were other considerations which influenced me. Pompey would have looked upon it as a contest with me, not for that man's safety, but for his own position...At this time of day, when I don't even care to be influential, and the Republic certainly has no power to do anything, while he is supreme in everything, was I to enter upon a contest with him?[1]

It was frustrating not to be free to attack one's enemy; to have to defend him was humiliating. Yet to this was Cicero brought by Pompey's insistence; for Gabinius had many enemies, and though he secured a narrow acquittal on the charge of treason, he was arraigned a second time for having taken bribes from Ptolemy. Cicero could not withstand Pompey's pertinacity, and to his angry shame he found himself defending his hated enemy, who was none the less this time convicted and forced into exile.

Pompey had suffered a defeat, against which could be set Caesar's victory in procuring Vatinius' acquittal. It was unfortunate for him that his protégé was so unpopular that a determination to bring about his condemnation insisted in spite of one acquittal on a second charge. For Pompey had quite openly succeeded once; and Domitius, one of the contestants for the consulship, had been happy to reveal for Pompey's benefit his vote of acquittal, hoping no doubt to be rewarded with Pompey's support. But elections for the consulship could not be held; Pompey could not control events sufficiently, and looked more keenly still at dictatorship to provide the necessary power.

The year 53 opened with only tribunes elected, and a motion for the appointment of a dictator was successfully opposed. Now Pompey was without resource; unable to impose his own choice upon the state he could only prevent Caesar imposing his, and the year drifted consulless into July, when Pompey in despair brought discipline sufficient to hold the elections; Domitius, who had toadied up to Pompey at Gabinius' trial, and Messalla, one of Caesar's candidates, became significantly the consuls. But dis-

[1] Q.F. III, 4, 2.

order soon again broke out in connexion with the elections for
52; for Milo was seeking the consulship, and Clodius the praetorship; Milo opposed by Pompey, and Clodius on Pompey's side,
but no longer enjoying Caesar's blessing. Milo's candidature
worried Cicero; anxious he was to lend what aid he could, but
what could he dare to do against an angry Pompey? Milo's cause
seemed doomed to failure, in spite of what force he could contribute to his cause, and Cicero could easily involve himself in
peril.

The defeat and death of Crassus at Carrhae in June of this
year added to the complications of the times. It was a disaster for
Rome which she deserved, in so far as Crassus represented Rome;
this first and catastrophic encounter with the powerful nation
of Parthia on her eastern frontier was to colour and in a sense
determine relations for a hundred years and more. More immediately it affected the scene at Rome, for now the balance of
power between the three dynasts was upset; no longer were there
three, all with large armies, jealous of each other, ready to prevent
the growth to dominance of one by a combination of the other
two; instead, Caesar and Pompey confronted each other, the one
determined to work his will unopposed, the other resolute that
none should stand on equal terms with him; the tension between
the two of 54 and 53 must necessarily increase.

There had already been grim foreboding of the antagonism
that might burst forth. In 54 Pompey's wife Julia, Caesar's
daughter, died, calamity itself enough; for loved both as wife
and daughter she was a bond between the two, preventing envy
getting out of hand. Her death was therefore of itself calamitous,
for now there was no bond; and Crassus' death had sharpened
the probability of feud when the tension was already mounting.
Caesar had marked uneasily his partner's growing antagonism,
and in this year had proposed a fresh alliance, he to marry Pompey's daughter, Pompey to marry his great-niece. In an age when
such marriages had significance sufficient that Cicero could divine
the permanency of the Triumvirate in 59 from Pompey's mar-

riage with Julia, the present proposal could have but one clear meaning: the final sealing of a compact between the two. Equally its rejection would spell the rejection of an offer and a compact; and Pompey refused. Not content with rejecting Caesar he with deliberation courted the nobles, and chose as his wife Metellus Scipio's daughter. This was the snub direct to Caesar and an indication of the point to which their mutual suspicions had advanced; the experiences of 54 and 53 had soured Pompey, and Caesar had known this fact; the climax could not be overlong delayed.

As in 54, the elections for 52 could not be held; riots and bloodshed once again disgraced the Roman scene as both contestants subtly manoeuvred for position. Pompey, who could, as he had in 53, have compelled the order needed to hold elections, preferred to provoke disorder to prevent them; Milo and Clodius would only cause disturbance, they could no longer command the day. At the beginning of the year Pompey prevented the appointment of an *interrex*, determined that the chaos should force the Senate to turn to his strong arm for discipline. Events soon played their mischievous part in his behalf.

On 18 January Clodius and Milo met on the road to Lanuvium; a squabble quickly became a fight in which Clodius lost his life. The body was brought to Rome and exhibited with all its wounds: riots ensued and the Senate House became its unintended pyre. A succession of *interreges* was unable to impose the order necessary to hold the elections, and the Senate empowered the *interrex*, the tribunes (the only magistrates) and Pompey to save the state, and Pompey to raise troops in Italy. But events continued critical, and Pompey still lacked the explicit power he sought; the Senate, powerless to act without his help, was forced to acquiesce, free only on detail to show some independence; they would make him not dictator, but sole consul. Thus after nearly sixty days of anarchy and a year of mischievous intrigue Pompey had compelled an invitation to assume exceptional power, however he was named; his dawdling and dark influence had achieved its object. It could be the first step towards his reconciliation with the nobles; if they could find agreement, the way was open for the solution of their common problem, Caesar; the nobles would have what they had so long lacked, a general with which to confront a general, and Pompey the mantle of the constitution.

Caesar's friends had put up a fight, demanding that Caesar too should hold the consulship; but Pompey had won this round and now was in command. The intenseness of their struggle in 54 and 53 had woken Pompey to his danger, nor had he yet defeated Caesar; Caesar's friends were strong in Rome, able to make demands in Caesar's interests; and none knew better how to force and how to prevent action at Rome. Caesar's position in the future would be critical, now that he could not put his faith in Pompey; he must have assurance for the time when his command in Gaul was ended, that he could hold the consulship without the need to sue for it at Rome, since he must be able to move straight from his province to his second consulship; if this were not to be, during the interval between the two, when he was *privatus*, his enemies would prosecute him, and that would be his end. His friends extracted from Pompey an undertaking that he would allow the passage of a law permitting Caesar to sue *in absentia* for the consulship; the law was passed, sponsored by all the tribunes, Cicero, persuaded by Caesar at Ravenna, having induced his young friend Caelius, a tribune, not to oppose the bill. This and this alone he had secured.

Pompey, endued with the power he had for long been seeking, now acted with a firm efficiency to bring order to the Roman scene. The rioting, bloodshed and lawlessness were instantly suppressed; a bill to deal with violence, and one with bribery, were passed, and preparations hurried forward for Milo's trial. This was in a sense a symbol of restored order; the two men whose activities had made so great a contribution to the disorder and whose final encounter had triggered off the recent tumult, requiring the threat of troops and the reality of a supreme magistrate to quell, must not be allowed to escape their due deserts; Clodius had lost his life; Milo must stand his trial.

But this was but a surface and a partial view. Milo had organised his private force to deal with Clodius in 57, and by that means had released Pompey from his shame and the government from intimidation. But after Luca, when Pompey in the Triumvirs' behalf was controlling the fate of Rome, had begun those tensions and divisions between Caesar and himself which we have witnessed; and in this struggle Milo's force had not been used more recently in Pompey's cause. Clodius had broken with Caesar and was on Pompey's side, while Milo had Pompey's hostility to his consular candidature; Pompey was pressing now not merely to see justice done but revenge taken.

He pursued his intention grimly; Cicero, deeply beholden to Milo, undertook his defence; but though he knew of Pompey's hostility, he was quite unnerved by Pompey's preparations 'to see fair play'; surrounded by soldiers, almost shouted down by Clodian supporters, he failed completely in what was probably in any case a hopeless task. Milo was condemned and retired to exile in Massilia. Having used the force of his position to be rid of Milo, Pompey allowed the other trials to take their course; M. Saufeius, involved in Clodius' death, was acquitted, while Sextus Cloelius and other Clodian supporters were successfully prosecuted for their part in the burning of the Senate House. And at the end of the year Pompey had the mortification of witnessing the successful prosecution by Cicero of Munatius Plancus Bursa, a tribune of the year, responsible for helping Pompey impede the Senate at the beginning of the year and for stirring up the agitation against Milo and Cicero, his counsel. It was not perhaps without significance that when in spite of Pompey's best endeavours he was found guilty, it was to Caesar that he betook himself, becoming from then on Caesar's man.

But Pompey, having brought order out of chaos, had more important work to do. For more than a year he had intrigued for this power in his silent struggle with Caesar, and now it was firmly in his hands; he had been forced to allow the ten tribunes to pass their law in Caesar's interest, against the advice of Cicero, according to his later claim, but now the stage was his. His refusal to ally himself a second time by marriage with Caesar had shown their growing estrangement and Pompey's dawning fear of Caesar's waxing power and influence; the struggle had been in these months keen, and now that he had with difficulty won this round, he must protect himself and his position. They stood now face to face, each too powerful to be acceptable to the other; yet before Pompey could dare risk an outright break, he must be sure of the nobles' support; for the nobles controlled the Senate, and the Senate government, and Pompey must have the constitution for his ally.

He now proceeded to other legislation. One of the most fruitful causes of disorder had been the elections, at which the bribery and rioting had become quite disgraceful; this behaviour was encouraged by the hope of the province which followed upon the senior magistracies; a gap between the office and the province would quench the ardour of the candidate to amass huge debts and of moneylenders to risk their money, when candidate and lender must patiently await the recovery of their money by the plunder of the province. He therefore made law a Senatorial decision of the previous year, by which an interval must stand between the office and the governorship, said by one source to be five years, though this period raises difficulties; in the meantime, provinces would be governed by former praetors and consuls who had not governed a province. He then reaffirmed the requirement that a candidate for office must sue in person. When it was pointed out that this conflicted with the concession made to Caesar by the Law of the Ten Tribunes, he made an explicit exception in his favour.

It is difficult to believe that so shrewd a schemer as Pompey had not realised the conflict between his and the tribunes' laws until some kindly friend remarked upon the fact. We recall that Caesar's friends compelled the original exception in his favour during the days of anarchy before they agreed to Pompey's sole consulship; was Pompey trying to undo what he had done, hoping that it would not be marked until later? This would explain this second law; for of all the causes of trouble during these years, suing *in absentia* had never provoked a riot; it had then no relevance to the present scene—except in terms of Caesar. Pompey had tried to outwit Caesar and been caught, so it would seem, and so the first law seems to prove.

For the first law would have consequences most serious for Caesar. For although the terminal date of his province was some time in 49, since it might not be discussed before March 50, the consuls of 49, elected in 50, were the earliest to whom it could be allotted, and they would not take it up until after their year of office, i.e. in 48. Since he had been permitted to sue *in absentia*, he had planned to move direct from his province to the consulship of 48 without having been for a single day *privatus* and hence open to prosecution; for his enemies had made it clear that they intended to attack him at the first opportunity.

Pompey's legislation now enabled the Senate to replace him as soon as the province was technically vacant; he could no longer expect any extension until 48, and even though he might be elected consul for 48, between the termination of his province and 1 January 48 he would be *privatus* and could be attacked. Pompey must have foreseen this possibility, and been content that it should be; it need not be employed, and he could himself be guarantor of Caesar's interests; but it gave him control over Caesar, and made him the dominant partner, able to dictate the terms of accommodation, if the crisis came. And this must have been the mainspring of his action, even though the reform might be desirable on other grounds; for though the separation of the magistracy from the governorship would reduce the allure of squandering a fortune and enlisting the help of force to gain election, yet this could have been achieved by other means. The use of force was Caesar's and Pompey's contribution to this decade, so too the bribery on its present scale; when Pompey wanted, he could end the chaos and compel elections, and were the Senate free, it too could have handled this, as it had done in the past, including 62, until Caesar intimidated it in 59. The struggle for supremacy of these two had forced them to these extremes; and now that Pompey had for the time obtained the mastery, he did not need this instrument to maintain the peace; he needed it, rather, to retain the mastery over Caesar.

He now took his father-in-law, Metellus Scipio, as his partner in the consulship, thus making a double gesture to the nobles, both by the very action and by the identity of his partner; for having established his control over Caesar he had no further need of his masked dictatorship. This final token of his readiness to reach accommodation with his former enemies seems to have clinched the bargain; he and the nobles were in need of one another against a common enemy, Caesar, and without a formal compact they realised that they had at last become allied. Without demur they extended the tenure of his province for a further five years, thus putting him beyond the reach of Caesar when the day of reckoning came, and voted him an annual 1,000 talents to support his armies. These two grants consolidated his ascendancy over Caesar against the time when the break might come; if that day came, Pompey would have the power and Caesar nothing. And in all these intrigues and machinations Cato had played a reluctant part on Pompey's side, still critical, but not obstructive any longer; for astringent though the medicine might be, it was the only cure for Caesar, and this he had come too late to realise. The situation for which Cicero had worked and risked so much was come to pass when it was now too late to be effective; had they been able to swallow their pride and listen to his wise advice in 56, they might have saved themselves and the Republic.

The year 51 saw the development of the crisis. Cicero, victim of Pompey's recent law on the government of provinces, having successfully avoided a province after both his praetorship and consulship, found himself now compelled to be the governor of

Cilicia, leaving Rome in early May and not returning until November of the following year. While he pined in this unwilling exile, he prevailed upon his young friend, M. Caelius Rufus, to keep him informed of happenings at Rome, and his shrewd letters are our main source of information for this period.

Of the two consuls, M. Claudius Marcellus was known to be Caesar's enemy. He first tried to pass a *senatus consultum*, which was vetoed, disfranchising some colonists of Novum Comum settled and given Roman citizenship by Caesar, thus making a first attempt upon the laws of Caesar's consulship; he then announced that he would on 1 June bring in a motion to deal with appointing a successor to Caesar. For some reason he did not bring his motion forward on that date; but meanwhile he had taken a further step to challenge the citizenship of the colonists of Novum Comum. One of these citizens, happening to be at Rome, was ordered to be flogged by Marcellus, who thus denied the wretch's citizenship. It was a cruel, humiliating and stupid act, which might, as Cicero saw, have had grave consequences even for his own side, since Pompey too was deeply interested; for his father it was who had founded the original colony and given Latin rights to the Transpadanes. Pompey, however, unable at this juncture to indulge the luxury of a quarrel with his new partners, chose to ignore the slight.

For Pompey's mind was surely made up by now. Cicero on his way to Cilicia paid him a visit at Tarentum and could thus report to Atticus: 'In Pompey I am quitting a noble citizen and one most thoroughly prepared to ward off the dangers which are at present causing us such alarm.'[1] To Caelius he could say: 'Only take this as certain, that Pompey is an excellent citizen, and prepared in courage and wisdom alike to meet every contingency that needs to be provided against in the political situation.'[2] Caelius, however, knew his Pompey: 'For he is accustomed to think one thing and say another, and yet is not clever enough to

[1] *ad Att.* v, 7.   [2] *ad Fam.* II, 8, 2.

conceal his real aims.'¹ True; but he seems to have convinced
Cicero now as he had always failed to do before. He announced
his intention of going to Ariminum to inspect his troops, in order,
probably, not to be at Rome when Marcellus raised the question
of Caesar's province; for he did not yet wish to be committed
openly. But the Senate, aware that it must pin him down, resolved
that he should return as soon as possible, in order to be present at
the discussion which they were determined to bring about. On
1 September at a very thin meeting of the Senate Pompey expressed his view that nothing at this time should be done, but
his father-in-law, Scipio, moved that the matter should be raised
on 1 March (50), as a separate piece of business.

The matter was finally raised in a House which had a quorum
on 29 September. A series of resolutions were then taken in connexion with the provinces, which, since they were vetoed by
tribunes friendly to Caesar, had no force; they none the less
showed the direction of the nobles' thoughts and their intentions.
First, it was resolved that on 1 March (50) the consuls should
bring forward the question of the consular provinces, and that
this should have absolute priority; this resolution alone remained
unvetoed. Two further resolutions, that no hindrance should be
offered by way of veto to a settlement of the question and that the
Senate should inquire into the cases of all the soldiers in Caesar's
army who had served their full time or claimed their discharge,
were naturally vetoed; the first would have exposed Caesar to
his enemies without the means of defensive interference, the
second, it was hoped, would weaken the allegiance of his army.
Finally it was resolved that Cilicia should become a praetorian,
instead of a consular, province; this too was vetoed. The object
of this was to reduce the available consular provinces for disposal to Syria; the two Spains were Pompey's for a further four
years; this left only the Gauls, one at least of which would then
have to come up for consideration.

Pompey declared that 'he could not without unfairness settle anything about Caesar's provinces before 1st March, but that after that date he would not hesitate'.[1] His mind was now made up; when asked what would happen if someone vetoed any decision reached on that occasion, he replied 'that it made no difference whether Caesar refused to obey the Senate, or secured someone to prevent the Senate passing a decree. "What if", said someone else, "he shall determine both to be consul and to keep his army?" To which he answered—with what mildness!— "What if my son should choose to strike me with his stick?"'[2] This could only mean that he was prepared at that date to see imposed a solution inimical to Caesar, and that Caesar must respect the government's decisions; to prevent the legalising of those decisions by a continued use of veto was tantamount to doing violence to the constitution, as terrible a thing as using force against one's parents.

Caesar's position had now become dangerous. Himself involved in Gaul, he had hitherto depended for the maintenance of his interests primarily on Pompey, kept up to scratch by Caesar's friends; and while he had sedulously cultivated friends and contacts and established a network of influence and intrigue in Rome, he was still anathema to the nobles, whose control of Senatorial government was still almost complete. Obstruction therefore was his only weapon now, since Pompey and the nobles had joined forces; and though both sides recognised the coming crisis, Pompey had given warning of the danger of obstruction, and Caesar perforce would use obstruction; the clash could hardly be avoided. Caesar must find a trusty tribune for his purpose, and his choice fell on C. Scribonius Curio, hitherto one of Caesar's keenest critics, who had but recently vowed continued opposition at every point. His father too was Caesar's enemy; but Curio himself was heavily in debt. Secretly these two conspired; Curio lost his debts, which Caesar paid, while Caesar gained an ally, who succeeded in becoming tribune.

Curio soon found occasion to reveal to a startled Senate his

[1] *Ibid.* VIII, 8, 9.   [2] *Ibid.*

change of loyalty by preventing the discussion on the provinces taking place on 1 March. In April it was suggested that Caesar should vacate his province on 13 November 49; an earlier suggestion that the date should be 1 March had been vetoed by Curio. The alternative suffered the same fate for the same reason, namely, that it left Caesar exposed to his enemies for a period of time, admittedly shorter, before entering upon his second consulship. Pompey was anxious to see Caesar deprived of his army—and hence his province—before he was elected to the consulship, fearing no doubt that if elected consul while he still had an army, he would dawdle or temporise until 1 January; for after all Pompey had shown the value of that technique. Pompey wanted the position clear; he did not wish Caesar harm, but Caesar must be unable to wish him harm. If Caesar were without his army while Pompey still had his, then he would be ready to revive his alliance with Caesar and protect him, if he could; but if Caesar did not need his protection, he would cease to be the dominant partner and might himself be insecure. But Caesar did not now trust Pompey, and would not put himself in his control, and would not agree to be stripped naked. There could not therefore ever be agreement; however narrow the gap might be contracted, a gap there must always be.

We should, however, recognise the terms of Caesar's thinking, namely an army by which his enemies could be controlled and, if it must be, crushed. For all the honey with which Caesar tried to sweeten his case could not obscure the bitter truth, that he would keep his army against the government's instructions in order to impose his will upon his country, to forward his career and to protect his *dignitas* against the attacks of his *inimici*. His determination to keep his army could have but one corollary, that he would, if he had to, use it; for an army that will not be used is not a threat. And it was this determination to flout the government, to use, if he must, his army against that government, that had so great an influence on Pompey; for Pompey, without precedent though his own career had been and in most ways unconstitutional, had always shrunk from using force against his country; his army's presence and his popularity had generally sufficed; faced in 62 with his own small crisis he had not for a moment thought to impose his wishes by the use of force; rather had he submitted to failure and humiliation.

He had expected Caesar to do the same, and as in 60 Caesar had helped him, so now would he help Caesar. Hence his words about persistent veto and taking a stick to one's parent reveal his understanding of the situation; and the clearer it became that Caesar would go to whatever lengths were necessary to achieve his ends, the further he found himself estranged from him and drawn towards the nobles and the Senate, to the very outbreak of the war incredulous that Caesar could ever bring himself to go to the length of war. Personal jealousies will have played a part in Pompey's calculations—Caesar's great military renown cannot have been welcome to him—yet what probably weighed more heavily was Caesar's easy readiness to go to any length for selfish reasons. For Pompey for all his faults was at heart Republican; *princeps* he wished to be, but in the Republic he had known and in his twisted way defended, not in a state that did not recognise the government, where power lay in the clutch of him who had used an army to wrest control from the proper hands.

M. Marcellus, one of the consuls of 51, tried to have Curio censured for his veto, but failed as the Senate did not dare yet to anger Caesar; Caelius could sum up the situation thus: 'They have come round to this—that Caesar is to be allowed to stand for the consulship without giving up army or provinces. How Pompey is likely to endure this I will write you word as soon as I hear.'[1] At about this time a further step was taken calculated to weaken Caesar. A Parthian army had crossed the Euphrates, and in consequence of Crassus' disastrous defeat Parthian reprisals could be expected. The Roman armies in those parts were certainly inadequate to contain a determined attack, and the

[1] *ad Fam.* VIII, 13, 2.

Senate required both Pompey and Caesar to contribute a legion each to the Syrian army's reinforcement. Pompey had in 52, when he was raising fresh troops, raised a legion in Cisalpine Gaul, which, since he had no immediate need of it, he had lent to Caesar; this legion was Pompey's contribution now for the Syrian army, with the consequence that Caesar effectively lost two legions, this and his own contribution. On reaching Italy they were encamped at Capua, the nearest they got to Parthia at this time; for the Parthians retired and Syria's immediate danger vanished. Whether there had been ever serious intent to send them to Syria we cannot know; but certainly Caesar had lost, and the Senate gained, two legions.

A grave illness of Pompey while he was at Naples caused him to offer the surrender of his province and army, though whether the gesture was sincere or intended merely for effect, we cannot know; it may be that in illness the lust for the struggle had grown weak, and a friendly surrender to Caesar seemed the preferable choice; or he may have done it for effect, shrewdly aware that the Senate could not dispose of him. So it turned out: the Senate refused his offer. His return to Rome was a remarkable demonstration of the unique hold he had upon the minds and loyalties of the Italians; his journey was marked along its route by crowds of cheering people, the roads were strewn with flowers, his passage was the passage of a much-loved hero. This incident strongly affected him: impressed by the depth of love and admiration shown he overestimated the influence and control he could exert on Italy. He had misread the meaning of the welcome; they were cheering Rome's greatest figure and one of her greatest soldiers, who had taken control to bring to an end the present disturbing series of events, whose firm statesmanship, they hoped, would remove the growing menace of civil war. Abhorring the thought of war they hoped they saw in him the minister of peace; when war came in his despite, they loathed it none the less and would not freely join. Here lay Pompey's miscalculation.

In August Caelius wrote as follows:

As to high politics—I have often told you in my letters that I see no hope of peace lasting a year: and the nearer the struggle comes, which must come, the clearer does that danger appear. The point, on which the men in power are bound to fight, is this: Cn. Pompeius has made up his mind not to allow C. Caesar to become consul, except on condition of his first handing over his army and provinces; while Caesar is fully persuaded that he cannot be safe if he quits his army. He, however, proposes a compromise that both should give up their armies. So that mighty love and unpopular union of theirs has not degenerated into mere secret bickering, but is breaking out into open war.[1]

The crisis, as Caelius saw, was clear: the resolves on both sides were incompatible.

Caesar meanwhile had procured the election of M. Antonius to the tribunate for 49, and had thus assured himself of someone to replace Curio. On 1 December the consul, C. Marcellus, moved that a successor be sent to Caesar, which was carried; the suggestion that Pompey be required to resign his command was decisively rejected. But a motion by Curio that both should be required to resign was carried overwhelmingly. It, of course, accomplished nothing except to make clear that the great majority of Senators were more anxious to avoid civil war than to face the consequences of confronting Caesar with his unconstitutional behaviour.

Events now moved quickly. A rumour that Caesar intended to march on Rome served as sufficient reason to Marcellus to propose that the two legions at Capua be brought to the defence of Rome, which Curio forbade on the ground that the rumour was baseless; and Marcellus' attempt to have Curio censured failed. Whereupon Marcellus went direct to Pompey, handed him a sword and charged him to take command of the two legions against Caesar, an invitation which Pompey did not decline, though for the moment nothing more was done.

At the end of this month of December, 50, Caesar made a fresh offer, that he should be allowed to keep Cisalpine Gaul and

---

[1] *ad Fam.* VIII, 14, 2.

Illyricum with only two legions until he entered upon his consulship. This was rejected, and Caesar then stated his final conditions, that he and Pompey should both resign their commands; otherwise he would refuse to resign anything, since to do so would put him at the mercy of his enemies. At a general discussion in the Senate, at which these proposals were not specifically considered, it became clear that the extremists would not have the willing support of everyone; many would prefer concessions to Caesar rather than civil war, and for a few days the issue hung in the balance; but on 5 January a suggestion by Caesar's father-in-law, Calpurnius Piso, and one of the praetors, L. Roscius, that they should report personally to Caesar the rejection of his offers, in case he was prepared to make a further gesture, was rejected by the anti-Caesarians; two days later Antonius and Cassius, the two Caesarian tribunes, were cautioned to leave the Senate, if they wished to avoid harm. They left Rome at once for Caesar's camp; the Senate meanwhile passed the S.C.U. empowering the magistrates and pro-magistrates to take whatever steps they thought proper and necessary to save the state.

Caesar at Ravenna as soon as he heard of the treatment accorded to his tribunes addressed his soldiers, pointing out the injuries done to himself by his enemies, and the constitutional wrong done to the officers of the people, the two tribunes. This speech and the one he made a little later in Rome, as reported by Caesar himself in his *Bellum Civile*,[1] reveal with crystal clarity what he regarded as the final justification for turning his arms against his country; they are shamelessly egocentric, yet seem to him to provide completely satisfactory grounds both for disobeying the government and then, because of their insistence on obedience, for civil war. Both sides must ultimately accept responsibility; but Caesar, who during these last ten years had been in deliberate opposition to the constitution, had so far successfully defeated his opponents; now that they had him cornered at the

[1] I, 7; I, 32.

last he showed his ruthlessness. The simple fact stands out that Caesar had given himself a province and an army for an unprecedented length of time; he had used this instrument to acquire vast wealth and military prestige, whether the Republic wanted the additional territory which he won or not; the Republic was given no chance to formulate a policy or to declare its wishes; both he and Crassus used the resources of the Republic for their own ends, Crassus fatally to himself, Caesar to the Republic.

There is no 'Rechtsfrage' to discuss; Caesar used the Republican constitution in the interests of his own power; when it would no longer serve his ends, he destroyed it. His so-called justification consists of nothing more than a legal quibble and a demand for treatment which would not derogate from his standing and his *dignitas*. The quibble is a quibble and nothing more; the fact of having been given permission to stand for the consulship *in absentia* was no reason why he must stand *in absentia*; it meant that, if it should be necessary, he might do so, in other words, he was enabled to stand for the consulship in 49, whatever his circumstances might be. It certainly did not mean that the government was under an obligation to see that he was *absens* at the time; if circumstances permitted his presence, that was the end of the matter. And if between the passage of the law and the time of his candidature, as a result of procedural changes instituted by the government, he was able to be present, this could not be a legitimate cause of complaint; he had been cheated of nothing at all except a chance to evade his enemies and to dominate the government.

And as to his *dignitas*, who was he to feel such tender concern for his *dignitas*? Had he, when at grips with the government in 59, shown any concern for Cicero's or Bibulus' *dignitas*, when Bibulus tried to prevent, and Cicero made strictures on, his unconstitutional behaviour? He had been content that Cicero, to whom the Republic owed so much, should be illegally hounded out of Italy by a guttersnipe made plebeian by himself, and had only consented to his return on promise of his abstinence from further criticism. Again in 56 without a scruple he had humiliatingly silenced Cicero when his own position was in jeopardy; why therefore should he expect others to show such sensitive regard for his *dignitas* when they could control events? One who was so quick to trample on the constitution and the susceptibilities of others had no just grounds for implying that he was victimised by the behaviour of others and their operation of the constitution; he was simply being asked to behave constitutionally; and if *dignitas* required that his behaviour should be unconstitutional, that is his final condemnation. If he felt that his enemies had schemed to bring him to this pass, he could also reflect that though in 59 he had brought his enemies to a comparable impotence, they had not threatened him with arms.

The Republic's failure, which ended in this ghastly civil war and inaugurated the authoritarian rule of the empire, had deeper causes than a quarrel between two dynasts, neither of them prepared to surrender his army; they were merely symptoms and symbols of the final struggle to resolve the problem first posed by the Gracchi, as to how the Roman world should be governed: whether government based on Senatorial power and authority should at all times be subject to interference and dictation by tribunes, and whether one man should have the right to use tribunes for legislation in his own interests or to oppose the government's will. For eighty years the struggle had continued, and in the process aims and methods had become more mean and sordid; neither side could now command great respect, and each could properly criticise the other; except in the hearts of a few such as Cicero ideals had withered in the light of selfish realism, with the interests of the group taking precedence of state, and self of group. But it can still be truly said that Caesar was the guilty party; he it was who had used the consulship and force to legislate without the Senate's concurrence or advice, ignoring or beating down all checks and opposition; had given himself an exceptional province for an unprecedented period of time, with the right to raise large forces; during this decade the constitution worked only on Caesar's terms; and now that the Senate had found the means to stand against him, he still insisted on the right to state his terms, and could complain of the government's unreasonableness in rejecting his terms, because he deemed them moderate.

When Marcellus flung himself out of the Senate to empower Pompey to assume the defence of the state, he was taking an initiative that should have drawn the whole Senate to his lead. For anxious though everyone would be to avoid a civil war, the price of peace can be too high; in the present instance the price was the surrender of the constitution and submission to the will of Caesar. For this, no less, was the price of acquiescence in Caesar's 'reasonable' demands; the right for one man to award himself a province for as long as he wished, to act in that province in a way completely uncontrolled by government, and then, when others wished to bring him to task for his conduct over many years, to have the constitution suspended, as it were, to enable him to proceed to a consulship under conditions granted to no one else, and, as an additional precaution, to keep his army and province beyond the legal term; and the Senate's refusal to agree to this would be met by force of arms. If this was the price of peace, then Marcellus was surely right to be prepared to fight; for peace, no less than war, spelt the end of the Republic, as he and now Pompey clearly saw.

CHAPTER II

CAESAR AND CICERO—49 TO 44 B.C.

CICERO left Rome on 1 May 51 for the province of Cilicia, whose governor he became as a result of Pompey's law. His governorship need not detain us. He bitterly resented the necessity to assume this—to him—distasteful task, which he accepted only as a loyal servant of the Republic; and throughout the year he pestered his friends and acquaintances to ensure the appointment of a successor at the first opportunity, in order that he should not be required to continue in the post for a moment longer than one year. He had always regarded time away from Rome as time wasted; to him government was seated in Rome, and it was at Rome that policies were made and things happened; to be away from Rome was to be away from the source of power and influence and to risk being forgotten; from the moment he left, therefore, his only anxiety was his return.

His letters are particularly interesting for the revelations they make about the standards of conduct common among Roman governors at this period, and also for the glimpses they give of the attitude of the average Roman of the governing class towards the provinces; one cannot help but pity the lot of the despised provincials, regarded as something inferior, from whom it is perfectly proper to extract by honest or dishonest means as much money as was possible or practicable, whose interests were neither known nor consulted, and who had no effective means of redress or appeal from persistent hard and unfair usage, nor the means with which to strike a blow in their own freedom. So much the more does Cicero's governorship stand out; determined to behave honestly and honourably and to require the same of his staff, he refused to make himself in any way a burden to the provincials or to allow them to be put to expense on his official account; his behaviour was regarded by the provincials as something quite exceptional and is one of his passports to greatness, far more than his rather trivial military excursions, which so excited him into hopes of a triumph. Yet he himself laid little store by the example he had set of honest government, nor did he see that the current standard of behaviour, of which he was rightly critical, was a damning condemnation of a system which made it possible and allowed its continuance. But this is part of another story.

A visit to Pompey at Tarentum on his way out reassured him as to that man's political views and his ability to keep the situation in control. He had always, as we know, regarded Pompey with respect and admiration, had marked him out as the man to preserve the Republic from the attacks being made upon it in the 60s; he had been strangely lenient over Pompey's part in the events of 59, and excessively grateful for his help in procuring his restoration. During his governorship every reference to Pompey was laudatory; Pompey seemed to stand for the same ideals as did himself, seemed ready also to defend them, and this belief gave Cicero confidence: 'For I perceive that the dangers ahead are at once less formidable than I feared, and the safeguards greater, if, as you say, all the strength of the state has devoted itself to Pompey as its leader.'[1] Thus Cicero wrote to Appius Claudius in June 50 when the question of Caesar's province had begun to be the subject of urgent and earnest intrigue, his confidence in Pompey unshaken. But this was only because of his identification of Pompey with his own ideals: 'Politics make me very anxious. I am fond of Curio; I wish Caesar to show himself an honest man; I could die for Pompey; but after all nothing is dearer in my sight than the Republic itself';[2] thus to Caelius in August of that year.

But as the crisis drew nearer, he found his position more and more difficult to enucleate. Since 56 and the threat to his future and his safety, he had withdrawn from independent politics and made it a principle of policy to be on good terms with both

---

[1] *ad Fam.* III, 11, 4.　　　　　[2] *Ibid.* II, 15, 3.

Pompey and Caesar—not, as we have seen, without success. But now this very policy brought anxiety in its train, since it seemed that the quarrel between the two must certainly grow worse, and he would be required to choose a side.

I think I foresee [he writes to Atticus in October 50] such a violent struggle...as there has never been before...It is my own particular problem that I would beg you to take up. Don't you see that it was on your advice that I sought the friendship of both?...Yet at length, after all, you did persuade me to embrace the one, because he had done me eminent service, and the other, because he was so powerful...My idea, in fact, was this—if I were allied with Pompey, I should not hereafter be compelled to take any improper step in politics, nor, if I agreed with Caesar, have to fight with Pompey; for their union was so close. Now there is impending...a mortal combat between them. Each of them, again, regards me as his own, unless by any chance one of them is playing a part. Pompey, of course, has no doubt; for he rightly judges that his view of politics has my approbation. From each, however, I received a letter, at the same time as yours, of a kind calculated to show that neither values any one in the world above myself. But what am I to do? I don't mean in the last resort of all—for if it shall come to downright war, I see clearly that it is better to be beaten with the one than to conquer with the other.[1]

It will be noticed that both Pompey and Caesar were most anxious to have the support of Cicero in the coming conflict, and for this there was sound reason. For Cicero's influence was great among large sections of the people of Italy; a country *eques* become Rome's greatest orator, whose career had attained its summit with the consulship, wherein he had led the Republic to safety through the dangers of Catiline's attempted revolution, he symbolised in the eyes of countless Italians their own middle-class attitudes and aspirations, and their impatience with the insults and pretensions of the nobles. His attempts to bring together Senate and Equites and the solid middle class of Italy, the foundation of his policy, won an approving sympathy from those who were anxious for a true unity which would assure them

[1] *ad Att.* VII, I, 2.

peace and orderly government. Support he had enjoyed through-out his career with the electors at Rome, as witnessed his constant successes at the polls, and among Senators, many with similar backgrounds to his own; and this support had given him power in Roman politics. Caesar's two vicious attacks upon him testify to his importance; he could not risk the consequence if Cicero called to judgement his unconstitutional behaviour, for he feared the possible success of Cicero's leadership in such a cause. For all the nobles' sneers against this *novus homo*, he was in truth a far more important figure than most of them, and could command support in Italy beyond anything that they could muster.

In December 50, as he neared Rome, his arrival was eagerly awaited; 'For as to what you say that my coming is awaited with astonishing interest, and that none of the loyalists, or even the semi-loyalists, have any doubt about what I am likely to do...';[1] here is proof of Cicero's importance even after five years of enforced silence in the arena of politics; and it was of this that both Pompey and Caesar were so keenly aware in their struggle to win Cicero's allegiance; himself in the game of power politics he was not important, since he had neither military skill nor *clientelae*. But a large part of Italy took its colour from Cicero; his sincerity was known, his courage proved, and his ideals of government chimed in with theirs; such a person was an impor-tant acquisition to the side that won him, and the protagonists were correspondingly concerned to number him among their supporters.

But by this time, though he was clear that, if the quarrel could not be healed, he must join Pompey, since Pompey represented the side more nearly identified with his Republic, yet he had no delusions about the personal ambitions of the two great men. In December he wrote to Atticus: 'It is for their own supremacy that these men are contending, but at the risk of the constitution. For if it is the constitution that is now being defended by Caesar, why was it not defended in his own consulship?' He then criti-

[1] *Ibid.* II, 7, 5.

cises Caesar's behaviour since 59 and the shortsightedness of those who allowed him to succeed; but concludes: 'The one hull for me will be that which has Pompey for statesman...Nevertheless, in private, I shall exhort Pompey to keep the peace.'[1]

He met Pompey on 10 December but found him pessimistic as to the chances of peace; Caesar's attitude towards himself, so Pompey thought, augured ill for hopes of peace. He was critical of the Senate's behaviour in having allowed Curio to succeed in his policy of obstruction; in fact 'the fountain-head of all these things is the same. We should have resisted him when he was weak, and that would have been easy.'[2]

The rest of 50 and the first days of the new year were taken up by proposals and counter-proposals on the part of Caesar and the Senate; but the leaders of the Senate were not disposed to make concessions; as Cato pointed out, the state should not have conditions laid upon it by a citizen; while Caesar's tribunes blocked any proposal inimical to Caesar. At last on 7 January the Senate passed the S.C.U., and Antony and Cassius fled to Caesar's camp, thus giving him the excuse of claiming to be defending the tribunes' rights, which had been trampled on by the Senate in ignoring their veto and threatening them with force.

Civil war had now come to the Roman world, destined for eighteen years to work its mad and furious will and to end for ever the last semblance of the Republic which had been Rome's form of government for nigh on five hundred years. It was not destruction but collapse the Republic suffered. While keeping its outward shape, within it had gone rotten, until finally its worm-ridden timbers could sustain the weight no longer. We have observed its earlier decline at the hands of powerful men's ambitions, the Sullan civil war, and the attempt at restoration through the Senate; the failure and the return to pre-Sullan ways; the age of Pompey and the Triumvirate; and we have witnessed these last ten years when, as Cicero so often and so bitterly remarked, the Republic was but a name, the fact a rule by force;

[1] *ad Att.* VII, 3, 4.   [2] *Ibid.* VII, 7, 6.

and finally we have seen these last three years, when the Senate successfully broke the grip about its throat by winning Pompey to its side, able at last to challenge Caesar on his own terms, with arms; the result not unexpectedly was war.

It is difficult to argue which side was right, nor can the issue be resolved in these terms; it was in essence the resolution of the problem raised by the Gracchi, whether the Senate was to govern Rome, or whether tribunes; whether the clique of noble families was to monopolise the reality and perquisites of power, or whether able men outside their circle should be found a place; and in the resolution of this problem there was neither right nor wrong. But in the narrower context we can discern responsibility; Caesar it was who raised the issue at this time in this particular way.

Caesar's ambition had at all times been ruthless to satisfy its appetite for power; during the 60s he had played with fire and revolution, with sufficient caution never to become inextricably embroiled; he had declared his opposition to the ruling class, endeared himself to the people, and used them as his instruments to power; and then in 59 had with Crassus' and Pompey's aid imposed his will upon an unwilling state, ready to use whatever force was necessary, and to trample on whatsoever laws and safeguards stood in the way of his selfish determination. If in 59 he went no further than he did, this was because he had brought his enemies to their knees already; further opposition to his schemes and legislation would have called down as much of force as was needed to suppress and silence it. From this time forward the Republic could not function freely; the open opponents of his laws were threatened, the elections hinged largely on force and bribery, and force, even if not employed, was never distant; and the Senate had had no power to act until it found someone it could oppose to Caesar's force, to call a stop to Caesar's claim to trample on the constitution for his ambition's sake and his convenience.

From 52 the Senate could act from strength; and though there was much of personal rancour in the manoeuvres of these last three years, yet two considerations prevent our reducing the whole issue to this level: first, that Caesar's behaviour had bred hatred and anger among many of his opponents, who now were burning to end his lawless and insulting ways; and secondly, that the Senate was right to address itself to the task of bringing to heel this proud proconsul, who had taken his province in their despite, continued himself in office to suit himself alone, and was now intending to adjust the constitution to suit his next whims. Caesar and the Republic were already contradictory terms; the Senate should not be criticised for trying to resolve the contradiction in favour of the Republic, even if this was what their own interests would recommend.

For Caesar there is little that can be said in his defence, little that he himself would say, except three things: that he was defending the tribunes' rights; that he was protecting his *dignitas*; that the people had given him the right to sue *in absentia*. We have considered these three pretexts—they were nothing more— and have seen that they have no substance; they were merely the flimsy excuses for marching his army against his country; and if we must find both sides morally guilty, at least Caesar had the law against him too.

And in this atmosphere Cicero found his own course of conduct difficult to decide. Many circumstances conspired to complicate his task: his real horror of civil war, the compound of his natural hatred of war and his memories of Sullan times; the embarrassment of being a friend both of Pompey and of Caesar; his natural futility in military affairs; and his emotional nature. His abundant letters to Atticus between now and June, when he finally joined Pompey in Greece, are full of anxious inquiry into what he ought to do; his philosophical mind could see objections to every course; he would be neutral and slink away to Malta or somewhere else; both Pompey and Caesar were selfishly seeking their own domination; to neither was the Republic a live, loved issue; whichever won would be a Cinna or a Sulla. Had Pompey and others but listened to his advice throughout the decade, they would not be in this dreadful crisis now—true observation, that only made crueller his dilemma. When Pompey withdrew to Brundisium, he was deserting Rome; when he crossed to Greece, he had abandoned Italy; he saw it as though the 80s were being repeated; Caesar, who was in Italy, would be a Cinna, Pompey would be an avenging Sulla. He could not evaluate Pompey's strategy except in emotional terms: Pompey was deserting his country and the Republic, Caesar was going to rape it.

These letters reveal a doubting and a tortured soul which, as he said, knew from whom to flee, but not whom to follow: 'Ego vero quem fugiam habeo, quem sequar non habeo.'[1] For Caelius it was easy; in peace one followed right, in war might; but Cicero's one and only love was the Republic, and this he regarded as utterly lost: 'I am therefore sustained by the purity of my conscience when I reflect that...the Republic has been wrecked by precisely the storm which I foresaw fourteen years ago.'[2] Both the contestants are at heart concerned for their own position and aggrandisement: 'The object of neither is our happiness; both want to be kings.'[3] Hence his tortured doubts; he wanted the restoration of the Republic, and neither leader offered this; why then join either side rather than stand between, ready to step in if he could forward the only cause he loved? And if he must join one side or the other, the choice would not be easy.

Yet amid all his doubts and difficulties there stood one rock, his deep friendship for Pompey and his gratitude for Pompey's help in 57. If it were to come to open war, never would his arm be raised against Pompey; finally, therefore, it was to Pompey's camp that he would go, however much he criticised his past and present actions. It followed that he could never be Caesar's ally, if he must choose between the two; for Caesar he held responsible for his own disaster in 58, and for the present state of the Republic and the imminence of civil war; he was the cause of all the troubles of the 50s, who could and should have been suppressed much earlier, when to do so would have been easy.

[1] *ad Att.* VIII, 7, 2. [2] *Ibid.* X, 4, 5. [3] *Ibid.* VIII, 11, 12.

During this time he never went to Rome; Italy was now in Caesar's control, and Caesar was trying to play the constitutionalist by persuading what was left of the Senate to give an air of legality to his actions. Some few respectable members had found themselves trapped into a semblance of support through appearance in the Senate; such was Sulpicius Rufus. But above all Caesar wanted Cicero's prestige to lend some decent authority to his behaviour; for Cicero's high repute in Italy and in Rome would hearten those who having joined were uncertain in their allegiance, and would encourage others to attach themselves to Caesar's cause. But this Cicero was at all costs determined not to do; and though he had, as a proconsul at the gates of Rome, been included in the Senate's S.C.U., and though he had accepted from Pompey the district of Capua and shore of Campania as his area in the defence of Italy, he had done nothing, and after Pompey's departure had made no pretence of helping actively the Senatorial cause. He preferred to stand as near to neutral as he could, and hope to be the means of bringing Caesar and Pompey together, a hope which Caesar nourished. In March he wrote to Caesar: 'If you are at all anxious to preserve our common friend Pompey, and reconcile him to yourself and the Republic, you will assuredly find no one better calculated than myself for supporting such measures.'[1]

But Caesar wanted more than neutrality; he wanted positive support. At the end of March they met, and Cicero described the encounter to Atticus:

I spoke in such a manner as rather to gain his respect than his thanks, and I stuck to the resolution of not going to Rome...He kept remarking that he was condemned by my decision, that the rest would be the slower to come, if I did not do so...After much discussion he said, 'Come, then, and discuss the question of peace.' 'At my own discretion?' said I. 'Am I to prescribe to you?' said he. 'My notion will be this,' said I, 'that the Senate disapproves of any going to Spain or taking armies across to Greece, and', I added, 'I shall make many

[1] *ad Att.* IX, 11A, 2.

regretful remarks as to Gnaeus.' Thereupon he said, 'Of course, I don't wish such things said.' 'So I supposed,' said I, 'but I must decline being present then, because I must either speak in this sense and say many things which I could not possibly pass over, if present, or I must not come at all.'[1]

A courageous answer, showing that, though neutrality was his preference, yet faced with a choice between the two, it must be Pompey; union with Caesar and his lawless ways was quite unthinkable. By the end of April his resolve is all but taken; Caesar's successes and his control of Italy have made his sick neutrality a sham; Caesar and the Republic are incompatibles, and Cicero's love has always been for the Republic, whose cause, it now was clear, was lost if Caesar won. Caesar heard rumours of his supposed intention and asked him in urgent terms to continue neutral, hoping that, since he could not bring him to his side, he might at least still keep him from the other. 'What can be more becoming to a good man, and a peaceable and quiet citizen, than to hold aloof from civil strife?...For yourself... you will find nothing at once safer and more honourable than to abstain entirely from active intervention in the fray.'[2] Early in June Cicero evaded the Caesarians and set sail with his brother, son and nephew to Pompey's camp.

From now until Pompey's defeat at Pharsalus Cicero remained with Pompey. It was not for him a happy or a pleasurable experience; he was deeply upset that the situation should have come to open war, for even an unfavourable agreement would in his estimation have been preferable to civil war; and now that it had come and he had felt compelled to abandon his half-hearted neutrality, he could find no stomach for the fight, and since neither his interests nor his talents inclined him to military pursuits, he became a disgruntled member of the Pompeian camp at Dyrrachium, by no means popular with Pompey and the nobles, and given neither important nor responsible work to do. His bitter disquiet found release in sarcastic epigrams at the expense of

[1] *Ibid.* IX, 18, 1.   [2] *Ibid.* X, 8B, 2.

those about him, which, while they may have won applause from others, did nothing to endear him to the victims. In truth he had no place in Pompey's camp, and Cato had told him that he should have remained in Italy to help effect a reconciliation between the contestants; hardly a hero's welcome for one who had given months of torturing worry to reaching his decision!

Nor was he buoyed up by the atmosphere and conversation of the camp; to Atticus he wrote after his return to Italy:

So bloodthirsty were their sentiments, so close their alliance with barbarous tribes, that a scheme of proscription was formed—not against individuals, but whole classes—and the conviction was universally entertained by them that the property of you all was the prize of victory. I say 'you' advisedly; for even as to you personally there were never any but the harshest ideas.[1]

The end of this phase came with Pompey's defeat at Pharsalus. Never in favour of the extreme policy of war he had yet felt finally obliged to share his fate with Pompey, his hero and the hope of the Republic; but now that he had gone, for Cicero the Republic too had irredeemably gone; sick with despair and heavy with a fatal acquiescence he had no further stomach for the fight. When the news of Pharsalus reached the fleet at Dyrrachium, Cato and Pompey's son tried to force the command upon him, as the only consular present. This he refused and came near to being killed, saved only by Cato; and thus with hope abandoned he gave up fighting for the Republic. He sailed away to Patrae, thence to Brundisium where he arrived about the beginning of November, having received permission from Caesar through the help of Dolabella, his son-in-law and a Caesarian, to return to Italy.

He spent in Brundisium nearly a year in misery and apprehension; to Rome he dare not go without Caesar's explicit sanction, especially since, when Caesar had earlier pleaded with him to lend his support to Caesar's government in Rome, he had de-

[1] *ad Att.* XI, 6, 2.

fiantly refused. He had still kept his lictors, the sorry trappings
of his Cilician command, for which he still hoped to be granted
a triumph; but at Brundisium he disguised them owing to the
presence of Caesarian troops, and they are no more in evidence.
Brundisium was not for Cicero a pleasant place to live, made even
less pleasant by the Caesarian soldiers; and the unhappy man had
all God's time to worry and to wonder how Caesar would treat
him on his return.

A further cause of great distress was the behaviour of his
brother and his nephew; at Patrae had blazed a violent quarrel,
they holding Cicero responsible for their unlucky fate of having
joined the losing side, and they had scuttled off as fast as they
could to make their peace with Caesar. Both of them, his nephew
in particular, behaved contemptibly in this matter, accusing
Cicero to Caesar and to others both directly and in letters; in
spite of which Cicero wrote to Caesar, before his own pardon
was assured, in these words: 'I beg you not to think that he [his
brother] did anything to diminish the constancy of my service,
or lessen my affection for you. Believe rather that he always
advised our union; and was the companion, not the leader of my
journey...I earnestly and repeatedly entreat you not to let me
stand in his light with you.'[1]

Apart from this source of grief and worry he had his own
position to cause him anxiety enough. His return to Italy and
refusal to continue with the fight had proclaimed his break with
the Pompeians; yet the Pompeians seemed to be recruiting their
strength in Africa, while report told of Caesar's difficulties in
Alexandria, and he himself could see the difficulties of Antony, his
Master of Horse, in Italy, with Dolabella mischievously agitating
as tribune against Caesar's debt-law, and Caesarian legions who
were awaiting discharge becoming mutinous and troublesome.
These harsh facts made his anxiety for the future yet more acute;
for if, as at this time seemed not unlikely, the Pompeians were to
be successful, Cicero's position would be even more unenviable

[1] *Ibid.* XI, 12, 2.

than if Caesar won; for they had never concealed their intention of wreaking vengeance on all who had opposed, or even not supported, them.

At long last this painful period of suspense was ended by Caesar's return to Italy in September, victorious over the Pompeians, the Egyptians and Pharnaces of Pontus. He landed at Tarentum, whither Cicero and many others from Brundisium and elsewhere had gone to welcome him; as soon as Caesar's eye fell upon Cicero, he alighted from his carriage and after a warm and friendly welcome walked for some distance in his company, talking alone with him. This generous gesture put an end to Cicero's immediate worries; he was, it seems, invited to return to Rome, whither he made his way in the early days of October, there to remain in greater or less contentment until Caesar's murder.

It was in many ways a difficult period for him, for although he enjoyed Caesar's respect and friendship and was at all times treated with the utmost consideration, his life was only possible on one of two conditions: either that he lent his support to Caesar's form of government, or that he abstained from political life. For opposition in political life to Caesar was impossible; yet the Forum and the Senate House had comprised two-thirds of his active life; this he must now forgo with rare exceptions, and try to find his satisfaction in all that was left to him, his books. Here he found consolation, but not complete; throughout this period his mind recurs to thoughts of the Republic which is no more, the Republic of which he had been a leading figure and which now, as never before, cried out to him for help.

He knew from the moment of Caesar's return that he had lost his freedom; after Thapsus, in April 46, the last hope of a successful challenge to Caesar's autocracy was gone; his choice, as he wrote to Varro, was clear:

And if anyone wishes for our services—not merely as architects, but also as workmen to build up the constitution—let us not refuse to assist, but rather hasten with enthusiasm to the task. And if, on the other hand, no one will employ us, let us compose and read 'Republics'.

And if we cannot do so in the Senate House and Forum, yet at least...
on paper and in books let us govern the state, and investigate its cus-
toms and laws.[1]

   The Republic, 'which for the present is most powerless of all,
but which hereafter must necessarily be powerful',[2] was at this
time only a name, not a reality. After Caesar's return from Africa,
Cicero attended meetings of the Senate, but, since he might not
express what he felt, preferred to be silent; and this resolve he
maintained until late in this year, when the question of restoring
M. Marcellus, one of Caesar's most bitter enemies before the
war, consul in 51, was raised. Caesar at first was not unnaturally
opposed to the request, but let himself be won over by the prayers
and entreaties of C. Marcellus, cousin of Marcus, and of others;
and this concession to the Senate's prayers Cicero found so
deeply moving that he broke his vow in order to address a speech
of thanks to Caesar.
   He describes the scene in a letter to Servius Sulpicius Rufus,
Marcellus' colleague in the consulship:

For in the first place Caesar himself, after inveighing against the 'bitter
spirit' shown by Marcellus...all on a sudden unexpectedly concluded
by saying that 'he would not refuse a request by the Senate for Marcellus, even in view of the character of the individual'. In the next
place the Senate had arranged, as soon as the case of Marcellus had been
mentioned by L. Piso, and Caius Marcellus had thrown himself at
Caesar's feet, that it should rise *en masse* and approach Caesar in a suppliant attitude. Ask no questions: this day appeared to be so fair that
I seemed to be seeing some shadow of a reviving Republic. Accordingly...I, when called upon (to speak), abandoned my resolution.
For I had determined, not, by Hercules, from lack of interest, but
because I missed my old position in the House, to maintain unbroken
silence. This resolution of mine gave way before Caesar's magnanimity and the Senate's display of devotion. I therefore delivered a
speech of thanks to Caesar at some length...[3]

----

[1] *ad Fam.* IX, 2, 5.   [2] *Ibid.* IV, 13, 5.
[3] *Ibid.* IV, 4, 3.

The speech is one of fulsome praise of Caesar, a panegyric on his great achievements, his great-mindedness, his clemency in victory; the origins and causes of the civil war are forgotten or passed by in gratitude for Caesar's generosity in victory; but something of Cicero's further expectation is discernible in his emphasis that victory has given the opportunity, generosity has laid the foundations, but the work still remains to recreate the Republic. The work, so far from being completed, is hardly yet begun: 'It is for you alone, C. Caesar, to reanimate all that you see shattered and laid low as was inevitable, by the shock of the war itself; courts of law must be set on foot, licentiousness must be checked, and the growth of population fostered; all that has become disintegrated and dissipated must be knit together by stringent regulation.'[1] Caesar's magnanimity on this occasion, triggered as it was by deference to the Senate, kindled for a few brief moments Cicero's hopeful expectancy that Caesar would listen to the Senate on other matters too, to himself perhaps, who would be always ready to lend his help, as he had told Varro, in the rebuilding of the Republic.

This optimistic mood was brief, for nothing had really changed; Caesar could be merciful to individuals, and in their cause could be won over; but this did not imply a deference to the constitution or to the views and wishes of others on matters constitutional. Cicero was one of the most important intermediaries between Caesar and former Pompeians; himself formerly of their side, he enjoyed the esteem and high respect of Caesar; he maintained a considerable correspondence over this period with various victims of the civil war, and was indefatigable in their cause, both directly with Caesar and also through the agency of Caesar's influential friends, Balbus, Oppius, Hirtius, Pansa, Dolabella and Matius. Towards the end of 46 he spoke on behalf of another Pompeian, Q. Ligarius, for whom he had already privately pleaded, together with Ligarius' brothers, before Caesar. Ligarius was then prosecuted by another pardoned Pompeian, Q. Tubero,

[1] *Pro Marc.* 23.

possibly for treason, and the trial was held before Caesar personally. According to Plutarch Caesar before the trial said to his friends:

'We know beforehand that the prisoner is a pestilent fellow and a public enemy; what harm can it do to listen once again to a speech of Cicero?' But soon he felt himself strangely stirred by Cicero's opening words, and as the speech proceeded...one might see rapid changes of colour pass over Caesar's face...At length, when the speaker touched on the struggle of Pharsalus, Caesar became so agitated that his body trembled, and some papers which he was holding dropped from his hand. In the end he was carried by storm, and acquitted the accused.[1]

Whether the story is true or not, it gives some indication of the effect the speech had upon the ancient world, an effect which we can still feel and admire today.

But none of this represented the first vestige of a return to the old Republic; and if Cicero could have occasional flashes of optimism, deep in his soul lay something close to utter, black despair. Early in January 45 he wrote to C. Plancius, an exiled Pompeian, thus:

You congratulated me because you had heard, as you say, that I was enjoying my former position...Well, certainly, if to entertain honest sentiments on public affairs and to get good men to agree with them constitute a 'position', then I do hold my position. But if 'position' depends upon the power of giving effect to your opinion, or in fine of supporting it by freedom of speech, then I have not a trace of my former position left; and it is great good fortune if I am able to put sufficient restraint upon myself to endure without excessive distress what is partly upon us already and partly threatens to come.[2]

This theme and that on the loss of freedom recur throughout this year; he knew that the old ways had not returned, and as the year progressed, becoming ever more convinced that they were gone, if not for ever, at least while Caesar lived, he betook himself to private interests, while the public calamities ate into his very soul. His letters betray the unconcern which he affects; but

[1] Plut. *Cic.* XXXIX, 5 f.   [2] *ad Fam.* IV, 14, I.

knowing his uselessness he did not seek to change what was beyond his power to influence.

Largely retired from public life, he now for diversion taught the younger Caesarians the art of oratory, learning from them in turn the latest fads in dining. 'Hirtius and Dolabella are my pupils in rhetoric, but my masters in the art of dining. For I think you must have heard, if you really get all the news, that their practice is to declaim at my house, and mine to dine at theirs.'[1] He was popular with these younger men, who could respect his genius and admire his qualities, while he found amusement and diversion in their company. Politics were not discussed, for between the generations was a gulf which even Caesar's murder would not close; but there was still much left for conversation, which served to occupy his time and lull his mind from his increasing sadness.

He was still, in March 45, depressed at heart and pessimistic; as he wrote to Atticus:

You urge me to reappear in the Forum: that is a place which I ever avoided even in my happier days. Why, what have I to do with a Forum when there are no law-courts, no Senate House, and when men are always obtruding on my sight whom I cannot see with any patience? You say people call for my presence at Rome, and are unwilling to allow me to be absent, or at any rate beyond a certain time; I assure you that it is long since I have valued your single self higher than all those people.[2]

During 46 he had divorced Terentia, from whom he had for some time been estranged, and very soon after married a young woman of considerable wealth, Publilia, who had been his ward. The marriage did not last and brought him no happiness. But at the end of February 45 he received the cruellest blow of all his life in the death of his dearly loved daughter, Tullia, the one person above all to whom he turned for spiritual strength and consolation in his doubts, uncertainties and disappointments, to whom he had never looked in vain for encouragement in his

[1] *ad Fam.* IX, 16, 7.   [2] *ad Att.* XII, 21, 5.

ambitions and pursuits. At first he could bear no company: 'In this lonely place (Astura) I have no-one with whom to converse, and plunging into a dense and wild wood early in the day I don't leave it till evening. Next to you (Atticus) I have no greater friend than solitude.'[1] His next letters to Atticus were full of a scheme for purchasing a piece of land near Rome on which to erect a shrine to her memory; but although certain plots were considered, nothing finally came of the scheme, which ultimately disappears from his letters. A more lasting consequence was his divorce from Publilia; a young person, she had naturally been both hurt and jealous at the unique place which Tullia held in Cicero's life, which, she understandably felt, should have been hers, his wife; she could not conceal a certain perverted satisfaction therefore at the catastrophe. Cicero at once divorced her and refused all attempts to effect a reconciliation; he never again saw or spoke to her.

He also sought consolation in his books, and this and the following year are the most prolific of his life for the production of those philosophical works which are no small part of his legacy to the Western world. Though they can claim little in originality, yet their influence has been greater than most of the originals of which they are translations; he created a philosophical language for the Latin tongue and thus made Greek philosophy accessible to the medieval world; the Church and the medieval world of thought owe a deep debt to Cicero's philosophical works.

But the thin vein of optimism which had persisted in his attitude to the present government and had served as an opiate to his pain at the Republic's misery disappears after Tullia's death. In reply to a letter of condolence from his friend L. Lucceius he writes:

And so I consider that I am even braver than yourself—who give me lessons in courage—in this respect, that you appear to me still to cherish a hope that things will be some day better; at least 'the changes and chances of gladiatorial combats' and your illustrations, as well as the

[1] *Ibid.* XII, 15.

arguments collected by you in your essay, were meant to forbid me entirely to despair of the Republic. Accordingly, it is not in one respect so wonderful that you should be braver, since you still cherish hope; in another it is surprising that you should still have any hope. For what is there that is not so weakened as to make you acknowledge it to be practically destroyed and extinct? Cast your eye upon all the limbs of the Republic, with which you are most intimately connected: you will not find one that is not broken or enfeebled...Therefore I shall bear my domestic misfortunes in the spirit of your admonition, and those of the state perhaps even with a little more courage than even you, who admonish me. For you are supported, as you say, by some hope; but I will keep up my courage though I despair of everything, as in spite of that you exhort and admonish me to do.[1]

In May of 45 he began to toy with the idea of writing a letter of advice to Caesar, recommending, as an elder statesman, the line of policy which he should pursue and the tasks to which he should set his hand; it was to have been, in fact, an elaboration of the advice given in the *Pro Marcello*. A draft of the letter was written and sent to Atticus for advice, with the proviso that, before it was sent to Caesar, it should be shown for approval to Balbus and Oppius. But they made so many suggestions for alterations that Cicero, unwilling to rewrite the letter, with a certain relief dropped the idea:

Now your friends have acted frankly, and have obliged me by not suppressing their opinion; but best of all by suggesting so many alterations that I have no reason for writing it all over again...There is no more to be said. I am extremely sorry I wrote it; nor could anything in this affair have fallen out more in accordance with my wishes than to find that my intrusion is not approved.[2]

After this Cicero abandoned hope and waited on events. Towards the end of 45 he pleaded in Caesar's house on behalf of his old friend Deiotarus, king of Galatia, who was accused by his grandson of having plotted to murder Caesar when Caesar was helping him against Pharnaces, king of the Cimmerian Bosporus; he was only partially successful. Towards the close of this year

[1] *ad Fam.* v, 13, 3 f.   [2] *ad Att.* XIII, 27, 1.

Caesar paid him a visit at his villa near Puteoli; an anxious business, since he was accompanied by 2,000 soldiers, apart from his
staff and suite. However, Cicero coped to his own and Caesar's
satisfaction: 'It was a very good dinner, and well served...The
upper part had a really recherché dinner. In fact, I showed that I
was somebody. However, he is not a guest to whom one would
say "Pray look me up again on your way back." Once is enough.
We didn't say a word about politics. There was plenty of literary
talk.'[1]

It is clear that Caesar was no longer concerned, as he had been
earlier, to win responsible opinion to his side. He knew what he
had in mind to do, he was resolved to do it, nor was he any longer
worried, if he had not the support of good Republicans. Cicero
he admired as orator and master of the Latin tongue; but he
knew that his plans were so opposed to Cicero's political ideals
that a discussion with him could not be of the slightest help; if he
needed to talk about these things, he sought the company of his
supporters, realists like Oppius and Balbus, who saw the naked
facts of Roman government and politics, who felt no love or
respect for the Republican traditions, and were in consequence
ready to think in Caesar's terms and to approve the concepts
in which he dealt. Caesar's determination to pursue his plans,
the confidence which now was his as the result of defeating all
his enemies in the field, and his increasing indifference to the
views of those who had been on the opposite side, all these
factors contributed to his present attitude and led him fatally
along the path whose end was the Ides of March.

For in these last months of life he accepted powers and honours
which were hardly human and were certainly un-Republican.
A dictatorship for ten years, which in 44 became for life, *Dictator
perpetuus*, was as insulting a denial of the Republic and its officers
as could be devised; so long as he lived, he was to have powers
such that he could rule Rome as a king; and he showed by his
behaviour that he regarded the Republican officers as meaningless

[1] *Ibid.* XIII, 52, 1 f.

symbols; for when one of the consuls died on the last day of 45, he had a suffect consul appointed for the remaining hours of the year. Whatever his wishes and intentions with respect to the name of *rex*, he had made it possible for men to believe that he hankered for the title; and his ostentatious protests at the offer of a diadem lacked any of that ruthless determination which at other times characterised his actions where he was resolved that his own interests should predominate. Even though he may not seriously have considered the assumption of the title, those close to him knew that he could be flattered by its offer, and he allowed his mind to play deliciously about the notion.

The setting of his statue with those of the seven kings and the adoption of a golden throne could have one meaning only, that after 500 years Caesar was to join their number and to enjoy the power which they had had. If *rex* and its connotations were hateful to other Romans, they certainly seemed to find a warm welcome in Caesar's heart; one does not set up one's statue among one's enemies. He tampered with ideas of his more than human qualities and nature, allowing his statue to be carried in procession with the images of the gods; he had a Flamen in his honour, attached to the Luperci, and a statue inscribed 'invicto deo'. All this was un-Roman and was odious to Roman sentiment, and Caesar, who knew it was, cared not. No wonder that Cicero felt the pain of shameful acquiescence, as he watched one by one the lights extinguished which had served him as beacons on the road to consulship.

What Caesar intended, whether he had formulated intentions even to himself, we cannot know; but if he had, he kept his counsels strictly to himself, content to let things for the present depend on himself alone. He despised the Republican form of government, an empty sham without substance, and was satisfied that he was a shrewder man than Sulla, who had shown his ignorance of his ABC when he resigned from the dictatorship; Caesar would not make that mistake; he had taken it for life. But to men of true Republican sentiment both the present and the future seemed insupportable; at first it had seemed that Caesar might respect their deepest wishes; during the war his behaviour was of necessity somewhat dictatorial, but now that the war was ended, it was supposed that the quarrel too was ended; *inimicitiae* and differences had been avenged, those who had tried to bring about his political extinction were defeated, if not dead; what reason, therefore, to delay the full restoration of the constitution, making only such changes as recent experience had shown to be desirable or necessary? Sallust possibly had sent him letters of advice; Cicero, we have seen, had toyed with the same idea, but had found the task impossible, since tact must have precedence of sincerity. Caesar did not particularly want to hear what advice these men might have to tender, since he had no mind—at least as yet—to restore the Republic; and at last men had come to realise that so long as Caesar lived, the Republic was dead.

Now he was making plans for a Parthian campaign, ordering the government of Rome for the duration of his absence so that Senate and consuls had no independent part to play; perhaps he was going to take the name and style of *rex*; certainly he would be gone for some time, and any change would be impossible. Cicero had become by now utterly hopeless and downcast; any hopes he might in 46 and 45 have cherished were dead by the end of 45; he knew now the truth, that Caesar was determined to exercise sole and complete control and that he despised the Republican form of government. At the beginning of 44 he wrote thus to Manius Curius:

No, I now neither urge nor ask you to return home. Nay, I am longing myself to fly away and to arrive somewhere where 'I may hear neither the name nor the deeds of the Pelopidae'. You could scarcely believe how disgraceful my conduct appears to me in countenancing the present state of things. Truly, I think you foresaw long ago what was impending, at the time when you fled from Rome. Though these things are painful even to hear of, yet after all hearing is more bearable than seeing;[1]

---

[1] *ad Fam.* VII, 30, I.

then comes a description of the appointment of a suffect consul for half a day.

Cicero's mood of deep and sullen resentment, of shame at his enforced acquiescence, and of utter hopelessness, was shared by many others. Other motives of discontent and hatred of Caesar and his form of government fired others; and of all this mixture was the conspiracy compounded. From petty jealousy to high principles, all was represented in this cauldron, but most of the emotions, however perverse, were deeply felt; above all was felt the harsh insult to the Republic and to the families whose life for generations had found itself in public service, who had been the effective rulers of the Roman world, and now were Caesar's servants, their offices depending on his whim. To them the removal of Caesar, it seemed, would free the constitution which gave them their power and their position. Others, among them chiefly Brutus, could regard their duty without nice calculations of their own advantage; to them the Republic was the freedom won by courage and resolution from the tyranny of kings and now again enthralled, this time to Caesar's domination; to restore the freedom required the removal of the tyrant, Caesar.

None of the conspirators had paused to weigh the problem and the consequences of what they planned to do. The problem was vast and deep, to provide the Roman world with responsible government, and to make impossible the recurrence of the intestine struggles that had twice exploded into destructive civil war. Caesar had not ridden lightly to dictatorship, nor could the Roman world of which he was the ruler be compared to those earlier cities which had endured their age of tyranny. The situations were quite incomparable in size and depth; to apply to the one the standards of the other was to reveal a failure of understanding of the Roman problem, which was seen in the consequences. Caesar's murder freed nothing, it simply restored the *status quo ante*, and opened the way to thirteen further years of civil war. Such now was the complexity of the Roman world that the constitution of the city-state, unable further to regulate its governance, must painfully evolve some better suited form of government; to the conspirators these issues were obscured beneath the outer semblance of a tyranny which their studies had taught them to regard as evil in itself; and thus without thought for what would happen they schemed to remove the tyrant, hoping that all would revert to what it had been before. It did; but these dreamers, inhabiting their ideal world, had hoped by murdering Caesar to translate themselves and Rome to a perfect world which had never been, and were vexed and disillusioned when they found themselves in Rome without the strong arm of Caesar to keep the peace. Their impetuous deed brought neither them nor the Roman world a single step towards the solution of Rome's great problem, how was the Roman empire to be governed.

The histrionics of the tyrant slayers revealed at once their paucity of understanding of the problem, the keenness of their emotions, and the bitterness of their resentment; it revealed also their failure to understand the meaning and the consequence of their action. They supposed that when the usurper was struck down, the people would cheer the gallant deed, and government would continue on its normal, proper course without the tyrant to impede its stately progress; in consequence their plans had never gone beyond the actual deed; there was no plan to take control themselves and so lead the government back along its proper path. Yet had they had that amount of common sense commingled with their high ideals, they would have realised how many of the important offices were occupied by Caesar's friends; they might have reflected on the events of 88 and 83 and those again of 50 and 49, to see that either side is likely to have opponents, and that unless the one side seizes power at once with a strong, sure grip, the other will certainly take advantage of the pause or failure. Failure it was in this case, fatal to the liberators, disastrous to the Roman world.

CHAPTER 12

CICERO'S LAST FIGHT FOR THE REPUBLIC

THE Senators were appalled at the bloody deed, the people stunned and fearful of what portended, while the murderers betook themselves dramatically and apprehensively to the Capitol, thus at once yielding leadership to others. Antony, Caesar's fellow-consul, was now the chief man in the state; Dolabella, who almost at once assumed the vacant consulship, and Lepidus, the Master of the Horse, were also in a strong position, Lepidus particularly, for he had a legion on the spot with which he and Antony kept order in Rome. But at first the Caesarians were far from confident; their leader lay murdered, nor could it yet be known how far the conspiracy was spread. Two days of anxious negotiations led to a meeting of the Senate on 17 March, at which, however, the Liberators did not dare appear. Here was struck an agreement between the two parties on the basis of a suggestion by Cicero, who, like the Liberators themselves, looked to Greece for inspiration; he proposed an amnesty by which the Liberators were freed from the possible consequences of their deed, while at the same time were ratified Caesar's *acta*. Both steps alike were necessary, if there were to be any hope of preventing civil war, since the omission of either would have been tantamount to pronouncing on the illegality of the side not thus protected. Further, the acceptance of Caesar's acts as valid was essential in the interests of law and order, since the alternative, to undo all his work, would lead to chaos uncontrollable and stir up so many bitter animosities among persons and communities who were his beneficiaries, not least his soldiers and veterans, that civil war must certainly have blazed out on the instant.

At the same time Caesar's friends procured from the Senate permission to publish Caesar's will and hold a public funeral; the Senate, in view of its attempt to compose rather than to exacerbate differences, had little choice, since refusal would be construed as admission that Caesar was an enemy of the state. None the less the consequences were serious; the people were roused to sympathy with the Caesarians by the reading of the will, in which all of them had been remembered and D. Brutus named among the 'second heirs'; the sight of Caesar's body, mutilated by the assassins' knives, inflamed them further; and Antony's funeral speech fanned their passions to white heat, with the result that the Liberators were in fear of their lives. The veterans and the people continued their agitations and demonstrations in favour of Caesar, and became so menacing that Brutus and Cassius, as well as others of the conspirators, found it expedient for their safety's sake to withdraw from Rome; a marble pillar, inscribed 'To the Father of his Country', set up in the Forum, became the centre of prayers for Caesar, while a certain Herophilus, claiming Marius for his grandfather, made it a rallying point for violent tirades against the enemies of Caesar.

Antony meanwhile, realising that the murderers' plans had ended with the murder, slowly recovered confidence and, armed with Caesar's money, his papers and his secretary Faberius, began to employ these instruments to his own advantage. The Senate had agreed that Caesar's *acta* should be recognised as valid; and though early in April it had been ordained that no further decree of Caesar's should thenceforth be published, Antony found it easy to ignore this injunction, and continued posting up as laws what purported to be Caesar's *acta* or intended *acta*. He had wooed Republican sentiment by submitting a motion to abolish the name and office of dictator, and by showing a readiness to find an accommodation with Sextus Pompey, as well as by supporting the decree which should have ended his traffic in Caesar's *acta*; but all this was due to his uncertainty and his lack of means to be defiant; he had not yet obtained an army. The Senate assigned

Macedonia and Syria to Antony and Dolabella for the following year; and in Macedonia were six legions. But unless something could be done, these would not be available until next year. Caution he still must exercise, but popular sentiment and, of more importance, the veterans' support were on his side; and the Republicans were still without a plan.

Antony put Herophilus to death; late in April on a visit to Campania to superintend the colonies for Caesar's veterans he took the opportunity to collect some 6,000 of them to serve as his bodyguard. This force, the equivalent of a legion, put him in a stronger posture. The Liberators, without resource or resources, could only remain at a distance greater or less from Rome, preserve their pride by pompous edicts, and watch dismayed while Antony strengthened his position; nothing could better illustrate their inventive barrenness than their inactivity and futile activity in these months. Unable to perceive why the Roman people had not responded like sixth-century Greeks to a piece of melodrama borrowed from that century, they showed not only lack of initiative but also inability to comprehend the magnitude of the problem which Caesar had set out to answer, and which now they themselves must handle, unless they wished someone else to grasp the initiative. As Cicero later complained:

When, however, I had begun discussing what ought to have been done...without touching on the question as to whether someone else ought to have been attacked, I said that the Senate ought to have been summoned, the people already burning with excitement should have been still further roused, that the whole government of the state should have been taken in hand by them.[1]

He also found Brutus at this time lacking in the courage to act, and this judgment corresponds with their meaningless behaviour until they finally took the plunge by leaving Italy to prepare to fight; but to this they were driven by their earlier supineness, which had let Antony and Octavian arm themselves to pose a threat which must be answered equally by arms.

[1] *ad Att.* xv, 11, 2.

The situation had been complicated by the presence of Octavius, the young man adopted in his will by Caesar as his son. He was in fact his great-nephew, and he had attracted Caesar's notice and interest some little time before his death and had been sent to Apollonia in Epirus to learn oratory and the art of war. There he heard of Caesar's murder and after discussing the situation with his friends decided to return to Italy, and to accept the adoption and the legacy; for Caesar had made him his heir. His mother and stepfather counselled against accepting, but Octavian was firm; and the attitude of Caesar's veterans and the people encouraged him in his stand. After spending some days with his parents at Puteoli he went to Rome and before C. Antonius, a praetor and brother of Antony, formally accepted the adoption with all its fateful consequences.

Antony thought at first to smother Octavian by his greater age and wisdom, the strength of his position as consul and the possessor of Caesar's papers and his money, and he was vexed at this man's bold self-possession. Ready to help him if he acknowledged Antony's primacy, he would not be the means of ousting himself from his leadership among the Caesarians. Yet his position was difficult; Octavian, as Caesar's adopted son, could neither be ignored nor swept aside; he not only bore the magic name of Caesar, but insisted on assuming its responsibilities; and in these circumstances his 'mana' had greater potency than Antony's. At their first meeting, on Antony's return from Campania at the end of April, feeling himself in a strong position, he brushed aside the youth's request for Caesar's money, on the plea that it was public funds, not a private fortune; in reality because he had already spent much and had plans for spending more of it; also because he felt that this young man should have been more suppliant in his approach, and sought his counsel and his aid.

But Octavian was determined and young, so young that he did not take the measure of what he was attempting; greater age might well have cautioned him against the tremendous odds that were ranged against him; youth's sublime ignorance carried him along the path that would finally lead to victory over Antony and the empire. He borrowed money to pay Caesar's legacies, and by his persistent *pietas* towards his adoptive father, combined with his tender years, he stirred the people's sympathy. And not merely the people's; the veterans too were showing sympathy for Caesar's heir.

At the beginning of June Antony felt strong enough to take the next step. He had been given Macedonia with the six legions there; but to dominate Italy he must, like Caesar, have his force in Gaul. Cisalpine Gaul was held by D. Brutus, who had taken up his command soon after the murder; if, therefore, Antony took this province, it could only be with civil war; and Antony knew this. None the less he procured the passage of a plebiscite to give him Cisalpine and Transalpine Gaul for five years, while Dolabella's tenure of Syria was similarly extended; he also retained the Macedonian legions. Brutus and Cassius meanwhile were provided with an excuse for their absence from Rome during their magistracies by being entrusted with a trivial commission for organising the city's corn; the next month saw them provided with the equally unimportant and insulting provinces of Crete and Cyrene. Beyond, however, a protest meeting with their friends, where Cicero was present, when they expressed their indignant fury at the insult and a determination not to touch the corn commission, they were powerless. The initiative had slipped both from themselves and from the Senate, and was becoming daily more firmly established in the hands of Antony, the sitting consul, and Octavian, the heir of Caesar. Antony's seniority still gave him the upper hand, that and his bodyguard of 6,000; but Octavian was in prospect the more formidable, because the basis of his power would not be changed; Caesar's heir he was and would remain; while Antony, his year of office past, would be left with his governorship alone, and whatsoever else his skill could contrive for himself.

Friction between Octavian and Antony continued and increased until the veterans and Antony's bodyguard compelled them to compose their differences in the common interest. But in fact at this stage true harmony between the two was nigh impossible; if both were sincere in their anxiety to avenge Caesar's death, then agreement was easy and obvious. But Antony, far more concerned about himself than about Caesar's death, had been prepared to compromise on this and every issue earlier on, and now was urgent only to build himself to strength; whither from there, his unimaginative mind had not explored. Octavian's youth made all things simpler to his comprehension; here was a chance for greatness; his youthful dreams soared hardly beyond the simple vision of the great man ordering all the earth; *pietas* to Caesar would help him in this dream of boyhood. But had revenge for Caesar's murder been his true aim and purpose, his first encounter with Antony should have taken a different turn. To both of them Caesar was an essential pretext; both of them hoped to use dead Caesar for their own aggrandisement.

Throughout these months Cicero remained inactive. Since 56 he had taken no active part in politics. He had stood by helplessly while Caesar forced the state to civil war; having followed his convictions to the camp of Pompey, he had then again observed in anguish while Caesar won the Roman world, then gave it a dictator's laws; perforce he had played his small, humiliating part in Caesar's world, content, though shamed, to be his friend and inoffensively to watch. He had not been privy to the conspiracy, though, when the deed was done, his was the name on whom the murderers called, for he to them, as to most others, was the great champion of that free Republic which Caesar had crushed and which they were claiming to have restored. From the first news of Caesar's murder he never ceased to rejoice at the tyrant's fate; and though he was quickly disillusioned as to what in fact had been achieved, he still expressed a satisfaction at the deed which would be tasteless in one who had claimed a friendship with the victim, did we not know how very deep had sunk the agony which Caesar's mauling of the Republic had inflicted.

For twelve years and more he had stood unwillingly aside and watched the Republic's shame, compelled to find consolation in his books and in philosophy, though his whole being clamoured for an active part in the life of politics which alone to him was fit and proper occupation; all this was renounced perforce, because he was like to stand in Caesar's way; and if he reached some sort of accommodation with Caesar, and found that his surrender of independence enabled him to be the friend of Caesar, yet beneath the surface he could not but hate the man that had killed what he held most dear on earth, the Republic. It is not, then, a cause for surprise that Caesar's murder gave him a satisfaction which he never ceased to voice; on 10 April he could write thus to Atticus: 'But come one, come all, the Ides of March console me. Moreover, our "heroes"...by their unaided efforts accomplished it in the most glorious and most magnificent manner. The rest requires material resources and troops, neither of which we possess.'[1]

But rejoice though he might at Caesar's murder, he quickly perceived that the Republic was not restored thereby, and that this problem lay deeper than the Liberators had supposed. 'Good God,' he writes to Atticus on 18 April, 'the tyranny survives, though the tyrant is dead. We rejoice at his assassination, yet support his acts!'[2] On 27 April he writes, again to Atticus: 'For though the tyrant has been removed, I see that the tyranny remains.' 'Let us bestow all our care and power of protection on our heroes...Yet though [the Ides] gave our friends—those inspired heroes—an entrance to heaven, they have not given the Roman people liberty.'[3] And to Cassius on 3 May he says: 'Well then, as far as we have gone as yet, we seem not to have been freed from a tyranny—only from a tyrant; for though the tyrant has been killed, we obey his very nod.'[4] Antony, as we saw, could exercise control on government by reason of his consulship and his connexion with dead Caesar, which the Senate could not

---

[1] *ad Att.* XIV, 4, 2. [2] *Ibid.* XIV, 9, 2.
[3] *Ibid.* XIV, 14, 2 f. [4] *ad Fam.* XII, 1, 1.

resist; he held the power and the popularity, the result of the Liberators' failure to plan ahead.

As the situation improved not at all with the passing weeks, he continued in his pessimistic strain; in touch with the Liberators and others, among them notable Caesarians, he gave counsel, but took no other active part. When Octavian came to Italy, he met him and was pleased with his attitude towards himself; but he took little interest in what he did except to rejoice when his attempts to honour Caesar were frustrated. Throughout these early months he remained an interested onlooker, no more; the habit, forced upon him since 56, was slow to die; he continued now, as he had done then, to stand aside and pass his comments. These months are joined to that period of inactivity, not to his earlier spell of leadership in politics, as though he did not yet realise that, though the murder had not restored the Republic, it had given him back his personal freedom.

Since early June he had been disquieted by the attitude of Hirtius and Pansa, consuls elect for 43; Caesarians themselves, they would not commit themselves to the Liberators'—and thus, to Cicero, the Republic's—cause, and he was apprehensive as to what would happen then. But he felt that he might once again become more active in the counsels of the state, that, whether they were Caesarians or not, at least Antony's rule of force would end. Fearing, however, the possibility of further civil war, he formed the plan of visiting his son, now in his first year of study at Athens. He had been appointed at his own request to Dolabella's staff, who was soon to start for Syria, thus gaining an excuse to leave Italy until the new year came, and the chance, as he hoped, of taking an active part in the affairs of state. Though chided by some of his friends, including Atticus himself, with deserting his country, he satisfied himself as to his motives, and made a leisurely departure.

But he did not get far; having progressed as far as Syracuse, he was driven by contrary winds back to Vibo, which prevented his departure before receiving important and exciting news from

Rome. This consisted of a speech of moderate tone by Antony, an edict from Brutus and Cassius, one of several which they issued in the struggle for the support of Rome and Italy, together with an appeal to all Senators, including himself, to be present at a meeting of the Senate to be held on 1 August. He received the news too late for him to appear, for 1 August had passed; but he resolved to return to Rome and to take an active part in the business of the Senate. This moment marks the transition to the final phase of his career, perhaps the most glorious, certainly the most courageous, period of his life, in which he was to put forth all his talents, experience and prestige in one last desperate attempt to save the Republic from the flood that was overwhelming it in dark destruction. *Si fractus illabatur orbis, impavidum ferient ruinae.*

He returned at the end of August, to receive a splendid welcome on his entry to Rome from a large crowd of citizens. His standing as a senior consular was high; but this does not explain his welcome now or later. The fact was that throughout his career Cicero had commanded the support and confidence of the people, as well as of the Italian middle classes; they had always trusted him, and now again, as in 63, confronted with a crisis, they turned to him, looking for a lead and leadership; tribute indeed to the influence and prestige of him whose achievement could have been so great, had Caesar not removed politics to the field of battle.

He did not attend the meeting of the Senate on 1 September, on pretext of tiredness from his journey, in truth not wishing to give offence to Antony, who was intending to honour Caesar; Antony, angry at his absence, threatened to drag him there by force, but was dissuaded. The next day Cicero turned up, but Antony was absent; Cicero made a speech, which has come to be known as the first *Philippic*; a speech which, while moderate in tone, was unambiguous in intent and meaning. He readily acknowledged the acts of Antony which were, in his view, salutary; but against them he set the far greater bulk of his activities which were hostile to the Republic, pointing with a critical finger at his plundering of the treasury, his use of force, his abrogation of acts of Caesar which to uphold was his responsibility. It was the speech of one who had assumed the leadership of the House, and who knew exactly whither and against whom he intended to lead it. Antony was criticised for all he had done that was in conflict with the Republic's practice; the restoration of the powers of Senate and magistracies was the aim, and the stripping of the illegal powers taken by Antony the means to its attainment.

Its moderation did not conceal its intention, nor the author's hostility to Antony, who, furious, prepared his answer, which he delivered on 19 September, an abusive attack on Cicero which marked beyond doubt his deep hostility towards him; for the tone of Cicero's speech had made clear the censure which lay behind the comments on Antony's behaviour; and Antony felt strong enough to challenge these rebukes. This speech in its turn provoked a fresh outburst from Cicero which threw down the gage of battle between the two, a battle whose end could only be death or abject defeat for one of the contestants, namely, the second *Philippic*. A political pamphlet in the form of a reply to Antony's speech, in its scathing denunciation of Antony's whole public and private life, his boyhood, his politics and policies, his drunken harlotry, it made any future accommodation impossible. Here we need not discuss its literary or other merits; the ancients tolerated such abuse, and much of this to us is offensive and unconvincing; but as a venomous attack on an enemy, which was intended to show the hostility between the two, it closed the door surely to any reconciliation. Cicero had committed himself, and knew that he had committed himself, to lead the state against Antony; from now on he must bend his every effort to building the strength with which to smash Antony's military power; all depended on that, and on the Senate's ability to control the counterweight they must bring into being, if they were to succeed in crushing Antony.

Much hinged on Octavian. His influence among Caesarians had considerably increased; soldiers and veterans regarded him as Caesar's heir and were ready to look upon him as his avenger. He had collected a bodyguard, the nucleus of a private army, from Caesarian veterans settled in Calatia and Casilinum; and when the Macedonian legions, which Antony had brought over for use in Gaul, landed at Brundisium, Octavian set himself to tamper with their loyalty. Nor did his efforts go without reward; in late November the Martian legion declared for Octavian, and a few days later the Fourth legion followed suit. Octavian had been in close and constant consultation with Cicero; for in his uncertain and unconstitutional position, with Antony challenging his claims as Caesar's avenger, and his only hope for recognition of the forces he had collected lying with the Senate, it is not surprising that he should woo the Senate's leader, who was also the architect of the strategy to defeat Antony, and that he should wish to be associated—if only for a time—with the forces being conjured up against this enemy of the government. He was therefore full of deference to Cicero, and Cicero not wholly without hopes in this young man, who in spite of his name and associations seemed to pay heed to the elder statesman and to wish to conform his behaviour to the older man's advice. In November he wrote to Atticus: 'I quite agree with you that, if Octavian gets much power, the *acta* of the tyrant will be confirmed much more decisively than they were in the temple of Tellus, and that this will be against the interests of Brutus. Yes, but if he is beaten, you perceive that Antony becomes intolerable; so that you can't tell which to prefer.'[1] And shortly after, in complaining to Atticus of Octavian's behaviour and the tone of a recent speech, he adds: 'I have received—heaven knows—many a prudent word from you under the head of politics, but never anything wiser than your last letter: "Though that youth is powerful, and has given Antony a fine check, yet after all we must wait to see the end."'[2]

This young man had now become a military force of some consequence, and in the present posture of affairs the Senate could ill afford the luxury of turning a possible military ally into

[1] *ad Att.* XVI, 14, 1.   [2] *Ibid.* XVI, 15, 3.

an additional enemy; for the Senate could not lay its hands on any considerable forces of experienced men on whose loyalty it could rely. The Senate needed whatever it could come by; for Antony had demanded Cisalpine Gaul from D. Brutus, who had stoutly refused to hand it over, stating in an edict that he intended to govern it in accordance with the orders of the Senate and Roman people, from whom he had received it. Civil war was, therefore, inevitable, and it behoved a wise general to seek his allies where he could. Cicero had written to Brutus applauding his steadfastness, and to L. Munatius Plancus, governor of Transalpine Gaul, except Narbonensis, exhorting him to loyalty to the Republic and urging him to stand fast against Antony; and on 20 December at a meeting of the Senate he urged the Senate to make Brutus' position legal beyond all doubt, to commend Octavian for raising an army of veterans, and the two legions which had deserted to him, for thus rallying to the state. His speech, the third *Philippic*, made his plans and his sentiments clear; and immediately after this meeting he addressed the people in the fourth *Philippic*.

Of his position and influence at this moment there can be no doubt: 'Accordingly,' he writes to D. Brutus of this meeting of the Senate, 'I went to the Senate early, and when that was observed there was a very full House';[1] testimony indeed to his influence and leadership at this juncture, which he was to maintain and enhance until the final catastrophe. Writing to Trebonius in February he spoke of this speech as follows:

...I returned to that old courage of mine which along with that gallant citizen, your father, you ever had upon your lips and in your heart...I reviewed the situation as a whole, and spoke with the greatest fire, and tried all I could to recall the now languid and wearied Senate to its ancient and traditional valour, more by an exhibition of high spirit than of eloquence. This day and this earnest appeal from me were the first things that inspired the Roman people with the hope of recovering its liberty.[2]

[1] *ad Fam.* XI, 6, 3.   [2] *Ibid.* X, 28, 1 f.

He too, it will be noted, dated the final round from this day, the day on which he formulated a strong line of action against Antony; in September he had accused Antony and come to grips with his lawless conduct; now he stepped forth as the leader in the holy war on behalf of the Republic against Antony. Referring to his speech to the people on this occasion he said:

On that day [i.e. 20 December], Romans, the foundations of the commonwealth were first laid; for the Senate, after a long interval, became so entirely free that you were at length free. At that time indeed, even had that day been fated to bring an end to my life, I had earned a recompense sufficiently great when you all with one mind and voice shouted that the state had been a second time saved by me.[1]

Here is further testimony to his leadership of the people, whom he had generally been able to persuade, when he and they were free to speak and reveal their mind.

And so came the new year and the new consuls, Hirtius and Pansa. His doubts about their loyalty were quickly set at rest, for as the senior magistrates they assumed their responsibilities without ambiguity. At the meeting of the Senate on 1 January, although Cicero spoke strongly against Antony, the majority were not yet ready to proceed to extreme measures; as he tells us frequently at this time, the younger men were active and ready to follow his bold lead, the older members, particularly the consulars, were timid temporisers. On this occasion, to Cicero's disgust, instead of naming Antony a *hostis*, with all that that implied, they voted to send an embassy demanding that he abandon his attack on Brutus, quit the province and keep his forces at least 200 miles from Rome.

Events turned out as Cicero had forecast; Antony, so far from paying attention to the Senatorial demands, had the effrontery to send the emissaries back with demands of his own, whose acceptance would imply complete surrender. This was undoubtedly Antony's intention; Cicero had forced matters to a decision instead of the game of cat and mouse which had

[1] *Phil.* VI, 2.

occupied their time and energy since Caesar's death; one side must now surrender to the other, or they must fight it out in open war. The Senate had called on Antony to surrender, now he on them; both had refused, and this left no alternative to war. On 1 January Cicero had persuaded the Senate to give Octavian the *imperium* of a propraetor and membership of the Senate; now they passed the last decree, empowering the consuls and Octavian to protect the state. Attempts by some to prevent, or at least delay, the outbreak of war were swept aside as signs of cowardice or treachery by Cicero. His hand was strengthened by the arrival of dispatches from M. Brutus in Macedonia, whither he had betaken himself in 44 without authority. There he had gathered an army, the governors of Macedonia and Illyricum had placed themselves at his disposal, and he had assumed the province's control. C. Antonius, to whom it was on 28 November allotted, and from whom it was taken away on 20 December, was far too weak to establish his claim, and had been driven for refuge to Apollonia, destined soon to surrender to Brutus. Cicero now prevailed upon the state to ratify what Brutus had done, with the result that the Senate now had an army in Macedonia, and an army marching to the aid of D. Brutus in the north.

Later in this same month came serious news from the province of Asia, where another of Caesar's murderers, Trebonius, was governor. Here Dolabella, to whom Syria had been decreed, treacherously slew Trebonius; but when Cicero moved that Cassius, who had taken possession of Syria, should be recognised in his tenure of that province, and entrusted with the war against Dolabella, who had been proclaimed a *hostis*, the consul, Pansa, stoutly opposed the suggestion, which was not at this time accepted. The reason for Pansa's opposition was not far to seek; the alternative motion made the war against Dolabella the consul's responsibility; in the hope that their present task against Antony would be finished, he wanted some further cause to keep his army together; perhaps he too aspired to become the military lord of the Roman world. None the less Cicero could still flatter himself on having the people's enthusiastic support: 'I said what I could about you', he wrote to Cassius afterwards, 'in a voice loud enough to fill the whole Forum, and with such cheering and acclamation from the people, that I have never seen anything like it.'[1] In spite of his failure to win recognition for Cassius, Cassius none the less proceeded against Dolabella without interference from the Senate or consuls.

D. Brutus had withdrawn to Mutina when Antony began his northward march; here he was now shut in by Antony's army, and must look to the consuls and Octavian to extricate him by frightening off or overwhelming Antony. They were anxious days for Cicero; in January he could write to Cornificius in Africa, who had an army whose loyalty must be retained: 'I put myself forward as leader of the Senate and Roman people; nor have I since thus undertaking the cause of freedom lost a single moment in supporting the common safety and liberty.'[2] In February he told Cassius: 'Though our consuls are splendid, our consulars are utterly shameful. Though the Senate is courageous, it is the lowest in rank that are most so. Nothing indeed, can surpass the resolute bearing of the people, and of all Italy.'[3] Thus did Cicero regard himself as the leader, and evaluate his Senatorial support.

We need not describe in detail the siege of Mutina; it was a time of strain and worry for Cicero, who spared no efforts to rally what support he could, and to maintain the loyalty of persons such as Lepidus, Plancus and Cornificius. Difficult and anxious it was, and we can but admire the vigorous energy with which Cicero assuming the leadership conducted affairs in the absence of the consuls, haranguing Senate and people, keeping Brutus and Cassius informed of events, writing countless letters, and generally maintaining single-handed the momentum of the policy and co-ordinating the diverse aspects into the grand design. His efforts seemed crowned with success; for after a false alarm that Antony was victorious, there arrived on 20 April news

---

[1] *ad Fam.* XII, 7, 1.   [2] *Ibid.* XII, 24, 2.   [3] *Ibid.* XII, 4, 1.

of Republican success before Mutina, and of Antony's discomfiture, which put an end to tense uneasiness in Rome, when 'three or four days before this glorious news, the city, struck by a sudden panic, was for pouring out with wives and children to seek you i.e. M. Brutus', as he wrote on 21 April to Brutus; 'on that day in very truth', he continues, 'I reaped the most abundant harvest of my great labours and my many sleepless nights...For I was surrounded by a concourse of people as great as our city can contain, by whom I was escorted to the Capitol and placed upon the Rostra amid the loudest cheers and applause.'[1]

Cicero with many others thought that the Republic now was safe and its enemy disposed of; and the news a few days later that Antony had suffered a second defeat served only to confirm their sanguine hopes. Antony was now at last declared a *hostis*; a public funeral was decreed for Hirtius and Pansa, who had lost their lives in the war, honours and a triumph were decreed for D. Brutus, to whom was given also the command of the former consuls' troops, while to him alone was entrusted the war to complete the defeat of Antony. Cicero proposed an *ovatio* for Octavian, but this was rejected by the friends of M. Brutus, who, like Brutus himself, resented these signs of honour to the man whose father they had murdered; though they had used his influence with the veterans in the interests of the state, they did not intend to allow his growth to strength when the danger was gone; for, whatever his behaviour and demeanour now might be, Caesar's adopted son could only look with hate and enmity upon his father's murderers; much better now to curb his growing strength while they had, as they thought, the opportunity and the means; if Antony were defeated utterly, and Octavian forced to be a common citizen, with danger of civil war removed, the Roman world would once again be safe for the Senate's domination and for the murderers of Caesar.

But again they had miscalculated. Antony was too shrewd a soldier to hazard needlessly defeat; having sustained before

[1] *ad Brut.* I, 3, 2.

Mutina two repulses, he withdrew to effect, if possible, a union with Lepidus in Narbonensis. D. Brutus, now released, was handicapped by the poor condition of his army; the pursuit of Antony, which was urgent in order to prevent his junction with Lepidus or with Ventidius Bassus, who was advancing with three legions to meet him, demanded the help of Octavian and his army. But this Octavian would not give; slighted by the Senate, determined not to co-operate with one of Caesar's murderers, and resolved not to be the instrument of his own downfall, he constantly assured Brutus of his good intentions, but took no steps to translate the intentions into deeds, intimating delicately the while to Antony that their enmity was neither necessary nor desirable.

All hinged on Lepidus. Even without Octavian's aid a resolute stand by himself and Plancus could destroy the forces of Antony; Lepidus, weak and colourless, pushed by events into the centre of the stage, must be persuaded or cajoled into doing his duty to the state; and what Cicero could do, he did. A stream of letters to D. Brutus and Plancus is eloquent proof of his anxiety at this time, and of his determined efforts to safeguard the state's safety.

Plancus, not himself a man of steel, was in a situation that called for qualities he did not possess. Whether Lepidus had from the outset an understanding with Antony, as Antony claimed, we cannot know; he probably had no understanding even with himself, but drifted weakly without the will to set himself a course. To the Senate he protested his loyalty, but did little to convert his protests into deeds. He and Plancus were in correspondence, agreeing a plan to deal with Antony; but Lepidus, having asked for Plancus' aid, as Antony drew nearer, deeming himself sufficient for the task, told Plancus not to come. Plancus did none the less approach more closely in order to lend aid, should Lepidus find himself in difficulties; but in the end the difficulties were his. For as Antony drew nearer to Lepidus' province, his legate made no attempt to oppose his entry, and the soldiers began to fraternise; Lepidus, averring his inability to prevent these happenings, when the soldiers admitted Antony to their camp, let himself be persuaded to meet him, then agreed to join him, and thus betrayed the Republican cause which he was claiming to uphold. In a letter to the Senate explaining these events, he protested that his troops' humane considerations had constrained him to take a course which avoided unnecessary bloodshed; he said nothing of the bloodshed his action had now made inevitable. In charity to Lepidus we may say that, if his behaviour seems to us contemptible, it was only because the weakness of his character was contemptible; that he had probably written as shiftily to Antony as he did to the Senate, and that it was the events which determined his actions, not the reverse; Antony was nearer and commanded the respect of many of Lepidus' troops.

Antony, from the defeated enemy, had now again become an important force, with whom the Republic was engaged in outright war, and with whom agreement was now impossible. Plancus, extricating himself from the difficult situation created by Lepidus' treachery, was now joined by D. Brutus with such forces as he could still command; for somehow they must block Antony from entering Italy with his now considerable army. The Senate, led by Cicero, had declared Lepidus a *hostis*, and had resolved that M. Brutus should return to Italy with his army; Cicero himself poured forth a flood of letters to both Brutus and Cassius, exhorting and beseeching them to come to the salvation of Italy and the Republic.

For the Republic was threatened on all sides. After the near-success which had seemed to reward at Mutina Cicero's gallant efforts, when he thought he saw the Republic's future assured and himself hailed as its hero, the situation had grown steadily worse; Antony had escaped and not been pursued; Lepidus had ratted; Octavian had failed to give the help he could have given to ensure Antony's defeat, and now was showing symptoms of a yet more dangerous malaise. He had not followed D. Brutus against Antony, for he nourished more ambitious hopes, and could in any case not fail to see the danger of his own position. His un-constitutional behaviour had been recognised by the Senate only because Antony had posed the greater and more immediate danger; the moment they thought that danger lessened, if not removed, they had shown their true sentiments and ignored him in favour of D. Brutus. If he collaborated with Brutus and Plancus in the defeat of Antony, he would then be at the Republic's mercy, which hated him as it had his father, and did not intend to let him be their master, if it could be prevented; either he must sub-mit or oppose by force; and this would be risky with M. Brutus and Cassius powerful in the East. At this moment his interests urged agreement with Antony rather than his destruction; they had a common enemy, the Republic, and, further, he would have as ally his father's friend against his father's murderers.

But first he must use his advantage to make himself an ally acceptable to Antony. While Antony was sparring with Plancus, Octavian decided to grasp Rome and the consulship, thus feeding his ambition and increasing his attraction to Antony. A group of centurions sent to Rome to demand the consulship on his behalf—Hirtius and Pansa had not been replaced—when met with polite objections, left the Senate House, their leader hand on sword declaring 'If you will not make him consul, this will.' The report of this rebuff in Octavian's camp stirred the army to demand to be led to avenge the insult; with eight legions and supporting troops he marched on Rome, which capitulated without a struggle; a report, soon to be proved untrue, that some of Octavian's troops had deserted, stirred the Senate to a brief spell of vain activity, after which Octavian withdrew from Rome while consular elections were held; Octavian and his cousin, Q. Pedius, were elected.

Thus cruelly was shattered Cicero's last attempt to save the Republic. Dependent as he and the Senate were on finding per-sons loyal to themselves to trust with armies, he had of compul-sion steered a course between the ideal and grim expediency, using such tools as came to hand, if they seemed able to be adapted to his great design. Such was Octavian. Suspicious he was of him at first, but he had swallowed those suspicions owing to the need against. Antony of Octavian's help; had Octavian been driven at that time into Antony's arms, as the soldiers so greatly wanted, the Republic's days would have been fewer than they were. They had a sporting chance; and had M. Brutus done what Cicero asked and brought his army to Italy at the crisis, all might have yet been well; but like Pompey he left his enemies in control of Italy, Spain and Gaul, able to choose the moment for attack; and the side that held Italy had the better chance of keeping the empire.

Cicero had tried to lead a Senate largely untouched by the ideals which meant so much to him, and now in his bitter failure he withdrew from the counsels of the state. Octavian passed a law against Caesar's murderers, who were all condemned in absence to be interdicted from fire and water. The Senate annulled their sentence of outlawry on Antony and Lepidus, and showed an unwilling readiness to do what they were told. Octavian meanwhile advanced to meet Antony; he had now shown his independence and his not contemptible strength; he enjoyed the status of consul, and enjoyed it at an exceptionally early age; but he realised that, if his youthful ambition was to have the *pabulum* it desired, it must be with Antony against the state; union with the state had nothing to offer beyond the consulship he already held, and the dangers of a war against Antony, a tried and able general. Further, the state was identified with Caesar's murderers; sooner or later he must take issue with them, and better now with Antony than later by himself. Alliance with Antony was, therefore, the obvious course of self-interest to a young man of barely twenty, not old enough in any case to see far beyond the immediate advantage.

Antony's position too had recently become much stronger. Asinius Pollio, governor of Further Spain, had chosen to throw in his lot with Antony, and had persuaded Plancus to do the same. Pollio had been a close friend of Caesar, yet in correspondence with Cicero had been protesting his hostility to tyranny and complaining of the Senate's failure to use his resources to the best advantage. But having left his province with only two legions, when he reached the Rhone, where Antony and Lepidus were encamped, he would have realised the difficulties of his situation and the strength of Antony's; nor could he have felt so strongly for the side that harboured Caesar's murderers as to risk all on their behalf. Pollio was thus content to join with Antony, where his sympathies probably lay; and if Pollio now joined, Plancus had no choice. D. Brutus was left alone, deserted; attempting to escape to Macedonia, without resources, gradually deserted by his soldiers, he was caught by a Celtic chief and by Antony's order murdered. Such was the outcome of the campaign which had begun with such splendid hopes at Mutina.

And now the final scene ensues. Antony and Octavian needed each the other; they and Lepidus agreed to meet, and on a small island in a river near Bononia they met, themselves without escort, their legions by the river banks. Here they conferred for two whole days, deciding the fate of the Roman world. They would become Triumvirs, *rei publicae constituendae*, for five years, with proconsular powers; they would, put simply, rule as dictators the Roman world, and they gave themselves what provinces they could; for Brutus and Cassius controlled the eastern parts. One thing alone remained, to lay their hands on money and rid themselves of enemies who might be dangerous if they had trouble with Brutus and Cassius; and for this purpose what better scheme than Sulla's, a proscription? Sedulously they drew up their list, stoic in their sacrifice of friends and relatives to their great cause and each other's animosities; and among their victims was Cicero, demanded by Antony, defended possibly for a time by Octavian. Let Plutarch describe the pathos of his end:

Cicero was brought to Astura, and finding a vessel there he embarked at once and coasted along as far as Circaeum...From there his pilots wished to set sail at once, but Cicero...went ashore and travelled on foot twelve miles towards Rome. But again losing resolution and

changing his mind, he went down to the sea at Astura...Then, re-
volving in his mind many confused and contradictory purposes, he
put himself in the hands of his servants to be taken by sea to Caieta,
where he had a villa...

Meanwhile his assassins came to the villa where he was resting,
Herennius a centurion, and Popillius a tribune, who had once been
prosecuted for parricide and defended by Cicero, and they had helpers.
After they had broken down the door...Cicero was not to be seen,
and the inmates said they knew not where he was. Then, we are told,
a youth who had been liberally educated by Cicero, and who was a
freedman of Cicero's brother, told the tribune that the litter was being
carried through the wooded and shady walks towards the sea. The
tribune ran round towards the exit, but Herennius hastened through
the walks, and Cicero, perceiving him, ordered the servants to set the
litter down where they were. Then he himself, clasping his chin with
his left hand, as was his wont, looked steadfastly at his slayers, his head
all squalid and unkempt, and his face wasted with anxiety, so that most
of those that stood by covered their faces while Herennius was murdering him. For he stretched his neck forth from the litter and was
slain, in his sixty-fourth year.[1]

Thus died the Republic's last true friend, a defeated failure in
the simple calculations by which success is often measured; *felix
morte sua*, he was spared at least the spectacle of the next ten years,
nor could he know how Augustus would define *res publica
restituta*; the Republic he had known and loved and fought for
was finally dead with Caesar, nor could his murder bring it back
to life; for a brief season it might seem to breathe and live, while
different parties strove and schemed for advantage; and in this
time Cicero could give a lead, because from time to time it suited
the one side or the other to use his influence for their purposes.
But behind this front of seeming obedience stood armies ready
to pounce if so their leaders should command, knowing allegiance
only to that leader, not to Cicero's Republic; and all his leadership and oratory, all his statesmanship and his appeals could
avail nothing against the legions' grim and surly dominion. How

[1] Plutarch, *Cicero*, XLVII, 3 ff.

many tens of thousands looked to him in these last months, supporting and cheering him, ready throughout the length of Italy to enlist in the cause he sponsored! But a match in their enthusiasm, they were outclassed in military experience; time and again in these fatal months the Republican commanders shrank from battle, knowing their armies inferior to Antony's trained legions; and so the better army won, as it did with Caesar. But not of necessity the better cause; if Cicero's efforts in these last months of life must be counted a failure, at least they showed how large a part of Italy accepted his ideals and leadership; they and Cicero alike succumbed to greater force, and either died or made a bargain with the victors; ten more years of bitter misery made even Augustus' Republic seem like heaven; no wonder Cicero was proscribed reading in his imperial republic!

There is a fatal quality in history, and he who tries to fight against that fate must needs be loser. We at this great remove in time can see so clearly the many failings of Rome's republican government: its inadequacy to its imperial tasks, its attitude towards the provinces, its lack of control and policy, and much else; but it carried none the less within itself the seeds of freedom, as the Imperial system never did; the *libertas* that Cicero cherished and defended was a truer and a finer thing than anything that Tacitus could know; and Caesar begat Domitian, Cicero left no political issue but a memory and a name.

SELECT BIBLIOGRAPHY

Adçock, F. E. *Caesar as Man of Letters.* Cambridge, 1956.
—— *Roman Political Ideas and Practice.* Ann Arbor, 1959.
Altheim, F. *A History of Roman Religion,* translated by H. Mattingley, New York, 1937.
Arnaldi, F. *Cicerone.* 2nd ed. Bari, 1948.
Badian, E. *Foreign Clientelae.* Oxford, 1958.
Bennett, H. *Cinna and his Times.* Menasha, Wisc., 1923.
Bloch, G. and Carcopino, J. *Histoire romaine,* Vol. ii. *La République romaine de 133 avant J.C. à la mort de César.* Paris, 1929, 1935.
Boissier, J. *Cicéron et ses amis.* 10th ed. Paris, 1895.
Broughton, T. R. S. *The Magistrates of the Roman Republic,* 2 vols. New York, 1951, 1952.
Cambridge Ancient History, vol. ix. Cambridge, 1932.
Carcopino, J. *Sylla, ou la monarchie manquée.* 4th ed. Paris, 1947.
—— *Les secrets de la correspondance de Cicéron.* Paris, 1947. English translation by E. O. Lorimer, London, 1951.
Carney, T. F. *A Biography of Marius.* An Inaugural Lecture given in the University College of Rhodesia and Nyasaland, 1961.
Cary, M. *A History of Rome down to the Reign of Constantine.* 2nd ed. London, 1954.
Ciaceri, E. *Cicerone e i suoi tempi,* 2 vols. 2nd ed. Naples, 1939, 1941.
Cichorius, C. *Römische Studien.* Stuttgart, 1922.
Cobban, J. M. *Senate and Roman Provinces,* 78–49 B.C. Cambridge, 1935.
Cowell, F. R. *Cicero and the Roman Republic.* London, 1948.
Degrassi, A. *Inscriptiones Latinae Liberae Reipublicae.* Florence, 1957, 1963.
Drumann, W. and Groebe, P. *Geschichte Roms in seinem Übergange von der republikanischen zur monarchischen Verfassung.* 6 vols. Leipzig, 1899–1929.
Frank, Tenney. *An Economic History of Rome.* 2nd ed. Baltimore, 1927.
—— *Roman Imperialism,* New York, 1929.
Frisch, H. *Cicero's Fight for the Republic.* Copenhagen, 1946.
von Fritz, K. *The Theory of the Mixed Constitution in Antiquity.* New York, 1954.

Fuchs, H. *Der geistige Widerstand gegen Rom in der antiken Welt.* Berlin, 1938.

Gabba, E. *Appiano e la storia delle guerre civili.* Florence, 1956.

—— *Appiani Bellorum Civilium Liber Primus.* Florence, 1958.

Gelzer, M. *Die Nobilität der römischen Republik.* Leipzig, 1912.

—— *Vom römischen Staat,* 2 vols. Leipzig, 1943.

—— *Pompeius.* Munich, 1949.

—— *Caesar, der Politiker und Staatsman.* 2nd ed. Wiesbaden, 1960.

Giannelli, G. and Mazzarino, S. *Trattato di storia romana,* vol. I, Rome, 1953.

Hardy, E. G. *The Catilinarian Conspiracy.* Oxford, 1924.

—— *Some Problems in Roman History.* Oxford, 1924.

Haskell, H. J. *This was Cicero.* London, 1942.

Heinze, R. *Vom Geist des Römertums.* Leipzig, 1938.

Heitland, W. E. *Agricola.* Cambridge, 1921.

Heuss, A. *Römische Geschichte.* Braunschweig, 1960.

Hill, H. *The Roman Middle Class in the Republican Period.* Oxford, 1952.

Kroll, W. *Die Kultur der ciceronischen Zeit,* 2 vols. Leipzig, 1933.

Lange, L. *Römische Alterthümer,* 3 vols. 3rd ed. Berlin, 1879.

Laurand, L. *Cicéron,* 2 vols. Paris, 1933–4.

Lepore, E. *Il princeps ciceroniano e gli ideali politici della tarda reppublica.* Naples, 1954.

Marco Tullio Cicerone, scritti commemorativi pubblicati nel bimillenario della morte. Florence, 1961.

Marquardt, J. *Römische Staatsverwaltung,* 3 vols. 2nd ed. Leipzig, 1881–5.

Marsh, F. B. *The Founding of the Roman Empire.* Oxford, 1927.

—— *A History of the Roman World from 146 to 30 B.C.* 2nd ed. (revised by H. H. Scullard). London, 1953.

Mattingley, H. *Roman Coins from the Earliest Times to the Fall of the Western Empire.* 2nd ed. London, 1960.

Meyer, E. *Caesars Monarchie und das Principat des Pompeius.* 2nd ed. Stuttgart, 1919.

Meyer, Ernst, *Römischer Staat und Staatsgedanke.* Zürich, 1948.

Meyer, H. D. *Cicero und das Reich.* Cologne, 1957.

Mispoulet, J. B. *La vie parlementaire à Rome sous la République.* Paris, 1899.

Mommsen, T. *Römisches Staatsrecht,* 3 vols. (I and II, 3rd ed.). Leipzig, 1881–1885.

Mommsen, T. *The History of Rome*, 5 vols. translated by W. P. Dickson. London, 1894–1901.

Münzer, F. *Römische Adelsparteien und Adelsfamilien*. Stuttgart, 1920.

Pareti, L. *Storia di Roma e del mondo romano*, 6 vols. Turin, 1952–61.

Paribeni, R. *L'età di Cesare ed Augusto*. Bologna, 1950.

Passerini, A. *Caio Mario*. Rome, 1941.

Pauly–Wissowa, *Real-Encyclopädie der classischen Altertumswissenschaft*. Stuttgart, 1893– . (Important biographical and historical articles; particularly important are: M. *Tullius Cicero* (M. Gelzer); *Cn. Pompeius Magnus* (F. Miltner); C. *Julius Caesar* (P. Groebe); *Nobiles* and *Optimates* (H. Strasburger); *Populares* (C. Meier).)

Peterson, T. *Cicero, a Biography*. Berkeley, 1920.

Piganiol, A. *Histoire de Rome*. 4th ed. Paris, 1954.

Pöhlmann, R. v., *Geschichte der sozialen Frage und des Sozialismus in der antiken Welt*, 2 vols. 3rd ed. Munich, 1925.

Pöschl, V. *Römischer Staat und griechische Staatsdenken bei Cicero*. Darmstadt, 1962.

Premerstein, A. v. 'Vom Werden und Wesen des Prinzipats', *Abh. der bayer. Ak. der Wiss., phil.-hist. Abt.*, N.F. 15 (1937).

Rambaud, M. *Cicéron et l'histoire romaine*. Paris, 1953.

Rice Holmes, T. *The Roman Republic and the Founder of the Roman Empire*, 3 vols. Oxford, 1928.

—— *The Architect of the Roman Empire*, vol. I. Oxford, 1928.

de Ruggiero, E. and Cardinali, G. *Dizionario epigrafico di antichità romane*. Rome, 1886– .

Schmidt, O. E. *Der Briefwechsel des M. Tullius Cicero*. Leipzig, 1893.

Scullard, H. H. *From the Gracchi to Nero*. London, 1959.

Shackleton Bailey, D. R. *Cicero's Letters to Atticus*, Books I–IV, 2 vols. Cambridge, 1965. (Books V– to follow.)

Sherwin White, A. N. *The Roman Citizenship*. Oxford, 1939.

Smith, R. E. *Service in the post- Marian Army*. Manchester, 1958.

Stein, P. *Die Senatsitzungen der ciceronischen Zeit*. Münster, 1930.

Strachan-Davidson, J. L. *Cicero and the Fall of the Roman Republic*. New York and London, 1898.

Strasburger, H. *Concordia Ordinum*. Frankfurt, 1931.

—— *Caesars Eintritt in die Geschichte*. Munich, 1938.

Sydenham, E. A. *The Coinage of the Roman Republic*. London, 1952.

Syme, R. *The Roman Revolution*. Oxford, 1939.

—— *Sallust*. Berkeley, 1964.

Taylor, L. R. *Party Politics in the Age of Caesar*. Berkeley, 1949.

—— *The Voting Districts of the Roman Republic*. Rome, 1960.

Thiel, J. H. *Caesar*. Hague, 1962.

Tyrrell, R. Y. and Purser, L. C. *The Correspondence of M. Tullius Cicero arranged according to its chronological order*, 6 vols., vol. I, 3rd ed., vols. II–VI, 2nd ed. Dublin and London, 1904–33.

Vogt, J. *Ciceros Glaube an Rom*. Stuttgart, 1935.

—— *Römische Geschichte*, vol. I. *Die römische Republik*. Freiburg, 1951.

Volkmann, H. *Sullas Marsch auf Rom*. Munich, 1958.

Warde Fowler, W. *Julius Caesar and the Foundation of the Imperial System*. New York and London, 1900.

Willems, P. *Le Sénat de la République romaine: sa composition et ses attributions*, 2 vols. Louvain, 1878, 1883.

Wirszubski, Ch. *Libertas as a Political Idea at Rome during the late Republic and early Principate*. Cambridge, 1950.

INDEX